Chicken Soup for the Soul

Our **101** BEST STORIES

for the Soul®

Preteens Talk

westland ltd
Venkat Towers,165, P.H. Road, Opp. Maduravoyal Municipal Office, Chennai 600 095
No.38/10 (New No.5), Raghava Nagar, New Timber Yard Layout, Bangalore 560 026
Survey No. A - 9, II Floor, Moula Ali Industrial Area, Moula Ali, Hyderabad 500 040
23/181, Anand Nagar, Nehru Road, Santacruz East, Mumbai 400 055
47, Brij Mohan Road, Daryaganj, New Delhi 110 002

This edition first published by Chicken Soup for the Soul Publishing LLC

CSS, Chicken Soup for the Soul and its Logo and Marks are trademarks of Chicken
Soup for the Soul Publishing LLC
www. chicken soup.com

The publisher gratefully acknowledges the many publishers an individuals who
granted Chicken Soup for the Soul permission to reprint the cited material.

First published in India by westland ltd 2009

ISBN: 978-93-80283-69-2

This edition is for sale in India, Pakistan, Sri Lanka, Nepal and Bangladesh only

Cover and Interior Design & Layout by Pneuma Books, LLC

Printed at Radha Press, Delhi

Cover photos courtesy of: *iStockPhoto.com/-M-I-S-H-A-*, *iStockPhoto.com/bsauter*,
iStockPhoto.com/JBryson, and *iStockPhoto.com/sjlocke*

Chicken Soup for the Soul.

Preteens Talk

Our 101 BEST STORIES

Inspiration and Support
for Preteens from
Kids Just Like Them

Jack Canfield
Mark Victor Hansen
Amy Newmark

westland

Chicken Soup for the Soul

Contents

❸
~Family Matters~

❹
~Heartbreak and Growing Up~

⑤
~The Popularity Game~

⑥
~Everyday Superheroes~

❼
~Tough Stuff~

❽
~Life's Little Lessons~

Chicken Soup

or the Soul

A Special Foreword

by Jack & Mark

For us, 101 has always been a magical number. It was the number of stories in the first *Chicken Soup for the Soul* book, and it is the number of stories and poems we have always aimed for in our books. We love the number 101 because it signifies a beginning, not an end. After 100, we start anew with 101.

We hope that when you finish reading one of our books, it is only a beginning for you too—a new outlook on life, a renewed sense of purpose, a strengthened resolve to deal with an issue that has been bothering you. Perhaps you will pick up the phone and share one of the stories with a friend or a loved one. Perhaps you will turn to your keyboard and express yourself by writing a Chicken Soup story of your own, to share with other readers who are just like you.

This volume contains our 101 best stories and poems for preteenagers. We share this with you at a very special time for us, the fifteenth anniversary of our *Chicken Soup for the Soul* series. When we published our first book in 1993, we never dreamed that we had begun the creation of what has become a publishing phenomenon, one of the best-selling book series in history.

We did not set out to sell more than one hundred million books, or to publish more than 150 titles. We set out to touch the heart of one person at a time, hoping that person would in turn touch another person, and so on down the line. Fifteen years later, we know that it has worked. Your letters and stories have poured in by the hundreds of thousands, affirming our life's work, and inspiring us to continue to make a difference in your lives.

On our fifteenth anniversary, we have new energy, new resolve, and new dreams. We have recommitted to our goal of 101 stories or poems per book, we have refreshed our cover designs and our interior layout, and we have grown the Chicken Soup for the Soul team, with new friends and partners across the country in New England.

Being a preteen is harder than it looks—we remember! School is more challenging, your bodies are changing, your relationship with your parents is different, and new issues are arising with your friends. But you are not alone. This new volume represents our 101 best stories and poems for preteens from our rich fifteen year history.

The stories that we have chosen for you were written by kids just like you who have been through the same things. They wrote about friends, family, love, school, sports, challenges, embarrassing moments, and overcoming obstacles. We hope that you will find these stories inspiring and supportive, and that you will share them with your families and friends. We have identified the 15 Chicken Soup for the Soul books in which the stories originally appeared, in case you would like to continue your journey among our other titles. And as you get older, we hope you will also enjoy the additional titles for teenagers in "Our 101 Best Stories" series.

With our love, our thanks, and our respect,
—*Jack Canfield and Mark Victor Hansen*

Preteens Talk

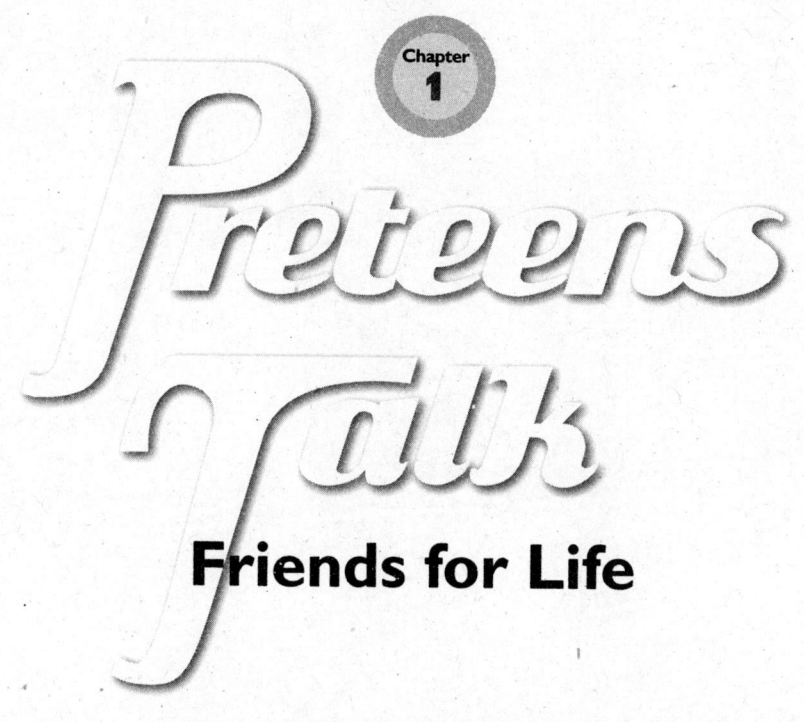

Chapter 1

Preteens Talk

Friends for Life

The most beautiful discovery true friends make is that they can grow separately without growing apart.
~Elisabeth Foley

Thanks, Y'All!

Remember, the greatest gift is not found in a store
nor under a tree, but in the hearts of true friends.
~Cindy Lew

I have distant friends, neighborhood friends, basketball friends, and friends online. However, I have one group of friends that has really been special to me.

In the fifth grade, my twin sister, Monica, and I transferred to a new school. Without any hesitation, I went. I didn't argue. Since my mom taught there, I would no longer have to ride the bus with a bunch of rowdy boys and worry about stuff like getting kicked in the head. No kidding—they actually accidentally kicked me in the head one day!

At my old school, I hadn't made any real friends. I was treated like a complete dork because of the way I looked. I had glasses, baggy clothes, pimples, and blemishes. I rarely smiled and hardly ever laughed, wore a belt, and was overweight. I was also dealing with the reality of my parents getting a divorce.

So on the first day at my new school, I just hoped that I would make friends. For a few weeks, I was always alone. Monica ended up having a different lunch period than I did, so I would just read during recess and lunch.

Then one day, a girl in my class named Cori came up to me at lunch and asked if she could sit by me. We began to talk, and since we both are twins, it gave us a lot to talk about. Soon, Cori introduced me to friends of hers—Adriane, Hannah and Toni—and I introduced them to Monica. Then Cori's twin, Cole, and his friends Matt and Ross started hanging around with us. We became one big inseparable group. At recess we played basketball and other games. We did everything together.

Ever since we've been together, my friends have always been there for me—even the boys. They liked me for me. Having them in my life changed the way I felt about myself. Their friendship gave me a sky-high feeling. We barely ever argued! We were really tight. They seemed to understand how hard it was to change schools and stuck with me through the tough times, like dealing with my parents' divorce.

One time, when Monica and I couldn't go outside with our friends after school, Toni supplied us with a pair of walkie-talkies to keep us all in touch!

I became more outgoing, like getting involved in student council and entering writing contests—some that I even won! Then came the sixth grade, our last year of elementary school and the last year for all of us to be going to the same school together. Adriane, Hannah, Toni, Matt, and Ross were going to Tison. Monica and I would at least still be seeing Cori and Cole since the four of us were all going to Hall Junior High.

I'd also be seeing my "old" classmates from the other elementary school, including some I had run into recently. Boys who had teased me in my old school stood staring at me not even knowing who I was. The girls who previously had treated me like vapor now paid attention to me and called me by name. I couldn't figure it out. I didn't know why. I thought that I was the same old me. But then when I looked in the mirror, I realized that I was a lot different than I had been before.

I wasn't short and stubby anymore. I had grown tall and slender and my complexion had cleared up. The glasses were gone and my belts were pushed to the back of my closet. I realized then that my friends had done more than just make me feel good—they had made me feel confident because they had supported me, and slowly my appearance had changed.

With their help, I had pushed my weight off. Toni helped me with that by encouraging me not to eat some of the more fattening foods and telling me that I could do whatever I set my mind to. I had been trying to lose weight since I was nine, when the doctor had said to my mom, "Michelle has a weight problem."

I learned to properly wash my face with the help of my friend Hannah and her magical beauty tips. "Just wash your face every night, it doesn't take too long!" she instructed.

With the help of Cori, my belt was gone. "Believe me, it's a lot less painful on your stomach. I used to tuck all my clothes in, even sweaters!" she exclaimed.

Adriane suggested that I wear my glasses only when I really needed them. "If you can see how many fingers I'm holding up, you are okay," she said. "Just wear them when you need to see the homework assignment on the board."

My sister, Monica, loves clothes and helped me pay attention to how I dressed. She would give me feedback about what looked good and what didn't. It really helped to hear her say, "Wow, Michelle, that looks FANTASTIC on you! Man, why couldn't I have gotten that?"

With the help of Cole, I learned a little bit more about athletics. "No! No! The receiver receives the ball! No! No! The quarterback doesn't flip the quarter! That's the referee!" he explained.

With the help of Matt, I learned to smile. "It won't hurt you," he encouraged.

With help from Ross, I learned a laugh a day keeps the frown away.

"B in math? Awesome! That's not failing—it's just not perfect," expressed my friends.

As I gaze into the mirror, I turn to the left and then to the right. I smile at my reflection, because I now realize that these people, my true friends, never saw me as a dork. They saw the beauty in me. They brought my personality out.

The best friends that anyone in the world could ever have will be missed when we go to junior high. But I will cherish the memories that we have created, and whatever happens, I'll always remember that my friends helped me become who I am. In conclusion, I have to say... thanks, Cori, Cole, Hannah, Matt, Adriane, Ross, Toni, and Monica.

Y'ALL ARE THE BEST!!!

~Michelle Strauss
Chicken Soup for the Preteen Soul 2

Stubbly Dooright

or years, my wife Teresa taught physical education at the elementary school level. Traveling on a regular schedule to the six schools in her district, she had a chance to get to know most of the kids in the area and see them at their best—and their worst.

Childhood is tough enough, but gym class strips away all the veneers, exposing the unvarnished truth beneath. There's nothing like P.E. class to display your strengths or frailties, your bravado or timidity, your blue ribbon winning athletic skills or complete lack of coordination. Worst of all, with people choosing sides, there's no doubt where you stand in life's pecking order. Some of us have been, and all have suffered for, the person picked last.

At one of the schools, whose gray facade and asphalt playgrounds reflected the mood of the depressed downtown area in which it stood, Teresa noticed a third grade child who was one of those always picked last. The girl, let's call her Meagan, was short and grossly overweight, with a closed and hopeless look on her face. Meagan always sat alone in class, played alone at recess, and ate alone from a recycled paper sack at lunch. The teachers and staff were kind to Meagan, but the students were not.

The stories made your shoulders drop. Teresa heard that when the playground supervisors turned their backs, kids would run up and touch Meagan on a dare, then run off to "infect" others with her "cooties." Mockingly calling her "Meagan the Munchkin," they did far worse than isolate her; they filled her school days and walks home with physical and emotional torment. Teachers who had met with Meagan's single mother, a hard-working woman who was trying her best to "make two ends that had never met each other meet," were told that weekends were special for Meagan—not because she had sleepovers and was invited to movies or parties, but because being away from the other kids, in the privacy of her room, meant the misery would stop, at least until Monday and the long walk to school.

Meagan's situation disturbed my wife deeply. After talking with the principal and other teachers, Teresa came up with an idea. She knew from talking to Meagan that the child had never had a pet. Teresa was sure a pet would be the perfect way to inject some high-powered love and acceptance into Meagan's life. Teresa told Meagan that she needed to talk with her mom about something important and asked her if she'd have her pick her up from school one day soon. Anxious that something was wrong, Meagan's dutiful and caring mother came the very next day.

Teresa recounted Meagan's school problems to her and, finally, broached the subject of a pet for Meagan. To my wife's surprise and delight, Meagan's mom said she thought it would be a great idea. She agreed to come down to the veterinary hospital where I practiced so she could look at the various strays and castoffs we'd accumulated, selecting from among them the perfect pet for Meagan.

The very next Saturday afternoon—after we had closed, but before we'd left for the day—Meagan and her mom walked in the back door as we had arranged. When the door buzzer sounded, the dogs engaged in a predictable and vigorous clinic-chorus of barking.

Getting down on one knee, I introduced myself to Meagan and welcomed her and her mother to my office. I noticed that Meagan, like any creature that has been abused, had a lot of hurt in her eyes—so much, in fact, that I had to look away momentarily to compose myself.

I escorted them to the back runs, where the homeless pets were kept. I fully expected Meagan to fall for one of the mixed-breed terrier puppies who had been dropped off in a box at our door earlier that week. The puppies had spiky hair, huge, liquid brown eyes and pink tongues that ran in and out like pink conveyor belts on overtime.

But, while Meagan really liked the puppies, she didn't love them. As we moved down the row to examine some more "used models," out sauntered the clinic mascot, a tiger-striped American shorthair cat that had lost one leg to a hay mower while he was out mousing in an alfalfa field at first cutting. With a stub for a right hind leg, he had been given the name Stubbly Dooright.

Stubbly had a peculiar habit of rubbing up against you, purring, and then biting you hard enough to get your attention but not enough to break the skin. It was love at first bite when Stubbly clamped onto Meagan's pinky finger, and she playfully lifted the cat almost off the ground. You could plainly hear Stubbly purring in his vertical position.

Meagan left the clinic that Saturday afternoon, glowing with happiness. Now she had a living, breathing friend who wanted to play with her, who loved to cuddle up next to her on the sofa and sleep next to her on the bed. Her mother later told us that when Meagan came home from school, Stubbly would rush to the door, Lassie-like, and follow her from room to room through the house. Like a feline boomerang, Stubbly would leave to do "cat things," but would always find his way back to her side.

Energized by Stubbly's unconditional love, limitless affection and loyalty, Meagan began to blossom. Though she still might never be Homecoming Queen, she did find fellow pet lovers who befriended her, and things began to improve for her—physically, emotionally, and socially.

Ten years later, Teresa and I received an invitation to the high school graduation ceremony from Meagan, whom we were thrilled to read was one of the co-valedictorians of her class.

On graduation day, we joined the throngs of family and friends seated in the auditorium watching the seniors get their diplomas. When Meagan strode to the podium, head high and beaming, I hardly recognized her. Now an attractive young woman of average height and athletic build, Meagan gave a speech on the importance of acceptance and friendship that kept the crowd riveted. She was going to be a communications major in college and clearly was gifted in this regard.

At the conclusion of the speech, she talked about the special friend she'd met in the third grade who had helped her climb the steep and treacherous slope of her childhood. The friend who had comforted her when there wasn't enough to eat in the house because her mother had been laid off from work, and who had stayed by her while she sobbed her heart out after a boy had asked her to a dance on a dare with no intention of taking her. The special friend who had been there to mop up her tears or to make her laugh when she needed it most.

With the gymnasium full of people in the palm of her hand, Meagan said she'd now like to introduce this special friend, and she asked her friend to come to the stage to be recognized. Meagan looked to the right; no one was coming down the aisle. Meagan looked to the left; still no one approached the stage.

It was one of those moments when you ache for the speaker, and people started swiveling in their seats, craning their necks, buzzing with conversation. After what seemed like an eternity, but was actually less than a minute, Meagan suddenly said, "The reason my friend didn't come to the stage is because he's already here. Plus, he's only got three legs, and it's hard for him to walk sometimes."

What? There wasn't anybody new at the stage, and what kind of person has three legs?

With high drama, Meagan lifted her hands high—displaying a photograph of Stubbly Dooright. As she described her beloved cat, the crowd rose to their feet with cheers, laughter, and long, thunderous applause.

Stubbly Dooright may not have been there in person, but he was definitely there in spirit—the same spirit that had made all the difference in the life of a very lonely child.

~Marty Becker, D.V.M., with Teresa Becker
Chicken Soup for the Cat Lover's Soul

Best Friends

I thought she was my best friend
The best one I've ever had.
Instead I found out the truth
And what I learned was sad.

We still call each other friends
But I feel we're far apart.
Though we see each other every day
I have a broken heart.

She has made new friends
And I have made some, too.
We are talking less and less
And inside I'm cold and blue.

Each and every night I pray
That she will finally see
How much I want our friendship back
And how much she means to me.

~Whitney M. Baldwin
Chicken Soup for the Preteen Soul

Right in Front of Me

When I was in the sixth grade, I met my new best friend. Her name was Courtney, and she was tall, pretty, and smart. She was also one of the most popular girls in school. That same year, I met my worst enemy, this awful boy named David. Every day he would call me names and pull my hair. I couldn't stand him.

When we graduated to seventh grade, Courtney ran for student body president. One night, she invited me over to her house to make posters and buttons for her campaign.

When I arrived, I was horrified at what I saw. It was David! Apparently, Courtney and David had been friends for some time. David and I looked at each other as though we were two cowboys in an old Western movie ready for a showdown. Our eyes locked and each of us frowned at the other. After what seemed like an eternity, Courtney broke the stare by telling us to get to work on the posters. We sat in silence for a few moments, and then David said, "Hey, we haven't gotten along in the past, but let's call a truce for the sake of Courtney." I was stunned at his suggestion, and I also couldn't refuse.

Once we decided to stop being enemies, we hit it off almost immediately. David and I found out that we had the same sense of humor and laughed at the same jokes. We both loved the same music and going to the same movies. We could talk about anything. I couldn't believe that a few hours before, I couldn't stand to be near

David, and now here we were, covered in glue and glitter and laughing so hard our stomachs hurt. I never even had this much fun with Courtney. But even after I realized that I had this connection with David, when I went home, I kind of dismissed it. After all, he was a boy and Courtney was my best friend.

A couple of months later, my grandfather died. A week after his funeral, my parents decided that we should move. I was terribly upset because I loved my school and my friends, especially Courtney. But she promised me she would call me at least once a week and we would get together as often as possible. There was no doubt in my mind that we would stay friends through this difficult time in my life—dealing with my grandfather's death and, on top of that, moving to a new town. I gave David my new phone number, too, and told him to call me.

A couple of weeks went by, and I never even got one phone call from Courtney. On the other hand, David had already called me several times to ask how I was doing and tell me what was happening at my old school. I was so upset that I hadn't heard from Courtney that I finally decided to call her. When she answered the phone, she apologized for not calling me and told me that she was going to be in a play and that I should come and see it with David. Courtney said we would all go out to dinner afterward. I was so excited that I was going to see my best friend again.

My mom dropped me off at the theater, and I ran into David right away. We had been talking so much on the phone that I felt like I had just seen him the day before; it was a great feeling. After the play, David and I waited for Courtney to come meet us so that we could go to dinner. But Courtney never showed up. She left without even saying hello or goodbye. I was heartbroken and I started to cry. I had wanted to see and speak with my best friend, who hadn't even called me since I had moved. I needed her to be there for me, to ask me how I was holding up, and she wasn't even interested.

After I had finished bawling my eyes out, I looked up and there was David. I realized something at that moment; my true friend wasn't at all who I had thought. During a rough transition in my life, the person that I had thought was my best friend couldn't even make time for me, and the person who was once my enemy became my closest friend in the world.

I have never spoken to Courtney again. But every week, David and I talk on the phone. To this very day, David is my best friend.

~Heather Comeau
Chicken Soup for the Preteen Soul 2

One Is Silver and the Other Is Gold

A lie may take care of the present, but it has no future.
~Author Unknown

"What? We're moving AGAIN?" I asked in disbelief after hearing my mother's "news." "I'm only in fifth grade, and this is my eighth school! It's not fair! I just finally made some friends!" I ran into my room, threw myself on the bed and cried.

By mid-January I had started yet another school. It wasn't quite so hard moving in the summer, but I hated moving during the school year. By then, everyone had made friends, and it always took a while to be included.

My first day at Mitchell Elementary was hard. Even though Mrs. Allen introduced my classmates, nobody ate lunch with me or said hi at recess. I sat alone, watching everyone on the playground having fun. Boys were running around trying to catch each other; girls huddled together, whispering and giggling. I noticed that everybody was wearing nice clothes and shoes, far nicer than my hand-me-down dress and tennis shoes that were ripping near my toes. I told myself that everyone here was rich and snobby, so I didn't care about being friends anyway, yet I did want to make friends. I was already missing the girls at my old school.

The next morning when my mother left for work, she reminded me not to be late for school. I decided to wear my best dress and shoes that day, the ones I usually wore to church or birthday parties. I figured not only would the other girls notice me, they would want to be friends. I looked in the mirror and decided to add one last touch for good measure.

I slipped into my mother's bedroom, opened her jewelry box and took out an expensive, beautiful bracelet that she had promised to give me when I was older. It was made of sterling silver beads that were hand-carved into roses. I looked in the mirror again, smiled and felt confident enough to start a conversation with even the most popular girl in school.

Walking into my classroom, I sensed many eyes on me. I held my head high, believing that everyone was thinking how pretty I looked. Instead of sitting by myself again on the steps during the morning recess, I marched right up to a group of girls from my class and said hello. I introduced myself, asked everyone their names again and played with my hair so they would notice the beautiful bracelet I had on—the one I wasn't supposed to wear until I was older. "So, what are you guys talking about?" I asked.

"Just about riding our horses last weekend," Tammy replied.

"I was right!" I thought to myself. "They ARE rich!"

The girls kept talking about their horses, their riding lessons, the new saddle they wanted...

"I have a horse, too," I suddenly blurted out.

There was silence. I couldn't believe that I'd said such an outright fib, but it was too late now.

"Well... I mean, I used to have a horse," I continued, trying to undo the lie a little. "But we had to sell him when we moved here."

"What a shame! You must be so sad!" everyone chimed in together. "What was he like?"

Instantly, I had everyone's attention! I told them all about Red, a stallion that actually belonged to a family friend. I became so caught up in describing "my" horse that I almost started believing the lie myself.

When the bell rang, signaling the end of recess, we headed back to class. "Wanna join us for lunch?" Jan asked with a smile.

"Sure, thanks!" I answered, thrilled that I'd found a way to fit in so quickly. I snuggled into my desk, glancing down to admire my beautiful bracelet that surely impressed those rich girls.

"Oh, no!" I heard myself gasping aloud. The bracelet was gone!

"Did you say something, Karen?" my concerned teacher asked. I burst out crying, and everyone turned to stare.

I don't know if I was more upset over losing that beloved bracelet or fearing my mother's reaction after she learned what I had done. "I... I lost my silver bracelet," I stammered. "It must have fallen off during recess."

I was so visibly shaken that Mrs. Allen took sympathy on me. She told me not to worry, quickly scribbled a note and told me to take it to the office. The instructions said, "Please read this on the PA system." Within seconds, the secretary's voice boomed over the loudspeakers: "Someone lost a very special bracelet this morning. Mrs. Allen has a Good Citizen Award for whoever finds it during the lunch recess."

I went back to my classroom, feeling relieved that my prized possession would certainly be found. At noon I joined the other girls in the cafeteria. We gobbled down lunch so that we could race outside and start hunting. Within twenty minutes, it seemed that all 300 kids in that school were helping me look, searching every inch of the girls' restrooms, the hallways, and the playground. I kept nervously glancing around, waiting for someone to yell, "I found it!" When the school bell rang, alerting everyone to return to the building, the bracelet was still missing.

I sat down at my desk, fighting back the tears. My kind teacher asked the secretary to announce another search. I just couldn't believe that it hadn't been found with all those kids looking for it! I developed a horrible feeling that someone secretly picked it up and decided to keep it. After all, it was the most beautiful bracelet in the world and obviously worth much more than some Good Citizen Award.

Again, during the afternoon recess, it seemed that everyone was looking for my bracelet instead of playing tag or standing around talking. Again, the bell rang, signaling that recess was over. Again, those silver beads were nowhere to be found.

Trying not to cry, I put my hands over my face. Several girls all gathered around me in the yard, and they all promised to help me look again tomorrow. I couldn't believe how caring and supportive they were!

"Thanks, everyone. You are so nice," I said, forcing a smile. "It's just that I shouldn't have even worn that bracelet this morning. It belongs to my mother." Then, without knowing why, I suddenly added, "And I'm sorry. I lied to you guys this morning. I've always wanted a horse, but we've never owned one. Red belongs to a friend of my mother's. I guess I told you that so you'd like me. I even wore my best clothes today so I'd fit in better."

"That's okay!" they all answered reassuringly. "It doesn't matter whether you own a horse or what kind of clothes you have!" Rhonda gave me a hug, and two other girls offered to let me ride their horse sometime.

It felt so good to tell the truth and to learn that I had misjudged those girls as being snobby! I really did feel like smiling then... even before I happened to glance at the ground and discover an almost hidden sand-covered bracelet, smack in the middle of my circle of new friends.

~Karen Waldman
Chicken Soup for the Girl's Soul

Friends at First Sight

How rare and wonderful is that flash of a moment when we
realize we have discovered a friend.
~William E. Rothschild

Bam! The car door closed as I ran to the gate. There was Jesse, waiting for me. He was the only kid who was tall enough to reach the lever on the gate at our daycare sitter's, Mrs. Rogers. He greeted me with a smile and we ran inside. After my mom signed me in, she called me back over to give me a kiss goodbye. I kissed her as usual and said, "See ya later, alligator!" She replied as usual, "After a while, crocodile!"

Jesse and I always wanted to play outside. I was about four or five when Jesse and I discovered how to dig perfect tunnels; we even planned to sneak away down the tunnel to my house and then to China.

One day, while starting one of our digs, we lifted up this old rock and found two scorpions. It was very frightening, so we ran straight inside screaming, "It's Scorpion Invaders! They just arrived!" All the other kids followed us in, and until the "invaders" were gone, we played inside.

Just before lunchtime, Jesse jumped up and down on Mrs. Rogers' couch—something that we were forbidden to do. He got in so much trouble! During his time out, I sat by him. I wasn't supposed to but I did anyway. Then, at lunchtime, as usual, I pulled the sticker off my apple and gave it to Jesse. It was a tradition to give the sticker to your friend, so I always gave mine to Jesse and he always gave his to me.

After lunch, we finally got to go outside, since Mrs. Rogers' husband killed the two scorpions. Jesse got on the swing and I pushed him back and forth until it was time for our naps.

After what seemed to be the longest naps ever, Jesse and I stayed inside and played a game that we had just made up. It was called Kitty Transporters. We were small enough to fit under an old chest of drawers where we pretended we were in a time travel shuttle that was transporting us to our newest location. We were kitties following our instincts as to which way to go and when to get ready to fight. We played and played all through snack time and when everyone else left, Jesse and I went outside and played our game in the sandbox until my mom arrived to pick me up.

That was a typical day for us at Mrs. Rogers'. Somehow, Jesse and I always got along. We never got bored, because we used our imagination and we just loved playing together.

Flash forward: Jesse's in the seventh grade at the same school where I'm now in sixth grade. We usually don't get to see each other except in passing period or at lunch. I think I embarrass him a little by always saying hi and bye, but he never shows it.

As you can see, Jesse and I have always been friends. We went to the same babysitter every day since, well, forever. We know each other so well that I could tell you just about anything about him. For one thing, he's smart. He can build a whole computer in one day, so whenever I'm stuck on the computer I always call him for help and advice. Jesse loves jokes and he always has a joke that will cheer me up whenever I'm down. He's truly the most kind and generous friend anyone could ask for.

I thought it was really, really nice of him to show up at my twelfth birthday party this year. Except for Jesse, it was all girls, but he didn't seem to mind. Ever since I was three or four, I've always invited him and he's never missed one single birthday party of mine. He has always gotten me a Barbie every year. I love Barbies. I collect them still today, so he got me one this year. His face turned bright red when I opened his gift and said, "I got a Barbie!" After the party, I said, "Thank you. I can't believe you came!" He replied, "Hey, that's what friends are for." Then he grinned, gave me a hug and said, "Happy birthday!"

I know that some friends just come and go—but not Jesse. Even though he's a guy and I'm a girl and we're definitely growing up, we are friends to the core. Our friendship was meant to be from the first time we met.

Because of Jesse, I truly believe in friends at first sight!

~Stephanie Caffall
Chicken Soup for the Preteen Soul 2

A Friendship
Never Broken

*You can make more friends in two months by
becoming interested in other people than you can in two years by
trying to get other people interested in you.*
~Dale Carnegie

"Get out!"

Those were the first words I exchanged with Laura when I was only five years old. She had walked in on me when I was using the bathroom in our kindergarten room. I was so mad. I remember going home and telling my mom all about this "bad" girl who opened the door on me. Little did I know that by opening that bathroom door, Laura would step into my life and open many other doors for me. She would change my life forever.

Laura has Down syndrome and was being mainstreamed at my school. After the bathroom incident, my mother sat me down and explained that Laura was "special." She tried to get my five-year-old mind to understand about Laura's mental retardation. I went to school the next day and decided to try to become Laura's friend. It wasn't very hard. Laura was playful, adventurous and full of giggles. She followed me everywhere, and I doted on her constantly. A few weeks into the school year, we declared each other "best friends."

For the next two years, Laura and I were put into the same classroom. My other friends got to know her better, and every year she sat next to me at my birthday party. We went to each other's houses to play, hung out at the park together, and she even got her ears pierced like I did. Laura counted on me to take care of her more and more with each passing year. By the time second grade rolled around, the principal decided that Laura needed to be in a different class from me. She wanted Laura to expand her capabilities and rely less on me. We were upset about it, but we still remained "best friends."

Laura sparked an interest deep inside of me that I don't think I would have discovered without her friendship. I became very passionate about kids with disabilities. I spent a lot of recesses in the Physical Support Room at our school, playing with kids who were in wheelchairs or who couldn't communicate with words. I loved the feeling I got when these kids smiled at me because I came to see them. I volunteered at a Cerebral Palsy Center when I was seven years old. Every other Saturday, I would go there and interact with disabled children—singing songs or playing games. Spending time with these kids made me consider becoming a special education teacher.

When we were in fourth grade, Laura switched schools and was placed in a Life Skills class. I didn't see her every day, but a few months later, she moved into my neighborhood. Now I could walk to her house and see her whenever I wanted. This made us both feel better about her being at a different school.

As I have gotten older, I have become busier with soccer, field hockey and other friends. Laura and I don't see each other as often as we used to, but we are back in the same school. We are thirteen now and in middle school. She is still in a Life Skills class, and once a week I spend my lunch period volunteering in her classroom. And when it's time for me to leave, Laura always yells out, "I'll call you tonight, Nikki." She wants her classmates to hear this because she is so proud to be my friend, just like I'm proud to be hers.

Laura has taught me a lot, and by showing my peers that it's okay to have a friend with Down syndrome, I hope that I am showing others about being accepting and open to kids with disabilities.

Laura has been like any other friend of mine. Sometimes she makes me laugh; sometimes she makes me cry. Sometimes she even embarrasses me. But these are all things that my other friends do, too. Laura is really not that different from everyone else. She loves to try on clothes, watch movies and always talks about her latest boyfriend. While my mind will continue to grow, Laura's will stop where it is. But that's okay, because our friendship keeps on growing. And so does my perspective of children with disabilities.

~Nikki Kremer
Chicken Soup for the Teenage Soul: The Real Deal Friends

Big at Heart

Desire is the most important factor in the success of any athlete.
~Willie Shoemaker

My best friend's exceptionally small. We're in the fifth grade, but Larry's as short as a first grader. Although his body's small, Larry's big at heart. He has a sharp mind, too. All the kids who know Larry like him a lot.

Sometimes he gets his share of teasing, but Larry knows how to handle it. When some smart-mouth calls him Dopey, Sleepy, or Bashful, Larry just laughs and starts humming, "Hi, Ho!"

Larry loves sports, but he can't play some, like football. One tackle and he would be wiped out. But one sport seems to be made for Larry—baseball. He's our star player. The legs that are too short for track and hurdles can pump up and down, carrying him around those bases faster than you can see. He can slide to safety under a baseman before he's noticed. And when he's in the field, he catches and throws that ball like the biggest of us.

I remember when he first came to try out for our Little League team. The coach took one look and shook his head.

"No, I'm sorry, but we need big, strong players. Tell you what—we could use a batboy!"

Larry just grinned and said, "Give me a chance to try out. If you still think I'm a weak player, I'll be the best batboy you ever had!"

The coach looked at him with respect, handed him a bat, and said, "Okay, it's a deal."

Well, obviously no pitcher could aim the ball inside Larry's ten inch strike zone! He would be a sure walk to first base every time, and the coach knew how to take advantage of that. And when he saw how fast Larry's legs could travel and how well he handled the ball, he bent over, patted Larry on the back, and said, "I'm proud to have you on the team."

We had a winning season, and yesterday was our final game. We were tied with the Comets for the championship. Their pitcher, Matt Crenshaw, was a mean kid who never liked Larry—probably because he could never strike him out.

Somehow we held the Comets through the top of the ninth inning, and we were tied when it was our turn at bat. As Matt passed our bench on the way to the pitcher's mound, he snarled at Larry, "Why don't you go back to Snow White where you belong?"

I heard him and jumped up, ready to give Matt a punch, when Larry stepped between us. "Cut it out!" he yelled, pushing me away from Matt. "I can fight for myself."

Matt looked as if he was going to clobber Larry, but my friend held out his hand and said, "Let's play baseball, okay? I know you want your team to win and it must be tough to pitch to a shrimp like me."

"Chicken, you mean. You won't even swing at the ball!" Then he stamped off to the mound as Larry slowly dropped his outstretched hand.

We had two outs when it was Larry's turn at bat. The bases weren't loaded, but the coach told Larry to wait for a walk, as usual. Larry held his ground for three balls. One more and he would walk to first.

Then, for some reason—maybe because Matt had called him "chicken"—Larry reached out for the next pitch. It wasn't anywhere near his strike zone, but he swung the bat up and around. He connected. We heard a loud crack and saw the ball sail over all the outfielders. They had to chase after it, and Larry's legs started churning.

Like locomotive wheels, they went faster and faster, rounding second and third and heading for home. The Comets finally retrieved the ball and passed it to the catcher. Larry slid safely under him as he caught it.

We had our winning run, the game was over, and we were the champs. After we were presented with our winner's trophy, we gave it to Larry and took turns putting him on our shoulders and marching around the field.

I was carrying him when we passed Matt. "Put me down for a minute," Larry said. He walked over to Matt with his hand extended again for the handshake Matt had refused earlier.

"It was a good game," Larry said, "and you came close to winning it...."

Matt looked at Larry for what seemed like a long time, but finally Matt took Larry's hand and shook it.

"You may be a shrimp," he said, "but you're no chicken. You deserved to win."

Then Larry and I ran back to the rest of our team. We were all going to the pizza place for a victory celebration. I sure was proud to have Larry as a friend. Like I said, he's big in the ways that really count.

~Mark Schulle as told byBunny Schulle
Chicken Soup for the Preteen Soul

Melts in Your Heart, Not in Your Hand

*T*hough she had been in a coma for nearly six months, it was still a shock when my grandmother passed away. She'd had her third stroke the year before and had lapsed into the silent sleep afterwards, leaving her family to sit by her bedside at the hospital, to ache, to cry, and to pray. I was not yet thirteen when she died, and the first thing I clearly remember was the shock that she was gone forever. I'd understood that death awaited her, but in those first moments of knowing, I could not believe that "eventually" had finally come to pass.

What was to follow was the pomp and circumstance of a typical Catholic send off. First, there would be wakes. Four of them. Two on the first day, one from 2:00 P.M. to 5:00 P.M., and one from 7:00 P.M. to 9:00 P.M. The same schedule would be repeated the following day. The third day would be the funeral itself, the church funeral, then the final burial at the graveyard. It seemed like too much to take. For the next few days, my whole life would become death: staring at the body of my grandmother amidst the overwhelming scent of too many fresh flowers, feeling the eeriness of the funeral home and dreaming of her at night, her ghost hovering over me while I tried desperately to fall asleep. My real life, the life of an eighth grader who was almost done with grammar school and off to high school, had never seemed further away.

At the funeral home, friends and neighbors poured in to pay their last respects to my grandmother and to show support for my mother. Not knowing where to be or what to do, I stayed off to the side, not wanting to upset my mother. The awkwardness finally came to an end with the arrival of my friend Kelly.

She lived down the street; we'd been friends ever since she was three and I four. My mother had been so pleased when she discovered that a family with a little girl had moved in down the street—finally, a playmate for me! She and Kelly's mother, Patti, became fast friends, as did Kelly and I. Though I was a year older than her and we were in different grades in school, it didn't matter much. We were "home" friends, the kind who rode bikes together after school and made up plays for our Cabbage Patch kids to act out. When we got older, we grew more mischievous and began sneaking to a diner a few blocks away for ice cream sundaes, even though we weren't allowed to leave the block. When finally we were allowed to leave the block, we'd go around the corner for pizza, but stopped first in the alleyway to put on pink lipstick and eye shadow.

At the funeral home, Kelly's parents went to the coffin and knelt to pray. Kelly came right to me. In her hands were two packages of M&M's, original and peanut. Kelly knew that candy was one of my favorite things; we had often taken long trips to the local store for chocolate bars and lollipops. "I thought this would make you feel better," she said. For the rest of that wake and the others that Kelly attended, we sat in the back of the viewing room, eating M&M's and talking quietly. A devastating and unfamiliar experience had suddenly become easier to bear, with a childhood offering of chocolate candies and the company of a devoted friend.

When my other grandmother passed away two years later, Kelly was there once again for all of the wakes and the funeral, and came bearing M&M's for each one. It's a difficult thing, trying to come up with something to offer a grieving person.... What do you do for a person who has just lost one of the most important people in their lives? Kelly had understood, even at twelve, that there wasn't much she could do to ease my pain but be there with me and bring something that just might make me smile. When Kelly's grandmother died a year after that, I arrived at her wake with a one-pound bag of M&M's.

Now, whenever Kelly and I find ourselves at a funeral home for a family member of ours, the other has always shown up bearing M&M's, a small offering of cheer to take the edge off the hovering sorrow. We've joked that when we're old, whichever one of us dies first will have a crazy old lady throwing M&M's into her grave, while the other mourners will look on in confusion. It's a silly thought, but M&M's will always be significant to me now. They will remind me that even when something as painful and as powerful as death comes to claim what's most important to me, there will always be chocolate... and Kelly.

~Jennifer Stevens
Chicken Soup for the Girlfriend's Soul

Love Lives On

A horse is the projection of peoples' dreams about themselves —
strong, powerful, beautiful —
and it has the capability of giving us a wonderful escape.
~Pam Brown

Whatever happens inside of you that makes you fall in love with horses happened to me. I devoured every horse book I could get my hands on, checking them out of our library again and again. *Man O' War*, the true story about the greatest thoroughbred racehorse of all time, was my favorite. I must have read that book ten times. I pictured myself owning the huge red horse, loving him with all my heart, but knowing I could never ride him because he was a champion racehorse, not a pet.

I asked my parents if I could take riding lessons and they agreed. I learned to ride well, made many friends at the stable, and my love of horses and the sport of riding grew.

After a year of lessons, I decided that what I wanted more than anything on Earth was a horse of my own. I asked my parents, and they agreed—if I earned half of the money to buy the horse. I worked all summer and saved one hundred dollars, a fortune in those days. At last, my dad said, "Find your horse, girl!"

Two hundred dollars wasn't much to buy a horse, and the one I had my eye on was going for five hundred dollars. "A deal is a deal," said my dad, so I could only watch as the beautiful black mare was sold to someone else. Disappointed, but still determined, I was introduced to a woman who told me that she had a horse she would sell me for two hundred dollars, but she doubted that I would want him, explaining that she had rescued him from an abusive owner and that he hadn't been ridden in years.

As we walked to the back of the stables, I was so excited that my heart was pounding. The woman explained that she thought I was a good horsewoman and that when she heard that I was looking for a horse—on a limited budget, no less—she had thought that perhaps it was time for this horse to come back to the world.

We walked up to the stall and she opened the door, cautioning me "not to expect too much." I was trembling with excitement as the sunlight spilled into the stall. There he was, an old giant of a thoroughbred, with gray sprinkled through his shiny, flame-colored coat. He turned and looked cautiously at us, and as I stepped into the stall he flattened his ears and bared his teeth. The woman explained that he had been beaten and had a mistrust of strangers, but that he wasn't mean, just afraid.

"What's his name?" I asked.

"We call him Rusty," she said.

"Rusty," I called gently, and his ears came up at the sound of his name. The woman handed me a carrot, and I held it out to him. He stepped forward slowly, but before he took the treat, he turned his head slightly and looked into my eyes. We held the gaze for just a moment, and then he took it from my hand.

When he was done munching his carrot, we led him out into the sunlight. What I saw was the most beautiful horse I had ever laid my eyes on. What most others saw was a twenty-year-old swaybacked horse, sporting a potbelly.

"I'll take him!" I cried, startling him so that he jerked his head back and snorted all over me. I laughed and reached up to pet the long, white blaze that ran down the front of his nose, and he lowered his head and begged for more.

That summer we were inseparable, and I spent all my free time riding him. He grew strong and energetic for his age. I often saw the woman who had sold him to me, and she would tell me how good he looked.

That fall, we moved Rusty to a small stable near our home, so I could ride him as often as possible during the school year. I began getting involved in the world of competitive horse showing. Rusty thrived on all the attention and competition, and even though he usually was twice the age of the other horses, the judges loved him, and we took home many blue ribbons during the next two years.

But one morning, as I arrived at the stables to go riding, something was different. Instead of standing, ears pricked forward and bellowing a hello, Rusty was still laying down in his stall when I walked up. He rose when he saw me, nickering softly, and I figured maybe it was just his age getting to him. After all, he was twenty-two years old. We rode quietly that day, stopping for lunch to share the same sandwich and chips. How he loved potato chips! But he was not hungry, and when I told my dad about it, he decided to call the vet.

The vet came to see him, and what he said was a shock to us. He believed that Rusty had cancer, and he referred us to a specialist for further tests. My parents and I had talked about the situation, and we decided that due to his advanced age, if the specialist told us that he was suffering, that we would elect to have him humanely put to sleep. I understood this on one level; on my heart level I was crushed.

That morning we loaded Rusty into the trailer and I waved goodbye to him, pretty sure it was for the last time. My parents had thought it would be best if I didn't go with Rusty to the vet. I had spent the entire night before with him, crying and laughing, remembering all the things we'd done together and the lessons we'd learned. I'd thanked him for being there for me during a tough time in my life when I didn't think anybody cared, but I knew he did. Unconditional love, that's what he had given me.

Later that day, I was lying on my bed at home, all cried out, when my dad came in. He told me, "There is a guy out front who wants to see you." I was fifteen years old, and I figured it was just one of my school friends coming by to talk. I asked my dad to explain that I couldn't come out now, but he said, "Honey, you'll want to see this boy."

I rose up from my bed and looked out the window. There, backed up into our driveway, was the horse trailer, and inside was Rusty! I tore outside and jumped up next to him, hugging his neck and crying with happiness. He stood quietly and took in my love, and when I stepped back, he turned his head and looked into my eyes, as he had done years before, and winked.

Rusty stayed with me for another happy year before the cancer took him. By then, we were a little more prepared.

All these years later, I still miss him. But, even though he isn't here physically, I realize that love lives on, and that Rusty will live in my heart forever.

~Laurie Hartman
Chicken Soup for the Preteen Soul

A Friend Will...

A friend will not talk bad about you
    and will never lie.
Friends are always there for you
    if you need to cry.
Friends will be there for you
    through thick and through thin.
When the rest of the world walks out on you,
    a friend will walk in.

~Nicole Johnson
Chicken Soup for the Preteen Soul 2

Chapter 2

Preteens Talk

So Embarrassed!

You will do foolish things,
but do them with enthusiasm.
~Colette

Strapped for Cash

In youth we learn; in age we understand.
~Marie Ebner von Eschenbaach

The stereo was blaring when Deb entered my room. She stood beside my bed, hands on hips, piercing blue eyes focused on me intensely.

"What?" I asked nervously. Deb didn't usually come into my room, or even have that much to do with me.

"I need to talk to you." Deb was my sister, actually my half-sister, and older by ten years. She took it upon herself to look after us younger kids, and I suppose that is why she was the one to come to my room instead of my mother.

"What?" I asked again, fidgeting with my pillow.

"I've been noticing that you've been changing," she said.

"Changing?" I asked innocently, but I knew what she meant. I had reached puberty and wasn't too happy about it, even going so far as to wear oversized t-shirts to hide it. I was a tomboy and proud of it. I didn't want boobs like some girly-girl.

"Robin Lynn, it's time you got a bra."

I rolled my eyes in embarrassment.

"I was thinking we could stop by Dad's office today and get some money. Then we could go to the mall and see what we can find for you."

"I don't want to ask Dad for money," I whined. "He'll want to know what it's for."

"No, he won't. He never has before," she said, looking toward the ceiling in thought. "Besides, if he does, you can just tell him you need it for something. He won't ask. Now get going."

"Is this really necessary?" I asked, wishing the whole situation would just disappear.

"You are not a boy, and it's time you started looking and acting like a girl," she advised. "I'm not going to argue about it. Get ready!"

As Deb shut the door, I flung myself backward, hitting the mattress hard and bouncing slightly. I closed my eyes and continued listening to my music until a sappy love song came on. That's when I grabbed my tennis shoes and headed downstairs.

Our fifteen-minute drive to town was unusually quiet. I was too embarrassed to talk about it, but nothing else was on my mind. A bra. What would be next? A dress or pantyhose!? Womanhood was not something I was looking forward to.

"I'll wait in the car," Deb said. "Hurry."

"Yeah, yeah," I answered unenthusiastically.

Dad's office was on the second floor of a huge building downtown. The building was old, and the dark stairwell gave me the creeps. I always took the stairs three at a time to hurry to the landing at the top, but each step still left an eerie echo.

Once at the top, I went into Dad's office. Dad's secretary was sitting at her desk. "Your dad is with a client. Let me buzz him," she offered.

She announced, "Robin's here."

"Send her in" was Dad's happy reply. He always told us we were more important than anyone else and could always come right in, but I was glad she checked first.

Dad sat behind his huge desk, which took up at least half of the room in the office. One side held pictures of us kids. Yellow legal pads were scattered in front of him, and a sign that read "J. R. Sokol, Attorney at Law" clasped the edge of the desk for all incoming clients to read. The faint smell of leather from all the law books filled the room.

His client sat in front of the desk in one of the four green leather office chairs. He was a round man in a blue three-piece suit. His thick black hair was slicked to his head as if he had used glue.

"Hello there, Robs. Where's your mother?" Dad asked casually.

"At home. Deb brought me to town."

"What do you need?" he asked, removing his black-framed glasses and rubbing the corner of his eyes. He had a permanently tired look about him; trying to raise seven kids would do that to a person.

"I need some money."

"For what?"

I thought, "Oh no, now what?" I looked at Dad's client, who seemed to be interested in what I needed the money for, too. I looked back at Dad. "I just need some money, that's all." I felt my face start to heat up like a hot coal.

Dad's voice rose slightly, "What do you need the money for?"

I couldn't take it anymore, "Never mind," I yelled and turned to leave. I could feel the tears swell up in my eyes but tried to fight them and not be a sissy.

"Young lady, you come back here this minute and tell me what you need the money for!" From the firm tone of his voice, I knew I had to tell him.

I walked back to the corner of the desk, tears now running down my face, and yelled at the top of my lungs, arms waving, "I need a bra!"

Dad's eyes widened in surprise, "Oh, I see." The corners of his mouth curled upright, and he started to laugh. So did his client. They both roared with laughter, which only made me madder.

"It's not funny!" I yelled.

"Young lady, you settle down." Dad said firmly, trying to tone down the situation. He reached into his suit pocket and pulled out his wallet. He flipped it open and handed me a couple of twenty dollar bills. "Here Robs," he said, still chuckling.

I grabbed the twenties firmly, spun on my heels, ran out of the office, and bounced down the stairs.

I stopped on the landing at the bottom, cried a little more, and then wiped the tears away. I was not going to let Deb know what happened.

At the supper table that night, I waited for Dad to say something about the day's events. I knew once the rest of the family knew, they would tease me relentlessly. But he never said a word about it.

Later that evening, there was a knock on my door.

"Yeah?" I asked.

"It's me. Can I come in a minute?" Dad asked quietly.

"Yeah."

He opened the door and stood inside, glancing around my room like he had never seen it before. I sat on the edge of my bed thinking I was in trouble for acting up today.

"Honey, I have an idea."

"Yeah," I answered, trying not to look him in the face.

"From now on, if you need money for something personal, why don't you just say it's for 'girls' stuff.' Then I'll know."

I felt my face get flushed again. "Okay."

"It's a deal then," he answered, lowering his eyes, as embarrassed as I was.

"A deal. Good night," I answered trying to end the conversation.

"Night. Don't let the bed bugs bite."

We both smiled as he shut the door.

I took the two new bras out of my drawer and lay them on my bed. One had two bears, dressed in jeans, kissing. The other had a moon and a sun imprinted on the front.

I put one on and pulled a baggy t-shirt on over it, looked in the mirror and smiled. Deb thought getting me a bra would turn me into a girl, but with a baggy shirt on no one would ever even be able to tell. This won't be so bad, I thought to myself.

Not so bad, that is, until my brothers found out I had been bra shopping.

The teasing lasted for weeks.

~Robin Sokol
Chicken Soup for the Girl's Soul

Paybacks

Revenge is often like biting a dog because the dog bit you.
~Austin O'Malley

I learned the danger of revenge and letting a "payback" escalate out of control the day I woke up with a long, curled black mustache on my upper lip. My sister had ever-so-carefully drawn it with a permanent marker as I slept!

It all began when I was eleven, the summer before I started seventh grade. My family had moved across state and since my boyfriend, David, and all of my childhood friends were in another town, I was miserable and dreading the start of a new school year. My sister, Rose, who is two years older, was bored and angry. And so, that summer we shared a room and a lot of pent-up frustration toward our parents and our situation. I guess feeling so powerless about an unwanted move made us feel a need to reclaim our power—any way that we could.

Our emotions led us to play crazy "practical jokes" on each other, which then spiraled into getting even, or paybacks, as we called it. It was my sister who really started it all.

I had met our neighbors, Randy and Britt, who were close to my age and a lot of fun. One night, when it was time to go in due to our curfew, I stayed out talking to my friends after Rose went in the house. When I finally went in, I quietly crept upstairs without turning on any lights. My sister had anticipated my every move and had piled chairs in the entry to our room. Of course, I came crashing into them and had to bite my lip to keep from yelling when I smacked my knees!

My surprise and anger turned into a plan for payback the next night. So at bedtime when my sister went to brush her teeth, I turned off the lights and took out a hidden bottle of airplane glue, which I poured onto the middle of her pillow. I had a vision of her waking up with the pillow all stuck to her head. But my plan was destroyed when she came in and smelled the glue.

"What is on my pillow?" she asked with wide eyes as she turned on the light.

"I don't know," I said innocently. Then I started to laugh so hard that I couldn't breathe.

"Mel Ann, you are so stupid!" she said with controlled anger in her voice. "So now if you don't want me to tell Mom and Dad that you ruined my pillowcase, you'll go make me a sandwich."

"Fine," I answered with resignation. I didn't feel like getting grounded, so I quietly went downstairs to the kitchen without waking my parents. But once I got there, more thoughts of revenge got the better of me, and I mischievously added hot sauce to Rose's sandwich. Rose got a hot mouthful in the first bite, so she yelled, "That's it! Now I'm telling on you!"

"No, no!" I begged her.

"Okay, then you eat it!" she demanded. So I took a bite and instantly my mouth was on fire! I quickly and quietly went through the upstairs hallway to the bathroom for a glass of water.

When I returned, Rose said, "Okay, if you eat one more bite, we're even."

"All right, give it here," I said with a growing frustration about the mess I had created.

But this time when I took a bite, I gagged! I ran out of the room and back to the bathroom. Rose had put cold cream in the sandwich! That was it. I hit her really hard with a pillow and started chasing her around the room trying to whack her again. Finally, our yelling woke up our parents, who were not pleased about being awakened from a sound sleep late at night by ridiculous stunts—especially the night before the first day of school. We tried to explain, but in the end, my mom just sternly said, "I don't think this is funny. Now go to bed! And... you're both grounded!"

As she walked out of the room, Rose mumbled, "This is your fault! You got us grounded!"

"My fault? You started it with those stupid chairs!" I replied with anger.

Finally I went to bed and knew I'd think of an even better payback the next day. But little did I know what startling surprise the next morning would bring me. When I woke up, I went to the bathroom. As I walked by the mirror, I suddenly stopped to stare at my reflection. My sister had taken a black marker and drawn a long mustache on me that curled up onto my cheeks.

"Mom!" I yelled and ran to show my mother.

But my tired and grumpy mother was in no mood for more pranks. So, she simply grounded my sister (again) and told me to "go to school." I was horrified! I scrubbed my face until only a little marker still showed, but then the hard rubbing made raised, red welts in place of the marker! I showed up at school looking totally ridiculous and realizing that paybacks never end; they only escalate into bigger messes.

Even if you think you've pulled off the greatest joke on someone, like your sister being glued to her pillow, you've only invited trouble to find you next—like a big, black mustache.

~Mel Ann Coley
Chicken Soup for the Preteen Soul 2

The Moment I Knew I'd Never Be Cool

Every time I've done something that doesn't feel right,
it's ended up not being right.
~Mario Cuomo

My older sister was born to be liked. She came out of the womb with a cute face, blond hair, a sense of humor, athletic ability, and what my mom called the "gift of gab." She went through her childhood with lots of friends, lots of parties and lots of attention. I wanted what my sister had: popularity.

I studied her for years and never came close, so I turned to kids my own age for role models. Jen, the girl I always sat next to in school, threw her blond hair around, showed off her dimples, put her head to one side when she asked for favors and was easily voted most popular in class. "Okay," I thought, "I'll try her tactics." I threw my brown hair around, smiled without dimples, put my head to one side and asked my teacher for a pass to the bathroom. She looked at me and said, "Why are you doing that with your head? Don't you feel well?"

That was my cue to try for cool instead of popular. I'd do anything to escape my lack of social status. Cool kids always acted as though they had the world under control, maneuvering around obstacles and adults with ease, and never cracking under pressure.

My big chance came when a new girl moved to town and into my class. Nothing seemed to ruffle Tiffany. She was cute, trendy, and best of all, she liked me.

Our friendship lasted four weeks—just long enough for me to learn that Tiffany took European vacations, went skiing in Aspen, and bought clothes at Neiman Marcus. I'd never been outside Illinois, on skis or anywhere but the Sears preteen department. We were only eleven and she'd already picked out the car she'd get for her sixteenth birthday. Tiffany was way too much for me. I crawled back into my familiar invisibility...

Until I met Mandy. Mandy's middle name was "rebel." She and her brother, Kevin, smoked cigarettes and stole money from their mom's purse. "If popularity and cool are out of reach," I thought, "I'll take rebellion over facelessness." I was soon hanging out at Mandy's house, where no adults were ever around to notice what we were doing. I puffed cigarettes, pretended to shoplift and felt powerful for the first time in my life. I did crazy things my parents never suspected, and had a great time bragging about it to other kids. I could feel my status rising. Then Kevin was arrested and sent to a detention center. Never wanting to end up like him, I pitched my cigarettes and headed back into obscurity.

By eighth grade, I was desperate. I tried out for cheerleading at my small school, and by some miracle, made it onto the squad. My head swelled like a melon. "I must have absorbed popularity and coolness without realizing it," I thought. I took this tiny piece of status and ran with it.

At first, being popular and cool seemed to be easy. I tolerated, agreed with, or laughed at the nasty comments of the cool girls who stayed that way by pointing out the uncoolness of others. Things like, "Look at Dana's hair. Think she used a hedge trimmer?" or, "Can you believe those shoes Lauren wore last night? She must have borrowed them from her grandmother." Guys weren't spared. "Oh, Tyler. What a crater face!" and, "Yeewww. Bryce actually thought I'd be seen with him in public!"

The better they were at cutting people to shreds, the faster those girls seemed to rise above the masses. Like stand-up comics, they pointed out other people's flaws and made the crowds roar. Why, I wondered, were put-downs cool? They made my stomach cramp. Was it who said them? The way they were said?

"Okay," I decided, "I can say nasty things about other people for the sake of personal success." I picked a time and place for my initiation. A budding friendship with the Faris twins gave me a stage. Sara and Shauna were way cooler than I'd ever be. They'd been hanging with guys since seventh grade.

My debut came after church. The three of us were standing around waiting for rides home. I listened to them rip first on girls and then on guys. One guy in particular took the brunt of their hits: first his clothes, then his voice, then his brain, then his looks.

"I know what you mean," I volunteered, as Shauna turned up her nose at the mention of the poor guy's hairy arms. "Some guys are real apes...."

As the words left my mouth, a not-so-good-looking guy drove past in a blue convertible. "Perfect opportunity," I thought. I pointed to the driver, "...like that guy—red-haired and u-g-l-y." I made chimp sounds as I watched the car turn into a nearby driveway. Instead of agreement, I heard nothing from the twins. It was like I was standing on the ocean bottom with my ears plugged. I turned slowly to see Sara and Shauna with necks stiff and eyes impaling me on an invisible stake.

"What? What?" my confused brain was pleading. "What'd I say?"

The answer slithered out of Sara's mouth as the twins turned their backs and walked toward the blue convertible. "That red-haired and u-g-l-y ape is our brother."

The rest, as they say, is history. My journey to cool stalled right there in front of church. With face burning and ears ringing, I'm sure I heard an otherworldly voice whisper, "You'll never be popular, cool, or anything else your heart won't let you be. Start looking inside, instead of out."

It took me a while to get what those words meant. But once I stopped trying to be like other people, life got a whole lot easier. I'm even growing up to be someone I really like.

~D. Marie O'Keefe
Chicken Soup for the Preteen Soul

Tasting the Moment

*Laughter gives us distance. It allows us to step back from an event,
deal with it, and move on.*
~Bob Newhart

When I was twelve, I wanted to have a summer romance more than anything I had ever wanted before—more than being able to drive a car and more than having big boobs—I wanted to fall in love.

I had no idea what falling in love meant, though. I thought that a romance would make me feel different—older and experienced. My friends all had experience with boys. They knew how it felt to have someone else's hand squeezing their hand or to have somebody smile at them for no apparent reason. I was starting to feel certain I never would. And then I met Erik.

Every summer my parents and I would go on vacation to the same RV campground. The campground was a haven for potential summer romances. My friends and I would check out all the new campers, hoping there might be some new love interest. We would talk about romance and imagine what we would do if we did have a boyfriend.

"I'd sit with him at the campfire," Trish would say.

"We'd go for walks, holding hands," Kelly said.

And I never said anything. I didn't know what I would do if I met a boy I liked. I never had much to say to boys. I couldn't remember the punch lines to jokes and didn't know what kind of questions to ask to get a conversation started. Whenever I did meet a new boy, I'd stammer and mumble, tripping over my tongue as often as I tripped over my own feet.

Then that summer, three baseball teams with twenty fifteen-year-old boys on each team camped at our park.

Everyone was in heaven!

Everyone... except my father.

"You are to be inside at ten o'clock tonight," he said. In all those previous years, I never had a curfew at the campground. Neither had my brother. Except this time. My brother was still allowed out and I, like Rapunzel, was locked in my tower while the rest of the world (my friends) were being swept off their feet. Unlike Rapunzel however, I knew what I was missing. They were all going to have another romance while I, once again, was not.

"Oh Andrea," Kelly had said the next morning. "It was so amazing! The guys on this team are so cute!"

My stomach crashed to the floor as she listed off their names. Taylor, Matt, Anton, Erik... I had missed it again.

"And we're going to their game this afternoon!"

I was allowed to go to the game. The game itself wasn't great—they weren't the best players and they weren't even playing on a very good ball field. It was out in the country and it didn't have any bleachers. We had to sit under this old, wooden canopy that had a few picnic tables. It was sunny and hot and we were dying of thirst, but I LOVED it.

My friends pointed out each of the players that they had met the night before. We were sitting pretty far away, so it was hard to tell what they looked like, but I felt that this was what having a romance was all about—going to watch your guy play baseball and cheering him on.

"And that's Erik," Kelly pointed out this guy who was kind of skinny with a few loose curls that stuck out from underneath his baseball cap. He looked over at us girls, waved and smiled. My stomach was flopping around like a fish on dry land.

They lost their game and the tournament. We spent the rest of the day swimming and hanging out on the beach. Erik and I went for a walk on a road just outside our campground. He held my hand as soon as we were outside of the park. I hadn't thought about what a guy's hand would feel like holding mine.

It was fun walking with him, holding hands. We walked along a dirt road leading to a hill through a grove of poplar trees. In the midst of the trees, at the top of a hill, was a giant rock. We sat there for a few minutes, still holding hands. He kept smiling. His teeth were so white they were glowing in the early darkness. I could smell him—sort of a mixture of bug repellent and lake water. He slowly leaned his head closer to mine.

"This has to be what falling in love feels like," I thought. I was so totally nervous that my stomach was doing flip-flops.

His face was just inches away and then his lips pressed against mine. His lips opened just a little and I followed his lead, opening my own lips just a little. As I did, I felt this odd little gurgle creeping up in my throat. The next thing I knew, I let out this tremendous burp right into his mouth!

Mortified, I excused myself and looked away. I wanted to run away but he was still holding my hand.

Then, weirdly enough, he laughed. Then I laughed too, and the "romance" of my first kiss was over. We walked back to the campfire holding hands.

Finally tasting a kiss didn't change me, make me feel older or more self-confident around boys. But I discovered that sometimes people like Erik come into your life and can help make an embarrassing moment a little easier.

~Andrea Adair
Chicken Soup for the Preteen Soul 2

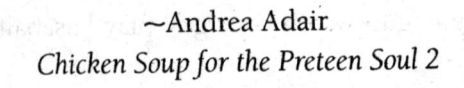

What's on the Inside

Attitude is a little thing that makes a big difference.
~Winston Churchill

I can still remember that boy in perfect detail. He had beautiful blue eyes that lit up whenever he smiled. And when his mouth smiled, half of his face would light up with shiny white teeth. He was the first boy who gave me that feeling that my heart was going to stop. When he walked by, I could see him out of the corner of my eye and smell the detergent he used on his clothes. My body would freeze, and my brain would stop ticking. Then he would flash that big smile at me and my breath would stop. I can picture myself standing in front of him like a fool with my mouth gaping open and my eyes melting with lust as this beautiful boy charmed me.

There was no doubt about it, I was head-over-heels, madly in puppy love. I might have only been in third grade, but this was real or at least I thought it was. I was constantly thinking about him and ways I could get closer to him. "Eric" was scribbled all over my notebooks with messy little hearts drawn around them. I adored him, and he knew it.

Then one Saturday, I got the chance to get closer to him. I was at a birthday party, and Eric showed up at the front door. The whole night I avoided him for fear that I would say something stupid.

As I was pigging out on potato chips, I turned around and saw him staring right at me. My stomach jumped and my cheeks blushed as he walked closer to me. He flashed his eyes at me and said, "Come here, Eleanor. I want to tell you something." My heart fluttered at the thought of being so close to him. Eric leaned closer and cupped his hand around my ear. He brought his face closer to mine, closer, closer. I moved my head away to give him more room, but he moved closer still. I felt his arm across my back and his hand warming my ear. But I didn't hear any words. I tilted my head away from him in an almost uncomfortable position and again his face moved closer to mine. I turned to look at him and there was his face, two inches from mine, with his eyes closed and his mouth pursed into a kiss. A wave of shock came over my face, and his expression copied mine as he opened his eyes.

"What are you doing?" he asked. He raised his eyebrows in a puzzled expression.

"What are YOU doing?" I shot back. I could only imagine what Eric was thinking right now. I'm sure he was thinking, "This girl, Eleanor, is a dork!" I desperately hoped that wasn't what he was thinking.

He looked right at me and yelled, "Geez, Eleanor, I'm just trying to kiss you!"

What? He was going to kiss me? I missed my chance! My one and only chance to kiss this boy of my dreams, and I ruined it.

"Oh, sorry," I said, very embarrassed.

He gave me a small kiss on the cheek then scrambled off to a group of boys who were laughing hysterically.

Then he yelled at his friends. "I'm NEVER playing Truth-or-Dare again!"

At the sound of his words, my sensitive heart crumbled into pieces. Tell me he didn't say what I thought he said. But I knew it was true. I could feel a sob starting in the back of my throat, but I promised myself to hold it in. Then tears came, filling up my eyes and spilling over my bottom lashes. My lip started to quiver, and I knew a flood of tears was only seconds away. I flew out of the basement with my head in my hands and retreated to the bathroom to cry alone for the rest of the night.

As much as I would like to, I can't say that this experience was easily forgotten. That night, I realized Eric didn't like me as much as I liked him. The next week at school, I would hear groups of kids talking about the incident when they didn't think I was listening. But I heard them and my feelings were hurt each and every time. While my heart ached for a while, I actually recovered rather quickly. I got over it in a couple of weeks, and the gossip stopped long before that. I did learn a lesson, though, and it still helps me to this day. There are a lot of cute boys out there, some even cuter than Eric, but just because a boy is cute doesn't mean he is necessarily nice. I still get crushes on boys who are cute, but I find out what their personality is like before I let my heart get involved.

~Eleanor Luken
Chicken Soup for the Teenage Soul on Love & Friendship

The Mysterious Book Bag

Love and kindness are never wasted. They always make a difference.
They bless the one who receives them, and they bless you, the giver.
~Barbara De Angelis

he homemade book bag was sprawled across my bed. It appeared to have taken over the entire room. I hovered in the doorway just staring at it, a little afraid to move toward it. I closed my eyes for a second, trying to imagine the large shoulder bag gone. I carefully visualized a nice, normal store-bought backpack in navy blue or black.

I opened my eyes again. It was still there. The large sack was the color of rust, and fuzzy, like a stuffed animal. I knew that my mom had spent all day happily sewing as she envisioned me proudly walking from class to class with it flung over my shoulder.

To make matters worse, I realized that the fabric was actually left over from a toy horse that my mom made for me when I was a baby. Now there was sentiment attached to it. I entered the room and picked up the gift. My mother had even quilted little running horses along each side. And, just to make certain that no one would be confused as to who owned this furry monstrosity, Mom had embroidered my name on one side.

If I had been eight and not twelve, I would have been thrilled.

The book bag was huge, with numerous pockets. The thing would easily hold all of my school supplies, and it was sturdy, too. It would last, so I couldn't hope that it would soon fall apart, giving me the perfect excuse to be rid of it.

"Do you like it?" my mother asked.

"Yes," I said in a halting voice. "Thank you."

"Well, if you don't like it, you don't have to use it," Mom said sadly.

"Oh no, Mom, I love it," I lied, picking the bag up and rubbing the soft fabric against my face. The last thing I wanted to do was to hurt her feelings. "You used the same fabric from Flaming Star," I said with a smile, letting her know that I understood the connection to my childhood stuffed animal. "Thanks," I muttered again and hugged her.

After a while, I got up the nerve to load the new bag with notebooks, pens and other school supplies. "It is kind of cute," I tried to convince myself.

The next day I was to start seventh grade at a new school, in a new state, in the middle of the school year. I was nervous and excited all rolled into one.

That first day at school I heard the whispers. "Have you seen the new girl? She's from California. Did you see that big furry bag?" Then there were giggles.

Because I started school in the middle of the year, all of the lockers had been assigned to other kids. There was no storage available for me, so I was forced to haul all my stuff around in the oversized fuzzy bag, making me seem suspicious.

I soon became known as "the weird girl with the huge, fluffy horse bag."

Wild stories flew back and forth about what I kept in the bag that never left my side. "Drugs?" some kids wondered. "Clothes? Is she homeless?"

There was nothing interesting in that bag, just my coat during cold weather, school books, papers and pens. Eventually, most students pretty much ignored me, but some of the kids teased me about the fuzzy horse bag. People grabbed at it, pretended to pat it like a dog, and tried to toss their trash into it. My teachers didn't seem to notice, probably because I didn't ever complain or ask for help.

As the year progressed, I started to hate that bag. I blamed all my problems on it. I felt helpless and alone, miserable, and homesick for California and my old friends.

One day toward the end of the school year, my math teacher assigned each student a partner to work with on word problems. I was told to work with Debbie, a popular redheaded girl who was in several of my classes. She smiled and waved me over toward her desk, so I grabbed my notorious bag and quietly moved toward her. As I sat down, I realized that I had never spoken to her before.

"So, what's in the bag?" Debbie asked loudly with a grin. The students working at the table next to us turned to hear my answer.

"Um, just books and stuff," I stammered, caught totally off guard.

"Can I see?" she boldly asked.

Then she held out a hand for my bag. I was so shocked that I simply handed it over without a word.

By this time, numerous other kids were watching us.

"So, why do you have clothes in there sometimes?" Debbie asked.

"Just my coat or a sweater or whatever I wore to school." I replied.

"But why?" Debbie tilted her head with the question. "And why on earth do you cart around everything, for all of your classes? Do they do that in California?"

"No, in California I had a locker!" Then I explained, "They were all out of lockers when I got here this year."

Then Debbie started to laugh—not at me, but at the situation. "You mean, you've just been carrying your stuff around all this time because the school didn't have enough lockers?"

I nodded.

"This happens every year. The school doesn't have enough lockers, so lots of us have to share." She started giggling again. So did I.

"There's, what, a week left of school," Debbie said through spurts of laughter. "But, you can share with me if you want. That bag is kind of funky—very chic when you think about it. One of a kind."

Then Debbie stood up, still grinning. "Hey everyone. Guess what? Laura's bag is just full of school stuff!" she exclaimed. "No locker," she said with her hands up and shoulders scrunched, as if to say, "What was she supposed to do?"

"All right, Debbie, that's enough," the teacher said loudly. "I'm glad that's settled. Now get back to math!"

Debbie rolled her eyes and handed me a piece of paper with her locker combination scrawled on it. "Wish I'd asked you about that bag months ago," she whispered. Then she asked me something I never thought I'd hear. "Do you think your mom would make me one?" When I nodded, bewildered, she started laughing again. "I think we're gonna be friends," she declared, loudly enough for the whole class to hear.

And we still are.

~Laura Andrade
Chicken Soup for the Preteen Soul 2

A Perfect Fit

When I was twelve, my summer consisted of getting into trouble on my family's farm. I spent hours on end swimming in a make-do livestock tank and climbing oak trees, getting my knees and elbows all skinned up. Thoughts of clothes, makeup, or boys were far from my mind. I was a tomboy.

I grew up in a rural Texas town. The only movie theater was forty miles away, and my parents didn't travel unless it was to go to the grocery store and back. I was fortunate to have the daily company of two sisters close to my age, which meant I could easily go an entire summer off from school without getting lonely and needing to see any of my girlfriends. So, I was basically out of touch with anyone but my family for two entire months. That is how the first day of sixth grade almost turned into the worst day of my preteen life.

Two weeks before school started, my mother took me shopping for the usual school clothes, just like she did every year. As usual, I had to be dragged to the bright, fluorescent-lit department store in the next county, and then practically forced to try on clothes. I never once glanced at the dresses on the circular silver racks or showed the slightest interest in any shoes other than those that could be tied with laces. I quickly learned to regret my lack of attention and enthusiasm for this particular back-to-school shopping trip.

The first day of school began like any other school year. I left the house dressed in my new clothes, carrying my purple notebook under one arm, eager to see my friends after two months apart. I couldn't wait to tell them about the new baby calf we were bottle-feeding or that I had nearly broken my arm in July climbing the tallest tree I'd ever conquered.

But from the moment I walked up those concrete steps to the junior high school, I knew something was horribly wrong... with ME.

My friends were huddled together in a circle, and the first thing I noticed was that most of them were carrying purses—some white, some hot pink, some brown leather. I didn't even own a purse. Four of them were wearing sandals with heels—we're talking lime green—with the tips of their pink-painted toenails peeking out! I immediately looked down at my plain white sneakers and felt out of place.

A boy we'd all known since kindergarten walked up and tapped my friend Morgan on the shoulder. She tossed her blond hair to the side just as he grabbed the back of her thin, frilly blouse. Then he popped the elastic on the back strap of her bra and ran away laughing. Morgan pretended to be mad, but I could tell she was somehow pleased. The other girls started laughing and teasing Morgan by saying that he liked her.

Somehow, without my even knowing it, over the summer our whole class had graduated from grade school to junior high—complete with new wardrobes, crushes on boys, and bra-popping. I no longer knew what planet I was on.

I hadn't given the idea of needing a bra a single thought. I looked down at the front of my shirt. It looked no different than it had this time the previous year. There was nothing there that needed support, for sure. I think the phrase "flat as a pancake" was one my mother had used to describe me.

The bell for first period rang before I could ponder this further. But already I was feeling like my whole world had changed overnight, and no one had bothered to clue me in.

My first class was P.E., but not the P.E. of my previous years. The gym of the junior high included locker rooms and showers, and we were issued polyester shorts and t-shirts to wear. The teacher informed us that from here on out, we'd be wearing these during gym class. In absolute horror, I clutched the uniform tightly to my body and numbly made my way to the locker rooms to change. I looked around me as all of my friends took off their shirts, gabbing about stuff the whole time like, "How cute is Devin this year?!" and "Did you know that he's going out with Chelsey?" All I could do was stare at the forty or so bras glaring at me from every angle. I was obviously the only girl in the entire sixth grade, perhaps the Entire World of Sixth Graders, who hadn't gotten the memo: Sixth grade meant girls wore bras.

I huddled next to a locker, hoping to get my shirt off and the uniform on without drawing attention to the fact that I wasn't wearing a bra. It didn't work, of course.

Morgan saw it first. "Where on earth is your bra?"

I swallowed and looked up as a group of six girls gathered around me.

"I... I...," was all I could muster.

Whispers rushed around the room and echoed off the tall ceilings, and I could feel my heart beating so hard against my chest I was sure everyone could see it, right there where my bra should have been.

"I forgot it," I said. Yep, I could really think on my feet.

"How could you forget a bra?" one of the girls asked, snickering over her shoulder at the others.

I didn't know the answer. All I knew is that I was now blushing in places I never thought possible.

As the day wore on, so did the rumors about what I didn't have on. Boys ran up to me and brushed their hands across my back in the hall between classes, shouting to each other that it was true. Nothing there to snap.

My so-called circle of friends closed their circle, and I was quickly on the outside looking in. I hung my head and hunched my shoulders as best I could to make viewing my chest as difficult as possible. And I secretly vowed to get even with my mother for not knowing about all this and for not preparing me like the other girls' mothers obviously had done. I had never felt this alone—or this foolish. I had missed the boat that carried the rest of my class to the shores of sixth grade, leaving me behind; me and my braless, boobless, purseless, high-heeled-sandal-less self.

Last period could not have come soon enough. I took a seat in the back and prayed the math teacher would not call on me for anything or draw attention to me in any way. I made marks on my spiral notebook, indicating to myself the number of people who had actually spoken to me since P.E.—and behind my back certainly didn't count. I was up to three, and one of those was the janitor.

That's when a redheaded girl named Maureen picked up a pencil that had rolled off my desk and handed it to me. I nodded my thanks without looking up or even really moving. In fact, I was beginning to master the ability of breathing without even the slightest rise and fall of my upper body.

"Listen, I heard what happened this morning."

So even Maureen had heard. She was the least popular girl in the whole class. She was taller than everyone else, weighed more than most eighth graders and had probably been wearing a bra since she was a toddler for all I knew. Her face was already covered in zits, something most of us girls hadn't begun to deal with yet. Most of the kids were either afraid of her or ignored her. I had always tried to be nice to her, but not in an overly friendly way that would get me cast out of the in crowd. A lot of good that had done me. One underwear mistake, and I was now on my own.

I allowed myself to slightly turn toward her. "I just forgot it, that's all." I was sticking to my story—it was all I had.

Maureen smiled at me. "Some people can be really mean." She probably knew that better than anyone.

"Yeah," I said, fully realizing that by now, some of the other girls had noticed I was carrying on a conversation with Maureen.

"I've got an extra one in my gym bag if you need it," she said.

I thought it was the nicest thing anyone had said to me in years.

Then we exchanged glances, each of us looking at our own chests, then at the other's. Let's just say Maureen's C cup wouldn't have been the best fit for me. My body wasn't even in training bra mode yet.

We began to laugh. In fact, we couldn't stop. Classmates around me rolled their eyes. The teacher gave us the look that said, "Quiet down or else," but we couldn't stop.

Sitting there, I realized I loved the way Maureen's laugh sounded, full and real. I liked her smile and the way she was far beyond caring about what others thought of her. I liked that nothing about her was fancy and that she carried a backpack. I liked that she wore jeans and sneakers like mine, and that her t-shirt was just like the ones I'd seen at Wal-Mart on the clearance rack. Her bra might not have been the right size for me, but everything else about her suddenly seemed like a perfect fit.

By the end of last period, I finally let the stress of the day fade away. I no longer cared what everyone else thought I should be wearing. I didn't really need a bra, so why should I be forced to put one on everyday until I was ready?

After class, Maureen and I walked down those junior high concrete steps, and I stood with her as she waited for the bus, our chests out and heads high.

And frankly, I didn't care who noticed—anything.

~Kathy Lynn Harris
Chicken Soup for the Girl's Soul

Confessions of a Four Eyes

Could we change our attitude, we should not only see life differently,
but life itself would come to be different.
~Katherine Mansfield

I made it all the way to fifth grade before anyone (besides me) realized that I couldn't see twenty feet in front of me. Our school had vision screenings every year, but somehow I had managed to fake good vision and pass the tests.

But then in the fifth grade, I got busted. It was my turn to go into the screening room, and I nervously took my seat in front of the testing machine. The nurse told me to look into the little black machine and tell her which direction the letter E's legs were pointing. Barely able to make out the black blob of an E, I strung together a guess: "Right, left, left, up, down, up, left, right." I looked up at her.

She squinted her eyes and studied my face for a moment. Then she said, "Could you repeat that?"

I panicked. I'd never been asked to repeat it. And I hadn't memorized the guess I'd just made up. I was trapped. So, I peered into the machine again and made up another sequence of guesses. I glanced over at the nurse, who was leaning forward with a stern frown on her face.

"You have no idea which way they're facing, do you?" she asked.

"Not really," I confessed.

"Can you even see the E at all?" she asked.

"Sort of... no," I admitted.

"Then why didn't you just say so?" she demanded.

I didn't respond. I thought the answer was obvious. Glasses in the fifth grade were a social death sentence. I assumed she knew this, but apparently it had been a very long time since she had been ten years old.

So she sent me home with a note for my mother that said I needed to visit the optometrist because I'd failed the vision test. The trip home that day was very slow.

My mother (who wears glasses) said it would all be just fine. It wouldn't hurt a bit, she said. But I wasn't worried about pain—I was worried about looking like Super Geek.

The next day, my mother dragged me to the eye doctor's office, where I flunked with flying colors. I picked out a set of frames and tried to believe my mother when she said they looked really good on me. The doctor said the glasses would be ready soon. But I wasn't ready, and I didn't think I ever would be.

When the glasses arrived, the eye doctor put them on my face and walked me out onto the sidewalk in front of his office. When I looked up from my shoes, I was borne into a whole new world—a world filled with crisp images, bold colors, and sharp detail everywhere I looked. Suddenly I noticed the beautiful outline of crimson leaves on trees. I could see the details of people's faces long before they were standing right in front of me. I could see my mother smiling as she watched me see the world in a whole new way.

"Glasses aren't so bad, are they?" Mom asked.

"Not bad at all," I thought to myself. On that first day, they were a miracle.

Then Monday morning came, and I had to face the kids in my classroom. And it happened, just like I feared it would. A mean kid pointed at me in the middle of math class and yelled, "Four eyes!" But at that same moment, looking through my new glasses, I could see all the way across the room that the kid who had said it had an awfully big nose.

Life has a way of balancing itself out sometimes.

~Gwen Rockwood
Chicken Soup for the Preteen Soul 2

Chapter
3

Preteens Talk

Family Matters

*Families will live on through the stories we tell our children
and grandchildren.*
~Carolyn J. Booth and Mindy B. Henderson

Perfect, I'm Not

> *Life is an adventure in forgiveness.*
> ~Norman Cousins

"Owwww!" Robert yelled, backing away from me. "That hurt!"

"What do you mean? I just hit you with my jacket!" I said, laughing. Robert was the cutest boy in class, and I had a major crush on him. I hadn't meant to hurt him; I wanted him to like me. Besides, it was just a lightweight jacket.

But Robert didn't act like someone who had been hit with a lightweight jacket. He was crying and holding his left shoulder.

"What's going on?" our sixth grade teacher, Mr. Mobley, asked.

"My shoulder... it hurts!" Robert groaned.

The next thing I knew, Robert was heading to the nurse's office. And I, bewildered, was marching back from recess and into our classroom with the other kids.

We started our spelling lesson, and I tried to pay attention as Mr. Mobley read the words for our weekly practice test.

Then someone knocked on our classroom door. When Mr. Mobley opened the door, a student volunteer from the office handed him a note. Every pair of eyes was riveted on Mr. Mobley. A note from the office usually signaled big trouble for somebody. This time, the somebody was me. Mr. Mobley looked up from the note and said, "Julie, Mr. Sinclair wants to see you in his office right away. He says you should take your belongings with you."

Oh, no! I was being sent to the principal's office. What would my parents say? With all eyes now turned in my direction, I dragged myself over to the coat hooks and grabbed the offending jacket. Embarrassment floated around me like a dirty cloud of dust.

How could a stupid jacket hurt anybody? I wondered as the door clicked shut behind me. I slid my arms through the jacket sleeves and slipped my hands into its pockets. Huh? My right hand closed over a hard, round object. I pulled it out. I had forgotten that my brand new Duncan Imperial yo-yo was in my pocket. I felt my legs weaken. So I had hurt Robert not with my jacket, but with my yo-yo. As I crossed the courtyard to the principal's office, I prayed, "Please don't let Robert be hurt too badly. And please don't let Mr. Sinclair call my mom."

When I reached the office, the school secretary ushered me in to see the principal without making me wait—not exactly a good sign.

"What happened, Julie?" Mr. Sinclair asked. He came out from behind his big wooden desk and sat on a chair next to me.

"We were goofing around... and... I hit Robert on his shoulder with my jacket. I... um... I guess I had this in my pocket." I opened my palm to show him the shiny red yo-yo I'd bought with my allowance. "I'm sorry. I'm really sorry. I was only teasing. I didn't mean to hurt him." Little snorting sounds were coming out of my nose now, and my shoulders were heaving with barely suppressed sobs.

"I know you well enough to believe you. But Robert has a knot on his shoulder that's about the size of your yo-yo. His mother is very upset. She's taken him to the doctor."

My head hung so low, it nearly touched my knees. More than anything, I wanted to melt into a puddle and trickle away under the door.

"I'm sure you didn't mean to hurt anyone," Mr. Sinclair went on. "But because Robert was injured, I have to send you home for the rest of the day. Please wait in the outer office until your mother comes to pick you up."

My eyes widened. "Now I'm going to get it!" I thought.

I had plenty of time to think while I waited for my mother. I was always trying to be the "perfect student." Straight A's and praise from my teachers were rewarded with more praise and affection at home from my parents. "What will happen now?" I wondered. I had never been in trouble at school before.

Ten hopelessly long minutes later, my mother opened the door to the office. Her face looked serious. "Come on," she said. "You can tell me about it in the car."

During our short ride home, I told her the whole story. I'd been teasing Robert because I had a crush on him. I hadn't meant to hurt him. We pulled into our driveway. "I'm s-s-sorry, Mom," I said. My body tensed, ready for the punishment I knew I deserved.

Mom leaned toward me, and I sucked in my breath, waiting to see what would happen. Would she yell? Would she slap me? I really didn't know what to expect.

My mother put one arm behind me and reached across in front of me with the other. Then she wrapped me tightly in a hug.

"I never told any of you kids this," she said, "but I did something even worse when I was in elementary school. I bit a boy on the arm—on purpose. I got called to the principal's office, too." What? My mother, who never did anything wrong, had bitten a boy at school? The thought was too funny. I caught her eye. "I guess we're just a couple of troublemakers, aren't we, Honey?" Mom said with a smile.

"I guess so," I said. In spite of the tears streaming down my face, I started to laugh. Pretty soon, Mom was laughing, too.

The next day, Robert was back at school, recovered except for a little tenderness. As soon as I saw him, I apologized, and our lives went back to normal.

But something important had changed. I had learned that life goes on, even when you make a mistake, and that a child can grow up to become a wise adult even after doing something foolish or hurtful. And to my great surprise and relief, I learned that I didn't have to be perfect to be loved.

~Julia Wasson Render
Chicken Soup for the Preteen Soul

21

My Brother, Ben

I am as my Creator made me, and since He is satisfied, so am I.
~Minnie Smith

When my brother was born he looked different from other babies. The doctors told my parents he had Down syndrome. Everybody, including my parents and relatives, started crying. I was only three at the time, so I wasn't sure what Down syndrome was, but I knew it wasn't good. I also knew that I finally had the baby brother I wanted, even if he wasn't perfect. The doctors said Benjamin might need help doing simple things such as walking, talking, eating, and interacting with people. I was told I would need to be extra careful with Ben, and that I might someday have to stand up for him and protect him. Of course, none of these warnings fazed me; I knew from the second I laid eyes on him that I loved him.

As Benjamin and I got older, we were always together, always helping each other. After Benjamin learned to walk, we wanted to get him to jump, run, and move around. Since Ben liked to follow my lead, his therapist or Mom would have me do the exercise first, and then Ben would try to do it. That procedure worked better than just anybody showing him how to move. Following me was Ben's way of saying he loved me.

A few years ago, I went away with some friends for the day. About five of us were just sitting in the van, and we started talking about our siblings. My friends were saying how stupid their siblings were and what they did to agitate them. I hadn't said anything; I was just listening in amazement. I had never thought there were brothers and sisters that just didn't get along. Suddenly I said, "I love my brother."

I said "love" proudly because it was true. All my friends thought I was a little weird, but they all knew Benjamin and how sweet he was. I was glad I told my friends I love my brother. He's the best little brother, and he loves me right back.

I would describe Ben as a very cute little nine-year-old boy that would do anything for anybody. If people tease him because he has Down syndrome he doesn't scream and call them names. Instead, he tries even harder to become their friend.

There are no second thoughts in my head when I hear people making fun of Ben. I go right up to them and explain that Ben has Down syndrome and that life isn't as easy for him as it is for us, that if you give Ben a chance he'll be the best he can be at whatever it is you want him to be.

I think Ben is perfect just the way he is. I will always love Ben, and he will always love me, no matter what.

~Donata Allison
Chicken Soup for the Teenage Soul IV

22

Our Christmas Secret

Oh what a tangled web we weave when first we practice to deceive!
~Sir Walter Scott

I was Christmas Eve when my sister and I decided to open our presents before our mom got home from work. She usually came home about an hour after we got home from school, which we thought was plenty of time to sneak a peek at the gifts under the tree. Since my sister was older, and that put her in charge, she opened the first gift while I was ordered to stand guard at the big picture window in our front room. I was to report any suspicious activity or persons, namely our mother.

I was so excited that I could barely stand still. I also couldn't keep my eyes on the window very long. My head moved from the window to my sister and back to the window again. I felt like I was watching a ping pong match.

"All right!" my sister shouted. She pulled out a jewelry box. "You know what that means, don't you?"

I jumped up and down. "Yeah, it's my turn!"

"No," she said. "It means that there must be some jewelry under here." I watched my sister rummage through the presents under the tree trying to find one she thought was small enough to be a necklace or earrings.

"Hey, that's not fair!" I whined, stomping my foot.

"Are you watching for Mom?" is all that she said. I couldn't do anything except stand guard as she opened present after present. Finally, when my sister's curiosity was satisfied and she had finished wrapping her last present back up, we traded places.

My heart hammered so hard that it felt like my chest was moving in and out. My sister reminded me to be careful so I wouldn't tear the paper, and to wrap the present back up the same way that I had found it.

After unwrapping a few presents, I found it faster to open one end of a present and peek inside. "Cool! Mom and Dad got me headphones for my stereo!"

I pulled the headphones out of the box and was about to put them on when my sister shouted, "Quick! Wrap it back up! Mom's coming!"

My heart hit the floor along with the headphones when I heard what sounded like glass crushing. I knew it was my mother coming down our gravel driveway. My body was as frozen as a snowman.

"Come on!" My sister's face was as white as the paint on the wall.

I shoved the headphones back in the box but my hands were shaking so much that I tore the paper trying to wrap it back up. My sister was yelling at me, which only made my hands shake more. I heard the jingle of keys and the doorknob rattle. I thought I was going to wet my pants! My heart pounded harder as I tried to get the tape to stick.

"Just shove it under the tree and put some presents on top of it!" my sister shouted as she ran to stall my mother.

I had just finished burying the package with my headphones in it when my mother came into the front room. I jumped up and said, "Hi, Mom!" She smiled at me and said, "Hi," back, but didn't appear to suspect a thing. My heart began to slow as I took a deep breath. That was close. Too close!

On Christmas morning, my sister and I smiled for pictures and gave award-winning performances when we opened our presents—again. "Headphones!" I exclaimed. "Thanks, it's just what I wanted." After everything had been opened, my sister and I looked at each other, and our eyes met. Our secret was safe, but somehow Christmas morning didn't feel the same.

My sister and I never opened our Christmas presents early again. I don't know if it was that opening our gifts for the second time just wasn't as much fun as the first time, or if we came too close to getting caught and didn't want to think about what our mother would have done to us.

I also learned something that year about my mother. I found out that she wasn't as dumb as I thought she was. Maybe it was the lack of squeals on Christmas morning or the torn wrapping paper that tipped her off. For some reason, all of the packages for our birthdays, which she usually hid at the top of her closet shelf, never appeared. I never did find out where she hid them.

~Lori Menning
Chicken Soup for the Preteen Soul

My Little Brother

It was a stormy Saturday afternoon when my mother took my five-year-old brother, Christopher, and me to a new enormous toy store she had read about in the newspaper. "So many toys," the advertisement had shouted in full and flashy color, "that we had to get a huge warehouse to fit them all!" Christopher and I couldn't have been more excited. We ran across the parking lot, through the cold and biting rain, as fast as our little legs could carry us. We left our mother outside to battle with the frustrating umbrella, which never worked when she wanted it to.

"Christine! I'm going to find the Lego section! There's a new pirate ship I want, and I have four dollars! Maybe I can buy it!" Christopher exclaimed and ran off excitedly. I only half heard him. I took a right turn and, to my wide-eyed delight, found myself in the midst of Barbie World.

I was studying a mini mink coat and doing some simple math in my head when suddenly an earthshaking clap of thunder roared from the storm outside. I jumped at the noise, dropping the accessory to the floor. The warehouse lights flickered once and died, covering the stuffed animals, matchbox cars and board games in a blanket of black. Thunder continued to shake the sky and whips of lightning illuminated the store for seconds at a time, casting frightening shadows that played tricks on my mind.

"Oh no," I thought, as my stomach twisted and turned inside of me. "Where's Christopher?" I ran up and down the aisles through the darkness, panic filling my small chest and making it difficult to breathe. I knocked into displays of candy and tripped over toys, all the while frantically calling my brother's name. I needed to know he was all right, but I could barely see. Tears of frustration and fear trickled down my face, but I continued to run. I found Christopher in the Lego aisle. He was standing alone, perfectly still, tightly clutching the pirate ship set. I threw my arms around him and hugged him until he couldn't breathe. Then, I took his hand in mine and we went to find our mother.

Years later, on a beautiful Tuesday morning, I was leaving my computer class on my way to sociology. As I drove, the radio filled my ears with horrendous news: A hijacked plane had crashed into the Pentagon and two other planes had crashed into the World Trade Center. Fires, destruction, and chaos echoed across the East Coast from Washington to New York City. My first thought was of Christopher.

My brother had joined the Air Force just a year earlier, and he was stationed in Washington. I had grown used to seeing him for a few days every five months or getting 2:00 A.M. telephone calls just to let me know he was alive and well. But as the Towers collapsed and newscasters began to cry, I was overcome with the need to see Christopher, to hug him and make certain he was all right. I pulled over to the nearest pay phone and frantically dialed my grandmother's number. Christopher would call her to let the family know what was happening. The operator asked me to hold; it seemed as if everyone in the nation was on the telephone, trying to get through to loved ones. I felt the familiar panic steal my breath as I waited for a connection. Finally, I heard my grandmother's voice.

"He's fine. He's okay. They might have to move him out. He might be called to help somewhere in some way, but he's fine, Christine. He called and told us he was fine."

I spoke with my grandmother for a few more minutes. Boston was evacuating its tallest buildings. Schools were closing. Some workers were being sent home. All airplanes were grounded. The sky was silent and crystal clear. As I hung up the phone, I began to cry from relief. "It was silly of me to worry about Christopher," I scolded myself. He was an adult. He stood 6'2" while I, his big sister, never hit 5'5". He could fit both of my hands into one of his. Christopher could take care of himself. But I realized at that moment that there is still a piece of my heart that will always run to try to protect him, no matter how big he may be or where in the world he is located. That same piece will always remember the five-year-old boy standing in the dark toy store with the pirate ship clutched to his chest, saying, "I knew if I just waited here, Christine, you would find me."

~Christine Walsh
Chicken Soup for the Teenage Soul on Love & Friendship

24

I Love You, Lindsey

Sometimes, when one person is missing
the whole world seems depopulated.
~Lamartine

My heart drooped as I forced my unwilling body into the car. It would be miles and miles until we reached our painful destination, where we would have to leave Brandy, my older sister. Brandy was leaving home to serve as a volunteer in the Americorps.

My dad revved the car engine and we left the house. Soon, the streets turned into highways, and we were closer to having to say goodbye with every mile. My heart continued to sink lower.

All of the bittersweet memories of growing up with my sister flowed into my brain... from when I was young and Brandy telling me that my troll was evil, to when I copied her every move because I admired her so much, to when the painful teenage years came and her life was too busy for her younger sister. The anger came back to me too, the anger that came when suddenly my life was too immature for hers.

I didn't understand why my old companion only talked to me when I did something wrong or when I annoyed her. Why did her new clothes make my childish apparel look babyish? These questions and many more stayed in my head.

Now I knew that my time with her was very limited. Throughout the ride she made wicked remarks that hurt, but this time I knew what they meant. They still hurt me even though I knew that this was the agonizing way that she pulled herself away from us, in preparation for her leaving us at last.

When we reached the place where Brandy was to stay, we did everything that we could to stall the painful goodbyes that awaited us, until all that was left were the goodbyes. The tears began to stream down my cheeks as she hugged me and told me the words that I hadn't heard in a long time.

"I love you, Lindsey."

I sobbed an answer in response. The family was all tears. We all piled into the car and pulled away. Brandy, still crying, turned her back and walked off. In that one moment, I loved her more than anything in the world. She looked like an adult as she walked away, but as the light from the headlight lit her face, I saw the little Brandy that still wanted to be my friend and still wanted to be a part of the family.

On the long drive home that night I felt as though I had left my heart with Brandy. I couldn't imagine life without my big sister or the endless chatter that Brandy always supplied. Would life ever be the same?

It has taken some time, but now I know that life goes on, even though Brandy isn't here. She is always with me because a part of her is in me and always will be.

~Lindsey Rawson
Chicken Soup for the Preteen Soul

25

Pale Dawn of a New Day

I had always had a feeling of dread deep down within me. When it happened, it hit me with such surprise that you would never know that I predicted it.

At the time, I did not know how lucky I had been. I would lie awake at night before falling asleep, hearing my parents fight and yell at each other. Although neither hurt the other, it always ended up with my mother crying... and that always scared me. I suppose they never thought I could hear them, and they hid their tension from me as much as possible.

One afternoon, my mother told me she needed to talk to me. I never thought of the obvious. My mother sat down next to me on our gray couch with my father on the other side. My mother calmly explained that they no longer enjoyed each other's company and that they would be getting a divorce. As I fought back tears, my mother continued to tell me how they had tried so hard to make it work—for me. They said they never wanted to hurt me. They could never know how much it did. They said that even though they no longer loved each other, it did not affect how much they loved me, and that my dad would move to an apartment nearby, close enough for me to walk to.

I could no longer hold back the tears, and I ran sobbing to my room, slammed the door, and collapsed on my bed. I clutched my pillow to my chest. Everything flashed through my head, everything I could have done to make it work. I lay there, never wanting to leave the safety of my room, not wanting to accept my new reality. I stared for hours out my second story window, not really thinking... not really looking, just sitting out of the reach of my own mind.

I woke up the next morning and trudged to the bus stop. At school, my friends comforted me and I hated it. I was trapped, and everyone made it worse. My friends tried to make me feel better, but they always reminded me of how it had been before. I began to associate the pain of the situation with them and it hurt. I pushed them away, enjoying the solitude.

I found I loved writing, though I shared my compositions with no one. Everything had been turned upside down. No one knew. I only suffered internally. I hid inside myself, remaining the same person externally. My parents, in separate places, acted as though nothing had happened, and that outraged me even more.

My father did not move to an apartment nearby. Instead, he stayed in our house. It was my mother who left and moved to the other side of town.

I was informed my father had fallen in love with a new "companion." It hurt immeasurably to watch my father preferring to hold her hand instead of mine. My mother had found one as well, and moved in with him. I would spend long hours at her house waiting to leave, feeling alone and ignored. I thought I would die.

My writings began to be terrible stories of girls in far worse situations than I, making me feel more fortunate. I moved back and forth between homes every week, and when anything went wrong, it was always the other parent's fault. I woke up every morning to meet the dawn, which seemed to be paler and more frail than ever before. Alone, not allowing anyone into my reality, I cried.

Now, two years later, I almost never cry, for I feel that I have cried my share. I have accepted and moved on. I've become closer to both of my parents, and throughout the trials they go through, I now feel involved and helpful. My mother's companion recently left her and she came to me in friendship, looking for support.

But it still hurts quietly somewhere inside of me. I will never forget, and I will always miss how it was. Even though they fought, we were together and I never appreciated it when we were. As for now, I realize that there is nothing more beautiful than the dawning of a new day and that I must go on.

~Katherine Ackerman
Chicken Soup for the Preteen Soul

Best Friend

During sixth grade, the world seemed to be far from my fingertips. I was under the rule of my "evil" parents—my mom and my stepdad. Somehow, I felt like they thought I could never do anything right. I struggled with my grades in history class, and kids at my school thought I was a little bit of a nerd. Overall, I was lonely, disgusted with myself and felt like life had dealt me the worst hand of cards! Then, as if God had heard my cry of despair, I was sent some company—however, it was not exactly what I had in mind.

At Christmas, my stepsister, Courtney, moved in—my new so-called best friend. My mom and her dad had gotten married after my parent's divorce. Although I had known her for five years, I had only seen her a few times—but even on those rare occasions, each time, there had always been tension between us, and we had never gotten along.

For the first month after she came to live with us, I ignored her as much as I could and almost completely avoided getting to know her. I had made up my mind that I hated her from the second that she had walked through the door. I did not know how to live with another person my age. Frankly, I wasn't up for the competition. I had been an only child for eleven years, and I wasn't about to let some prissy blond thirteen-year-old girl move in and take away all of my hard-earned attention! Oh no, not me.

Of course, my parents forced me to talk to her, which didn't change how I felt at all. Without a thought about how she might have felt about having to move in with us, I went about becoming the most mean-spirited sibling in the history of mankind. I plotted and schemed about how I could make her life miserable and drive her away. I stole her possessions, ate her "secret" stash of chocolate, and even framed her, so that she would end up having to do more chores than me. I became her worst nightmare.

One day after school, we started fighting as we walked home. We entered the house and began our homework while we still argued over a topic I can't even remember now. Then she did it! She called me a name that I will not mention. Anger rose up into my chest, and I looked around for something to throw at her. I found a pile of my school textbooks nearby. I picked them up and threw them at her, one at a time, with a force that amazed even me. After I ran out of textbooks, I was still in a rage, so I searched for something else to throw at her that could cause damage. I saw our new telephone out of the corner of my eye. I ran to it, ripped it out of the wall and chucked it at her without even a thought of what could come later.

My parents were horrified to find two extremely upset girls when they arrived home, not to mention the debris of their brand new phone scattered on the floor along with my textbooks. That afternoon's occurrences were explained, and then Courtney and I were both sent to our rooms while they thought up a punishment.

Once I was able to calm down, I sat in my room and remembered all of the other times that I had lost control and injured Courtney physically and emotionally since she had come to live with us. I could not think of any legitimate excuse for me to treat her the way that I had, and I become conscious that I had acted out all of these heinous crimes for ridiculous, selfish reasons. I started to search my heart and recognized all of the wonderful qualities she possessed. With a shock, I realized that not only was I not lonely anymore, Courtney had actually brought a lot of fun into my life.

That night, my parents lectured me for hours. My sentence was that I had to pay for another phone, in addition to having lots of extra chores added to my normal duties. As I walked back to my room, I could hear Courtney crying in hers. For the first time in my life, I was sincerely sorry for the pain I had caused her. I stood in front of her door, trying to think of ways to apologize. Even though I was afraid I might be too late, I went in anyway. I found her in the dark, weeping on her bed. Because of her brokenhearted crying, she didn't hear me enter her room or my whispered apology. But when I lay down and wrapped my arms around her to comfort her, she knew how truly sorry I was.

After that night, she and I called a truce. Eventually, we began to get along better and even started hanging out together. Somewhere along the line, we discovered that we could get up on the roof of our apartment complex through a window in the laundry room. Having our own little private place to share secrets or just to talk, as we lay up on the roof looking at the stars or getting some sun, has been a special thing that we have shared for the past few years.

Over time, I have realized that it's really pretty nice having a sister and a friend to go through life with. Courtney and I have shared many triumphs and tragedies together, and she has been my rock through it all. Now, I can't imagine my life without her. She and I rarely argue anymore, and when we do, the disagreements are short-lived for we have learned that it is better to be happy and loved than it is to win the argument.

I can truly say that after all we've been through, my stepsister Courtney is my very best friend.

~Bethany Gail Hicks
Chicken Soup for the Girl's Soul

27

Tippy

How lucky I am to have something that makes saying goodbye so hard.
~From the movie Annie

I was late for the school bus and rushing to get ready. My dog, Tippy, ran past me. "What's your big hurry?" I wondered, annoyed. It wasn't like he was late for the school bus like I was. When he got to the front door, he lay down in front of it—his way of asking to be petted. I ignored his shameless begging for affection, hurdled over him and sprinted for the waiting yellow bus.

That afternoon, I jumped out of the bus and dashed up the driveway. "That's odd," I thought. Tippy was usually outside, barking an entire paragraph of "hellos" as soon as he saw me come home. When I burst through the door, the house was quiet and still. I dumped my coat and backpack on the floor. Mom silently appeared. She asked me to sit down at the kitchen table.

"Honey, I have some sad news that I need to tell you. This morning, while you were at school, Tippy was hit by a car and killed. He died instantly, so he didn't suffer. I know how much he meant to you. I'm so sorry," said Mom.

"NO! It's not true!" I was in shock. I couldn't believe her. "Tippy, come here! Come on, boy!" I called and called for him. I waited. He didn't come. Feeling lost, I wandered into the living room. He wasn't on the couch, so I had no pillow for my head while I watched cartoons. Mom called me for dinner and I rambled to my place. He wasn't hiding under the table, so I had to eat all of my dinner. I went to sleep that night, but I didn't cry. I still couldn't believe that he was gone.

When I got off the bus the next day, the silence grew deafening. Finally, my sobs bubbled up and erupted like lava from a volcano. I felt like I was also going to die from having my insides shaken apart, and I couldn't stop crying or end the thoughts that kept going through my head. *I should have trained him better. If I had been home, I could have called him away from the road. I didn't even pet him when I left. How could I have known that was my last chance?* I cried until I felt hollow inside.

My parents bought a new dog named Tinker Belle. I didn't care. I was busy giving hate looks to people speeding in their cars. *They shouldn't drive so fast that they can't stop when they see a dog in the road.* My parents still got the silent treatment from me. Why hadn't they made sure that Tippy was tied up? I was mad at Tippy for getting killed, and I was mad at the entire "dog kingdom" for not knowing enough to stay out of the road.

I didn't share my dinner with our new dog. She was too small to be my pillow for television, and her bark was squeaky. When she begged for attention, I pushed her away. I spent a lot of time alone, feeling sorry for myself and wondering, "Why did this have to happen to me? What am I going to do now? Why did Tippy have to die?"

Time passed, and against my will, I started to understand some things. It felt like waking up a little at a time. I realized what little control any of us have over what happens to a dog. Sure, we can train them and tie them up and do everything right, but bad things can still happen. And, in spite of us, good things can happen too. That's life. The best way to deal with the hard times is to figure out what I need to do for myself to get through them when they come, and to remember that hard times pass.

I also discovered that my capacity to love didn't die with Tippy. I became awfully lonely when I was trying to harden my heart. I began to realize that there were good things about Tinker Belle that were different from the good things about Tippy. I couldn't rest my head on her little body, or pretend to ride Tinker Belle the way I had done with Tippy, but I could fit Tinker Belle into my backpack and carry her around.

I learned that I need to pet my dog whenever I can—and to really enjoy my time with her! Now I pet my dog slowly when I have the chance and quickly when I'm in a hurry, but I never leave the house without petting her.

I now deeply understand the "Circle of Life." Everyone is born, everyone dies, and that's the way it is. If dogs never died, there would be no room for others like Tinker Belle... and her five cute puppies!

Best of all, I realize that Tippy left behind all of my good memories of him. And they come to me every time I call!

~Christine Armstrong
Chicken Soup for the Preteen Soul

28

The Bigger Man

What we see depends mainly on what we look for.
~John Lubbock

Although I am the younger brother, I have always felt like my brother's keeper. Even now that Brian is seventeen and I am sixteen, I still watch out for him because, though chronologically I lag behind, my parents have encouraged me to take the nurturing role.

You are probably thinking that my brother is either mentally or physically handicapped—he is neither. I'm not sure if his "nature" was born or created. My mom has treated him like fine china ever since his birth. Maybe it's because there were problems with his delivery. She often recounts how the umbilical cord became wrapped around poor Brian's neck, and how he could have strangled on it had the doctor not rescued him with a Caesarean delivery. Although Brian went full-term, his tiny size reflected his future fragility within the family.

After Brian's birth, my mom grew more religious. She made all sorts of deals with God to watch over her tiny infant in exchange for her spiritual devotion. A year later, I was born. I was the quintessential bouncing baby boy. From the way my mom describes it, I practically walked home from the hospital and was eating solid food by the time I was a month old—probably raw steaks.

My mom saw my larger size and strong constitution as a sign

from God that I was to be a kind of guardian angel for my older brother, Brian. It was not at all strange to see me reminding Brian to tie his shoes, or asking the waiter for another glass of water for him. No one ever thought our reverse relationship was odd, since by the age of five I was a head taller than him anyway.

I could never leave the house without my mom telling me to drag Brian along. He was smaller and fit in better, size-wise, among my group of friends. But defending and protecting him became tiresome. And then there were those luscious desserts my mom would bring home to fatten up poor little Brian. I would watch him longingly while he delicately sipped at chocolate milkshakes and critically picked at the strawberry cheesecakes I would have gladly scarfed down if given half the chance. And when my hand, through no power of my own, would drift toward a tempting slice, my mom would reprimand me, saying, "That's for Brian. You don't need that."

And so, though I loved my older brother, I began to resent him as well.

One day our school sponsored a pumpkin-carving contest. First prize was one hundred dollars, and I knew just how I would spend it. There was a brand new Sega game—*Dungeons and Dragons*—that I was dying to own. Realizing that my birthday and Christmas were nowhere in sight, I decided that the first place stash definitely had to land in my pocket.

I ran out to the market and picked out the nicest pumpkin I could find. Then I set out to draw on the most gruesome face. In my third grade mind, I had created a Pumpkin Freddy Krueger, of sorts. Now all I had to do was carve the face. That's when it dawned on me. With my big clumsy mitts I'd surely screw it up. I thought of Brian's smaller, delicate hands and knew he was the man for the job.

I pleaded with Brian to carve the pumpkin, but wise fourth grade businessman that he was, he asked for a cut.

"How does eighty-twenty grab you, Bri?"

"You mean eighty for you and only twenty for me? Forget it. It's either fifty-fifty or nothing."

Quickly doing the math in my head, I figured out that even if I split the first prize fifty-fifty, I'd still have enough cash for the game—and I knew this pumpkin had to win the grand prize. It was just so awesome. So I gave in to Brian's demands.

With skillful hands Brian carved the blood-slashed face, and then we sat back to admire our handiwork. Together, we had created the goriest Halloween pumpkin ever, which I was sure nobody could deny.

Then the unexpected happened: We came in second. Unfortunately, second prize was only fifty dollars, and I needed every penny of that to buy the game. The day of the awards ceremony, the principal handed over the money to me because Brian was home sick with some fragile kid's illness like a cold or something equally pathetic.

God, I thought to myself, if he really wanted to win, he would have been here today. And I need the whole check to pay for the game. I was able to justify stealing the cash from under poor Brian's runny nose. With hardly a thought, I ran over to my friend Glenn's house and his mom drove us out to the mall to buy the game. I felt no guilt that night as Glenn and I pounded away on our controllers having the time of our lives.

That night when I got home, I found Brian lying on the couch watching TV.

"Did we win?" he asked.

I tried not to flinch as I stared down at his cheesecake-eating, milkshake-sipping face, and I answered, "No."

I hid the game over at Glenn's and never told anyone in my family about it. I thought it was pretty pathetic anyway that Brian never found out. What a dork.

As Brian got older, he began to loosen up a little and Mom did, too. He actually had a growth spurt, and though I'm still a head taller than him, he's wider from side to side now—guess those milkshakes finally caught up with him.

With Brian's hearty physique and persistent begging, Mom even gave in to allowing him to attend college away from home. I played my usual role in helping him pack, although I had mixed emotions about seeing him go. I'd miss having the geek around.

As I rifled through one of his desk drawers, a photo of our gruesome pumpkin dropped to the floor. We both laughed as we looked at the ridiculous face we'd thought was so frightening. Then Brian said, "And we actually thought that squash was going to make us rich. We didn't even win third prize."

A kind of guilt rose up in my throat, and I felt a confession of sorts was needed.

"Brian, uh... hate to admit this, but we kinda did win. In fact, we kinda won second place."

"Huh? Is that so?" he said scratching his head. Brian rustled through his desk drawer again and pulled out another photo of our pumpkin with a blue satin second-prize ribbon flanked across its bloodstained face.

"I took this the day after the contest, Worm Brains. What did you think, I didn't know? I was the photographer for the school newsletter, Einstein."

"What? You actually knew and didn't say anything? Why?"

Brian looked down at his half-packed suitcase, and then up at me. "Don't you think I knew how Mom always forced you to watch out for me, and don't you think it made me feel really small? I'm supposed to be the bigger brother, Numbnuts."

Actually, I'd never thought about how Brian might feel; it just always felt like I was the one being put out. Everyone always seemed to care more about Brian. Everyone needed to protect poor, pathetic Brian—I was just the big, dumb bodyguard for hire.

"I wanted, just once, to do the same for you," Brain said, interrupting my thoughts. "Just once, I wanted to be the bigger man."

"It always looked to me like it would be way better being smaller," I confessed. "I wanted to be the one who everyone wanted to take care of."

"You're such a jerk," Brian said, shaking his head. "Do you know how lousy it feels when everyone thinks you're so lame you can't even take care of yourself? It sucks!"

We sat silently on Brian's bed, just staring at one another. As dense as we were, something finally sunk in. How pathetic. We'd each lived our lives secretly wishing to be the other.

"I'm sorry, Bri," I mumbled.

"For what? About that pumpkin? Forget it."

And then another uncomfortable silence lay upon us. I wanted to tell Brian how much I loved him and how cool I thought he was. But I felt really dumb saying it out loud. Then Brian kneeled over, scooped up his football and threw it at my head. I lunged for him and pounded him in the gut. This was the way we communicated our understanding.

~C. S. Dweck
Chicken Soup for the Teenage Soul on Love & Friendship

This Old Chair

"**M**om! I'm home!" John slammed the door and dropped his books on a nearby chair. "Something smells good." With his nose in the air, he followed the sweet aroma into the kitchen.

"Hi, John, home already?" His mom turned around. She had just placed a sheet of fresh-baked cookies on the counter near the open window.

John reached for a cookie and looked outside. Shafts of sunlight slanted through the clouds, tempting the flowers to bloom. A robin sang a bubbly song. It was the kind of day that made John feel warm inside. Pop-Pop, John's grandpa, who lived with them since Grandma had died, came shuffling through the door. With his face to the floor as if looking for something he mumbled, "When the robin sings..." He paused, trying to remember what he had started to say.

"Spring is here," John's mom finished the sentence. "And you know what that means."

"Sure," John volunteered. "Our annual fishing trip is coming up."

Amused, Pop-Pop winked at John while heading straight for the cookies.

"I was thinking more of our annual spring cleaning," John's mom suggested. "Tomorrow, John, you have no school and I can use some help, okay?"

"Okay, okay," John agreed reluctantly.

The next day John and his mom cleaned the house. They cleaned upstairs, downstairs, inside, outside, until everything was spotless. Exhausted, they sank into the couch. Wearily pointing to Pop-Pop's chair, John's mom exclaimed, "Oh my! That old chair has got to go. We'll buy Pop-Pop a new one."

It was true, John had to agree. The chair was unsightly. It was faded and worn and in some places even torn.

"John, come and help me." John's mom sprang to her feet. "We'll take the chair to the curb. Tomorrow the garbage truck is picking up on our block."

As they attempted to move the chair, Pop-Pop worked his way through the door. Seeing what was happening, he quickly blocked their way. "Oh, no!" he protested. "You can't take my chair."

"It's old... It's worn...," John's mom argued, a slight edge to her voice.

"No," Pop-Pop persisted, trying to push his chair back into place.

"But Pop, we'll buy you a new one," John's mom tried to persuade the old man.

"I don't want a new one," Pop-Pop's voice trembled.

"I give up." John's mom let go of the chair. "We'll discuss it tonight when Matt gets home." Matt, John's dad, was still at work. With a sigh of relief, the old man sank into his chair and closed his eyes.

"Pop-Pop, why won't you let us get rid of the chair?" John asked when his mother left the room. "It's so old."

"You don't understand, John." Pop-Pop shook his head from side to side and after a long pause he said, "I sat in this chair, with your grandma right here, when I asked her to marry me. It was so long ago, but when I sit in this chair and close my eyes I feel she is near." The old man tenderly stroked the arm of the chair.

"It's amazing," John thought, "how Pop-Pop can remember things from the past. In the present, he forgets almost everything." John sat down on the floor by Pop-Pop's feet and listened as the old man went on.

"And the night your father was born, I sat in this chair. I was nervous. I was scared when they placed the tiny babe into my arms, yet I was never happier." A smile now flashed across his old face.

"I think I'm beginning to understand," John said thoughtfully.

"Many years later," Pop-Pop's voice broke and he paused a

moment before he continued, "I sat in this chair when the doctor called and told me that your grandma was ill. I was lost without her but the chair gave me comfort and warmth." The old man's sadness seemed to grow as he recalled that fateful day.

"I'm sorry, Pop-Pop." John looked at his grandfather and said, "I do see now. This is not just any old chair. This chair is more like a friend."

"Yes, we've gone through a lot together." Pop-Pop fumbled for his handkerchief, and trumpeted into it.

That night, however, when John and Pop-Pop were asleep, John's mom and dad carried the chair out to the curb. It was a starless night. Spring had retreated and snow fell silently from the black sky and covered Pop-Pop's chair with a blanket of white.

The next morning, when John came downstairs, Pop-Pop stood by the window and looked outside. A tear rolled down his hollow cheek. John followed the old man's gaze and froze. Snow-covered, the chair stood at the curb out on the street. The clamor of the garbage truck pulling up to the house shocked John into action. He ran outside. "Wait! Don't take that chair," he shouted, flailing both arms in the air as he rushed to stop the men from hauling the chair away. Then he ran back inside and faced his mom. "Look at Pop-Pop, Mom. You can't throw out his chair." John swallowed hard before going on. "This is not just a chair. This chair has been with Pop-Pop for a very long time. This chair is like a friend."

John's mom turned and looked at the old man. Slowly she walked towards him. With her middle and ring finger, she wiped away a tear. And then she took the old man's face in both her hands and said, "I'm sorry, Pop-Pop. I guess... I just didn't realize how much the chair meant to you. John and I will bring your chair back inside."

They brushed off the snow with their hands and heaved the chair back inside. They placed it next to the fireplace so it could dry. John's mom stepped back then, and as if seeing the chair for the very first time she mused, "Mm, I guess it does give the room a certain touch of character."

And John and Pop-Pop wholeheartedly agreed that the living room had been rather dull without this old chair.

~Christa Holder Ocker
Chicken Soup for the Preteen Soul

Chapter 4

Preteens Talk

Heartbreak and Growing Up

Nothing is a waste of time if you use the experience wisely.
~Auguste Rodin

30

Broken Heart

If you're never scared or embarrassed or hurt,
it means you never take any chances.
~Julia Sorel

I was six years old when I experienced my first heartbreak. The boy's name was Matthew. He was older than me, a cool eight-year-old. His hair was the color of beach sand and, as it blew in the wind at recess, his bangs would fall over his dark blue eyes in exactly the right way. He played touch football with his friends while I watched him from the tire swing on the playground.

"Someday I'm going to marry Matthew," I told my friend Nicole as I pumped my legs, my golden ponytail flying behind me as I swung higher and higher.

Nicole sighed. She was my very best friend, content to follow me anywhere. It was always me who would drag Nicole along to a new adventure, her protesting and kicking, and me pushing on resolutely. I wasn't afraid of anything. Well, almost anything. I was terrified to let Matthew know that I had a huge crush on him.

I drew pictures for him every day at school. I liked to draw houses with big apple trees in the yard and a smiling yellow sun in the top corner. I dreamed of living in one of those houses with Matthew, where every morning we would go outside and pick apples from the tree and eat them for breakfast. My teacher, Madame LeBlanc, liked to look at my drawings.

"Très bien," she would say, admiring one as I stood by her desk, beaming with pride. "C'est pour qui?"

"Mon papa," I would answer, telling her it was for my father when in reality it wasn't. It was for Matthew, but I didn't have the guts to give it to him.

By the last day of the school year, I had made up my mind. Toward the end of the day, as jubilant and rowdy kids emptied out their desks and tidied up the classrooms, I quietly asked my teacher for permission to get a drink from the fountain. Behind my back, I clutched my very best drawing, with my name written in very small letters on the bottom.

I knocked on the door to the third grade class. The teacher opened the door and peered down at me, a little first grader with an earnest smile. She smiled back, looking mildly puzzled. She asked if she could help me with anything.

I thrust the picture at her. "Pour Mathieu," I said, using the French version of his name. Then I turned and scampered back to my class. My palms were sweaty and my heart was beating. I wondered what he would think of my drawing.

The school bell rang then, and laughing kids poured out of the school, with weary but relieved teachers waving goodbye and telling them to have a good summer. I gave Madame a hug before I left and waved goodbye to my friends. My grandpa was waiting for me outside.

He grinned as I slid into the front seat and reached over to help me fasten my seat belt. His blue eyes twinkled. "How was your last day, Ashleigh?"

I shrugged. "Fine." My stomach was turning somersaults and I still felt awed at what I had done. However, I didn't want to talk about it with my grandpa. It was my secret.

Our car slowly crept along the driveway in front of the school, behind the big yellow school buses waiting to take kids to their summer freedom. Our car stopped right in front of the big steps leading to the front door. On them sat Matthew and another third grader, a tough-looking girl named Alice with a messy black ponytail and dirt-smeared cheeks. Matthew was holding my drawing in his hands. My window was rolled down, and I could hear them laughing at it. A tear slid down my face, and I wished with all my heart that I had never given him that picture. My stomach felt like little green men were kicking it from the inside.

The car rolled forward, and we left Matthew and Alice behind. I could hear their cruel laughter ringing in my ears. Grandpa drove on in silence, glancing at me as I hunched up in a little ball on the seat, tears falling from my eyes.

"Ashleigh, what's the matter?"

I shook my head and a sob escaped. Out poured the story. Grandpa listened, trying hard to understand me through all my sobs and sniffling. He said nothing, just nodded and patted my knee.

"Come on," he said. "I'll buy you a milkshake."

Before long we were sitting in a booth, with me slurping on a vanilla milkshake and Grandpa stirring his coffee, deep in thought. He finally put down his spoon and took a sip. Looking me squarely in the eyes, he spoke.

"Ashleigh, I want you to know one thing and never forget it: I love you very much, and so does Grandma, and your mom and dad and your little brothers. No matter what happens, we will always love you," he explained. He took my small hand inside his larger, calloused one. "Forget about Matthew. He doesn't deserve you! You're a smart, pretty, and kind little girl, and someday, a long time from now, you will meet somebody very special who will love you, too. But you have to wait for it, until you're grown up."

I stared into my milkshake. "But how will I know?" I whispered.

Grandpa squeezed my hand. "You'll know."

I nodded, and we got up and left the restaurant. Already I was beginning to think ahead. Nicole was coming over the next day, and we were going to go swimming at the pool. Maybe my little brothers would want to build sand castles in the sandbox when I got home. I had the whole summer before me. I had my whole future before me.

~Ashleigh Dumas
Chicken Soup for the Teenage Soul on Love & Friendship

31

The First Day of Middle School

That's the way things come clear. All of a sudden.
And then you realize how obvious they've been all along.
~Madeleine L'Engle

My stomach was tied in knots, and I could feel the sweat soaking through my t-shirt. My hands were clammy as I spun the face of my combination lock. I tried and tried to remember the numbers, and every time I thought I had it, the lock wouldn't open. Around and around went the numbers, left, right, right, left... which way was it supposed to go? I couldn't make it work. I gave up and started to run down the hallway. As I ran, the hall seemed to get longer and longer... the door I was trying to reach was farther away than when I had started. I began to sweat even worse, then I could feel the tears forming. I was late, late, late, late for my first class on my first day of middle school. As I ran, people were watching me and they were laughing... laughing... laughing... then the bell rang! In my dream, it was the school bell. But as I sat up in bed, I realized that it was my alarm clock jarring me awake.

I was having the dream again. I started having the dream around the end of sixth grade, and as the start of seventh grade drew closer, the more I had the dream. This time the dream was even more real, because today was the morning of the first day of seventh grade.

In my heart, I knew I would never make it. Everything was too different. School, friends—even my own body.

I was used to walking to school, and now I had to walk six blocks to the bus stop so that I could take the bus to and from school. I hated buses. They made me carsick from the jiggling and the smell of the fuel.

I had to get up for school earlier than in the past, partly because of having to be bussed to school and partly because I had to take better care of myself now that I was in my preteen years. My mom told me that I would have to shower every morning since my hormones were kicking in—that's why I perspired so easily.

I was totally uncomfortable with my body. My feet didn't want to respond to my own directions, and I tripped a lot. I constantly had a sprained ankle, wet armpits, and things stuck in my braces. I felt awkward, smelly, insecure, and worried I had bad breath on a full-time basis.

In middle school, I would have to learn the rules and personalities of six different teachers instead of just one. There would be different kids in all my classes, kids I didn't even know. I had never made friends very easily, and now I would have to start all over again.

I would have to run to my locker between classes, remember my combination, open it, put in the books from the last class, and take out different books... and make it to the next class all within five minutes!

I was also scared because of some stories I had heard about the first day of middle school, like being canned by the eighth graders. That's when a bunch of eighth graders pick you up and put you in a trash can. I had also heard that when eighth grade girls catch a new seventh grader in the girls' bathroom alone, they smear her with lipstick. Neither one of these first day activities sounded like something I wanted to take part in.

No one had ever told me that growing up was going to be so hard, so scary, so unwelcome, so... unexpected. I was the oldest kid in my family—in fact, in my entire neighborhood—and no one had been there before me to help lead me through the challenges of middle school.

I was on my own.

The first day of school was almost everything I feared. I didn't remember my combination. I wrote the combination on my hand, but my hand was so sweaty it came off. I was late to every class. I didn't have enough time to finish my lunch; I had just sat down to eat when the bell rang to go back to class. I almost choked on my peanut butter and banana sandwich as I ran down the dreaded hallway. The classrooms and the teachers were a blur. I wasn't sure what teacher went with which subject and they had all assigned homework... on the very first day of school! I couldn't believe it.

But the first day wasn't like my dream in another way. In my dream, all of the other kids had it together and I was the only one who was the nerd. In real life, I wasn't the only one who was late for classes. Everyone else was late, too. No one could remember their combination either, except Ted Milliken, the kid who carried a brief-case to school. After most of the kids realized that everyone else was going through the same thing they were going through, we all started cracking up. We were bumping into each other in our rush to get to the next class, and books were flying everywhere. No one got canned or smeared—at least no one I knew. I still didn't go into the girls' bathroom alone, just in case. Yeah, there was laughter in the hallway, but most of it was the laughter of kids sharing a common experience: complete hysteria!

As the weeks went by, it became easier and easier. Pretty soon I could twirl my combination without even looking at it. I hung post-ers in my locker, and finally felt like I was at home. I learned all of my teachers' names and decided who I liked the best. Friendships from elementary school were renewed and made stronger, and new friends were made. I learned how to change into a gym suit in front of other girls. It never felt comfortable, but I did it—just like everyone else did. I don't think any of us felt very comfortable.

I still didn't like the bus; it did make me carsick. I even threw up on the bus once. (At least it was on the way home, not on the way to school.) I went to dances and parties, and I started to wonder what it would feel like to be kissed by a boy. The school had track tryouts, and I made the team and learned how to jump the low hurdles. I got pretty good at it, too.

First semester turned into second, and then third. Before I knew it, eighth grade was just around the corner. I had made it through.

Next year, on the first day of school, I would be watching the new seventh graders sweating it out just like I did—just like everyone does. I decided that I would feel sorry for them... but only for the FIRST day of seventh grade. After that, it's a breeze.

~Patty Hansen
Chicken Soup for the Preteen Soul

32

Ready or Not

I was wiped out. After two hours of grueling swim practice, the zipper on my bag felt like it had been cemented shut. I couldn't even lift the towel. I was starving, but how was I going to pick up a fork? I flopped down on the bench in the locker room, barely able to hold up my head. Breathing in and out took what little energy I had left. Maybe my skanky, bleach-smelling hair didn't need to be washed tonight? Couldn't I just dry off and shuffle home to dinner? I hauled my weary body to the mirror and tried to get away with "styling" my mop with the towel.

"Oh, no! What is that under my arm?" I wondered, quickly yanking my elbow down to my side before anyone else could see. Cautiously, with every attempt to appear calm, I slowly lifted my arm just high enough to peek underneath. Yep! It was there! A hair! A black, plain-as-day-so-everybody-could-see hair! I quickly scanned the locker room to figure out if any of the girls had noticed that my body had completely changed. Whew. No one seemed to have noticed.

Suddenly I had energy. I couldn't wait to run home, so I threw on only the most necessary clothes, which wasn't easy, since I wasn't willing to separate my elbow from my hip. Taking no time to chat, or even complain about the workout, I whisked out of the locker room and sprinted home.

"Mom! I'm home! I'll eat later!" I shouted as I flew up to my room. I almost ripped my shirt off and stood about a millimeter away from the mirror, carefully examining this newfound evidence that

I was becoming a woman. I was thrilled that I was actually, finally, growing up, but I was terrified that I was actually, finally growing up. The thoughts starting streaming through my brain...

Oh, I can't wait to swagger into the locker room and show the other girls the real bra I am surely going to need soon, now that I have armpit hair. It will be so wonderful to be allowed to shave my legs, which my mom will just have to permit now that I have armpit hair. But how long will it be before I absolutely have to wear deodorant so I won't gag the kids next to me in class? Armpit hair is kind of cool, but the thought of hair... um... down there, still freaks me out. Will that show through my swimsuit? And then there is the whole period thing, which is particularly a pain for swimmers. What if I get my period when I have a swim meet? What if it's the state championships? What if my first period comes and I don't know it until I get up on the starting blocks in front of the whole team, all their parents, all the other teams, and people start pointing and whispering? As all these thoughts whizzed through my head, I slumped down on my bed. Why couldn't I get all the cool stuff that comes with growing up and just say, "No thanks," to all the stuff I wasn't ready for?

"Hey, Snotwad," my older sister Elizabeth said cheerily as she walked into my room.

"Don't you ever knock?" I rolled over on my side to face the wall.

"What's up with you?"

"Nothing."

"Yeah, I believe that," she laughed. "Seriously, what's up? You look stressed."

I turned toward her and whispered into the pillow, "I have hair."

"Yeah, and your point is?"

"No," I rolled my eyes, "not the hair on my head!"

"Oh, you got a pube? Congratulations!"

I groaned. "No, not a pubic hair, thank goodness—an armpit hair."

"Just one? That's no big deal."

I jerked up to a sitting position and glared at her. "Yes, it's just one, but it wasn't there one day and suddenly today it is, and it's long and black, and I've never had one before, and I don't want hair anywhere else, and what if I get my period, and..."

"Hey, hey, slow down!"

My sister gently sat down on the bed next me and put her hand on mine. "It'll be okay. You got one hair under your arm, but it's not that big a deal. One hair doesn't mean you're suddenly going to have a triple-D chest and get all hairy everywhere. It all takes a whole lot more time than that."

"Yeah?" I looked at her.

"Yeah," she said softly. "It takes years for all that stuff to take place. Didn't you listen in health class?"

"Sort of. Mostly I was embarrassed, listening to Mr. Williams talk about breasts and stuff."

"Gross. At least I had a woman teacher, Mrs. Kilgore."

"Elizabeth, what was it like for you... you know, changing?"

"Don't you remember how I washed my face like ten times a day? My face was always a big grease bomb. At least no one can see your pit hair."

"That's true," I said. "When did you get hair?"

She looked at the ceiling, trying to recall. "I don't really remember. I got sort of wigged out when it happened, like you are now, but I got over it."

"Do you think Mom will let me buy a real bra?"

"For what? You don't have anything to put in one!"

My face turned scarlet, and my eyes started stinging. Elizabeth leaned over. "Hey, I'm sorry. Don't worry—you'll get breasts. I didn't really need a bra for a long time, but it might be different for you. Just don't go crying to Mom about 'When am I ever going to get breasts?' When I did that, she made up this totally lame little poem, 'Hush little pancake, don't you cry; you'll have cupcakes by and by.'"

We both fell back on the bed from laughing so hard. When we caught our breath and sat up, I looked at her in a new way.

"Wow, am I ever glad you're the oldest!"

Elizabeth tried looking serious. "Are you done freaking out now?"

"Yeah, I guess. It's just that I don't know what to do!"

"Don't worry, I'm here for you, and I'll bet your friends will be, too," she reassured me. Then she suggested, "If you start going nutty about something, go online and find the info you need."

"Going online would be good. And I suppose I could ask Mom about some of it, too. I can't stop all this body stuff from happening anyway, huh?"

"Nope, but then, you don't want to be a little kid forever, do you?"

"No, I guess not."

Of course I didn't. I was just freaking out about it all being out of my control. My body was going to do things, and I didn't get to say a thing about it! Growing up would be a whole lot easier if you could order the changes you were ready for, when you were ready for them.

I did change over time, and I was okay. My big sister and I are closer than ever before, and I think it all started with that conversation. She really helped me by being kind and understanding when I was panicking. I only wish that I had a little sister. I'd like to help her know that the first armpit hair is no big deal.

~Morri Spang
Chicken Soup for the Girl's Soul

Not My Boyfriend

There is only one thing more painful than learning from experience,
and that is not learning from experience.
~Laurence J. Peter

"Jason likes you," Kellie said, as she sat down next to me on the bus. "He wants to know if you'll go out with him."

"Jason?" I said, surprised. After all, I knew who he was since we rode the same bus to and from school, but I didn't really know him. He was in seventh grade—a year younger than me—and we had never even talked to each other. I had certainly never thought of him as a boyfriend or anything.

"I'll have to think about it," I said. I really couldn't imagine being his girlfriend. But, on the other hand, some of my friends had boyfriends and others had guys who liked them. I wanted one, too.

When the bus reached my stop, I practically danced down the street to my house. "You must have had a good day," my mother smiled when she saw me.

"I did!" I said. "Jason likes me! He wants to be my boyfriend!"

After explaining to my mother who Jason was and reassuring her that, no, I wasn't too young to have a boyfriend, I decided to say yes to Jason. "It will be the most romantic day of my life," I said to myself.

The next morning, I spent extra time on my hair and put on my favorite perfume. Kellie and Jason were both already in their seats when I got on the bus.

"Well?" Kellie asked, leaning over the back of her seat. I wondered why she, another seventh grader I knew only as someone on my bus, suddenly had such an interest in my love life.

"Yeah, I guess I'll go out with him," I responded, trying not to sound too excited.

She got up and headed to the back of the bus, where Jason sat with some other seventh grade guys. "She said yes," she told him. Suddenly, the bus erupted with chants of, "Whooooo... Carol and Jason." I didn't pay any attention. "I have a boyfriend," I thought to myself all the way to school. "I'm going out with someone!"

Before going into school, I stood talking to some of my friends. Of course, the topic of conversation was my new boyfriend. Every few minutes, I glanced over at Jason who was talking to his friends at the other end of the sidewalk.

I wasn't sure if I should go over and talk to him. I wanted to, but the only thing I could think of to say was "So, you're my boyfriend," and since I didn't want to sound stupid, I stayed put.

Finally, I saw him walking over. He was looking right at me, so I broke from my friends and smiled at him. He didn't smile back, though. Instead, he stopped and said, "I don't want to go out with you."

"You don't?" I choked out, trying to catch my breath.

"No," he replied. "Kellie was bugging me yesterday. She kept asking me who I like, so when she asked if I liked you, I said yes just to shut her up. Sorry if you thought I was serious."

Then the bell rang and everyone headed inside. I felt as if someone had punched me in the stomach. All the guys snickered as they walked by me and I wanted to just crawl into a hole—to go home, get into bed, and never leave my room again. I walked slowly into my classroom, wondering why the day that was supposed to be the most romantic of my life had turned into the most humiliating.

I couldn't concentrate all day, and I stared into space through most of my classes, but none of my teachers seemed to mind. The story had gotten around, so they probably all knew what was wrong.

When I got home I slammed the door of my room and cried for hours, not because that particular guy didn't want to go out with me, but because I felt so stupid to have created an entire romance with Jason based on a conversation with Kellie. When I realized that I wasn't upset about Jason not being my boyfriend, I stopped crying.

In the six months that remained until I graduated from eighth grade and moved on to high school, I never talked to Jason again. In fact, if we hadn't been on the same bus, I probably would have forgotten all about him. I'm glad I didn't, though. The next year, a girl I knew slightly told me that she knew a guy who liked me.

"If he likes me, he'll have to tell me himself," I replied.

And he did.

~Carol Miller
Chicken Soup for the Preteen Soul 2

Rediscovery

Seven. The age of ballet lessons and Barbie dolls, of learning to add and subtract simple numbers; the time when the family dog is your closest companion. Seven. The age of innocence.

I was a typical-looking child. I had long, straight brown hair that fell past my shoulders. My almond-shaped hazel eyes were always full of adventure and curiosity. And I had a smile that could brighten a bleak winter day.

I was a happy child with a loving family and many friends, who loved to perform skits on home videos. I was a leader in school, not a follower. My best trait was my personality. I had imagination. But what made me special was not seen from the outside: I had a special love for life.

At age twelve, my life had a huge breakdown. It was then that I developed obsessive compulsive disorder (OCD). OCD is a disorder that is the result of a chemical imbalance in the brain. People with OCD don't think the same way as people with chemically balanced brains. People with OCD do rituals. I started to wash my hands ten times an hour to avoid germs, and I constantly checked my kitchen oven to make sure that it was off. This way of life for me continued for four agonizing years, and by then, my OCD had led to depression. I was no longer the happy little girl I had been.

In the tenth grade I finally confessed to my mother that I was suffering from depression along with my OCD. I couldn't take the emotional pain anymore. I needed help if I wanted to continue living.

My mom took me to a doctor the same week. I started taking medicine that would hopefully cure my OCD and depression. Over the course of a few months, the medicine did help the OCD. I stopped doing rituals. I no longer took four showers a day to avoid germs. But one thing didn't change; I still was overwhelmed with depression. I still was constantly sad and I started to believe that my life no longer mattered.

One autumn evening two years ago, I hit rock bottom. I thought that my life no longer had meaning, because I no longer brought joy to other people like I did when I was little. I decided suicide was the only solution to my depression problem, so I wrote a suicide note to all my friends and family. In the note I expressed that I was sorry for deciding to leave them, but that I thought it was for the best. As I was folding the note, my eyes fell on a photograph. It was a picture of an adorable little girl with natural blond highlights in her brown hair from spending so much time in the sun. She was wearing her red soccer uniform and held a biking helmet in her small hands. She had a carefree smile on her face that showed she was full of life.

It took me a few minutes to realize who the girl in the photo was. The photo had been taken one weekend at my uncle's house when I was seven years old. I almost couldn't believe that smiling child was me! I felt a chill go down my spine. It was like my younger self had sent me a message. Right then and there I knew I couldn't kill myself. Once I had been a strong little girl, and I had to become strong like that again.

I tore up my suicide note and vowed that I would not rely only on my medicine to help my depression. I would have to fight the depression with my mind, too. I could make myself happy again.

It has been two years since I "rediscovered" myself. I am OCD- and depression-free. I still take medicine to keep my disorder at bay, but the real reason I am healed is because I took action and refused to let depression ruin my life. I learned a lifelong lesson: Never give up. Life is good. Everyone has challenges in life, but everyone can survive. I am living proof of that. Also, it is important to keep smiling, because in the end, everything will work out.

Of course my life can still be a struggle, but I pull through with a smile on my face. I know I can't give up on life. I am here for a reason. Sometimes, I think it was strange that I had to look to who I was as a little girl in order to regain faith in myself at age eighteen. But I think everyone can look back on their early years and see that it was then that they knew how to live in peace and happiness.

I have plans for myself now. Once I graduate from high school this spring, I plan on going to college to major in journalism. I want to be a writer someday. And I am prepared for whatever challenges life may bring. I have a role model to look up to for strength, and who is guiding me through life. My hero is a seven-year-old girl, smiling back at me from a photo on my desk.

~Raegan Baker
Chicken Soup for the Preteen Soul

35

Suffocating

I am suffocating
And I just need to breathe.
I'm smothered under pressure
I must be relieved.

Nothing I do is right,
Nothing they say is fair.
I cry and scream and throw a fit,
But no one seems to care.

Nobody will listen,
To what I have to say.
My life is not important,
Yet I'm living every day.

I can't do what I want.
I cannot stay out late.
Here I sit and write this poem
To release my pain and hate.

I'm confused and I'm alone
I'm lost inside my mind.
No one will search beyond my looks
To see what they might find.

So many thoughts confuse me,
Feelings I can't perceive,
In this time of adolescence
And I just need to leave.

None of it makes sense
None of this seems real.
And no one understands
The emotions that I feel.

I'm still suffocating
And I still need to breathe.
I'm smothered under feelings
Let me be relieved.

~Marion Distante
Chicken Soup for the Girl's Soul

36

Moving On

If you don't like something change it; if you can't change it,
change the way you think about it.
~Mary Engelbreit

It was an early November morning when we said our final goodbyes and pulled out of my grandparents' driveway. I was leaving my lifelong home in Wisconsin and heading to our new home in Arizona. Crying as I waved goodbye, I thought about all of the memories I was leaving behind. I already missed my friends and family and we hadn't even reached the main highway. They had been everything to me. I simply had no idea how I was going to survive without them. I knew this would probably be one of the most difficult journeys of my life.

For the next four days, we drove and drove and drove until, finally, we pulled into the driveway of our new home in Arizona. I was surprised to see that all of the houses in our neighborhood were the same and that there was barely any grass in the yards. When we got into the house, everyone chose their new bedroom. That part was pretty exciting.

Over the next few days we unpacked and moved in. About a week later, my brother, Nick, and I started school. When we got home and compared notes, we discovered that we both hated it there. Especially me. I had just started going to middle school in Wisconsin, and now I was going back to elementary school because there were no middle schools in my city. It was really awkward, and I felt like I didn't fit in. At first, my brother and I were totally depressed, but we pressed on and tried to adjust, and over time it got better.

I was too shy to ask anyone to come over to my house, so I just waited until someone invited me over to their house. Finally, one day, a girl in my class asked if I could come to her sleepover birthday party. I was so excited, I couldn't wait to finally go somewhere other than my house.

The night before the party, I went to bed early so I wouldn't be tired the next night. Well, around 1:00 A.M., I woke up to get a drink. When I opened my door, all of the lights in my house were on. I thought that was kind of weird, so I checked my clock again to see if I had slept into the afternoon. It definitely said 1:00 A.M., so I went to my parents' bedroom and found my mom packing clothes into a suitcase.

"Mom, what's going on?" I asked. She motioned for me to sit on her bed. Then she told me the worst news I had heard since we moved. My great grandmother, who had leukemia, was in the hospital. My mom said that she didn't have much longer to live.

My family and I were always very close to my great grandma, so in our minds, there was only one option for us. That same morning, my brother, Mom, and I got on an airplane and flew back to Wisconsin. Sadly, we got there too late. Great grandma had died that morning at 9:30. So we stayed in Wisconsin and attended her funeral and visited our friends. I was really sad about the death of my great grandma, but I was also happy that I was able to visit everyone that I had missed so much.

Well, after ten days, it was time for us to go back to Arizona. I was so sad on the plane ride home, I tried really hard to hold back tears. I missed my friends and family, but most of all, I missed my great grandma. I never even got to say goodbye to her, and that hurt.

When we finally got back home, I became really depressed again. I cried almost every night. Every weekend, I'd talk to my friends on our cell phone. They were always talking about how much fun they were having and how they wished I was there with them. Every time

I would even think about my friends, I'd get so sad that it felt like someone had ripped my heart out and stomped on it. I missed them all so badly.

Over the next few months, I realized that I couldn't have my old life back, no matter how badly I wanted things to be the way they had been. Realizing this, I gained a lot of courage, and I started to go up to people and talk to them, and I actually made a lot of new friends.

Now, almost a year later, I am a lot happier than I was when we first moved. I feel a lot better now, and I have a lot of friends. I still miss my friends and family, and I would much rather move back to Wisconsin than stay here, but I know we can't.

I learned a lot over the past year. I'm a lot less shy and a lot stronger now. I realized that when I moved, I wasn't leaving my memories behind; I would just treasure them now more than ever before.

~Ellen Werle
Chicken Soup for the Preteen Soul 2

37

A Life Once Lived

When I was thirteen, I found myself at home alone after school every day while my parents worked until seven or eight o'clock each night. I was bored and I felt somewhat neglected. So I started hanging around with other kids who were at home unsupervised after school.

One day, I was at my friend's house and she had some other friends over as well. There were no parents at her house and mine were in Nashville; we had total freedom! As we sat there doing nothing, one of the guys pulled some marijuana out of his coat pocket. In this crowd, I was the only one there that had never tried it, so, under pressure to be cool, I did.

As the weekend approached, everyone was talking about a party at my friend's house. I ended up partying with people I didn't even know and had my first experience of being drunk and high. I was now ruining my life, but as far as I knew, I was making more friends and hanging with a different crowd. The only thing that concerned me was partying on the weekends and looking for something to give me a better high.

One day, when I was in the eighth grade, my best friend and I were bored out of our minds. We thought that it would be really cool to go to my house where no one was home, find the keys to my dad's car, and drive all over town showing off to our friends. When we ran a stop sign with a cop car right behind us, we were taken in for stealing my dad's car.

Things at school were equally as bad. I was suspended from school twice for fighting. The second time I was out for three days. I no longer cared about my grades and was literally failing school. I never looked at my parents' opinions as being important anymore. It seemed like I was always grounded, but I would sneak out of the house at night to see my friends. When my parents discovered that I was sneaking out, my dad no longer had any type of trust for me. I had put myself into a position of having no freedom whatsoever. No matter what, I was never happy, and my parents and I argued constantly. My life was falling apart.

No longer was I the girl who got good grades; no longer did I have parents who trusted me, or friends that really even cared. I lost all that; it was gone.

So one night I sat with a bottle of prescription pills, sure these pills were going to get rid of all my pain. It was late at night so I thought, "No one's at home so who's going to stop me?" I stared at the pill bottle with a deep feeling of hate toward myself. I never thought that an emotion like this could take over my life.

I began sobbing and tears were rolling down my cheeks. I wondered if anyone was going to care. I told myself that they didn't care now, so why would they care when I'm gone?

Then I heard a car door shut, and I knew my parents had come home. I quickly took as many of the pills as I could with a couple of drinks of water.

I sat on the couch with my dad, stepmom, and one of their friends. They had no clue what was about to happen. We were watching my favorite TV show. Then, the weirdest thing happened. I laughed with my dad for the first time in what seemed like forever. Suddenly, I no longer wanted to die. I realized that I loved my family and that they really loved me. Now what was I to do? I ran to the bathroom and made myself vomit up all the pills.

I lay awake all night thinking. I realized that my priorities were all wrong and if I kept up this behavior and kept hanging around the same people, my life would never improve. I recognized that I was the one who made my life what it was, so I also had the power to change it.

The first thing that I did was stop taking drugs and hanging around that crowd. Within days, I noticed a huge improvement in my self-esteem. Then, right after the first of the year, I switched schools so that I could get away from my "friends" who only cared about partying all the time. It wasn't long before I had made new friends and my grades improved. (I now have a 4.0 grade average—straight A's!)

The new choices I've made totally beat waking up with hangovers and not caring about where my life was headed. I made cheerleading this year and I'm having so much fun. Drugs never made me feel this high.

I'll never know if I was going to die that night, but I do know one thing; I'm glad I didn't. I learned from my mistakes and found that ending life completely is not the way to go. It is never too late to change your direction. Every day, every hour is a new opportunity to begin again.

~Brandi Bacon
Chicken Soup for the Preteen Soul

38

Jimmy, Jimmy

When I was in the seventh grade, I broke my leg skiing. The doctor described my injury as serious—a spiral fracture of the tibia that was fragmented in three places—and just barely spared me the surgery to put pins in my leg. The tradeoff was that I had to wear a cast from hip to toe for four months, the first of them in a wheelchair. The weather that winter alternated between snowy blizzards and mucus-freezing-in-your-nose cold, so Mom or Dad had to drive me anywhere I wanted to go. Since sledding, skating, going to the local McDonald's, and hanging out were my friends' favorite pastimes, I didn't get out much.

That left plenty of alone time for me to daydream and develop the biggest crush on a new boy in my class. His name was Jimmy and he was gorgeous. He had thick brown hair, dreamy dark eyes, a perfect complexion, and a great body. His slight Texas accent could charm anyone, and he was soooo nice. If only he would notice me! But how could he? I hardly ever got to see him outside of the classroom, and he seemed to like one of my girlfriends, Kim. Besides, boys tended not to "like me" like me, because I was taller than all of them. I hoped Jimmy wouldn't notice my height thing since I was sitting in a wheelchair or slouching over crutches all the time. I didn't dare tell anyone about my crush, not even my best friend. I wanted to spare myself the misery of being teased. The crush on Jimmy was my big secret.

One Saturday evening, I got the phone call of my life. It was my best friend, Jodie, calling to say that someone in our class liked me and wanted to ask me out, but he wanted to know if I liked him first.

"Well, who is it?" I asked Jodie.

"Jimmy," was the unbelievable reply.

I felt goose bumps crawl up the back of my neck to the top of my head. I nearly dropped the phone.

"Well, do you like him? Would you go out with him if he asked you?"

Doubt quickly crept its way into my thoughts. Paranoia set in. Perhaps this was some cruel trick by my friends to find out who I liked. After all, how could Jimmy like me? We'd never even spoken so much as a word to one another.

"I guess so," I tentatively replied. My stomach was getting queasy. I waited for the teasing to begin.

"You guess so? Well, do you or don't you like him? It's got to be one or the other," Jodie pressed.

"Yes, I like him," I replied with a little more enthusiasm this time, my secret finally out.

"Great! Can we come over now? Jimmy wants to ask you out tonight!" gushed Jodie.

"Uh... sure. Come on over."

When the doorbell rang about fifteen minutes later—an absolute eternity—I answered the door to find my friends on the front porch. The guys were around the corner, waiting to send Jimmy over. I stepped out on the porch with the aid of my crutches and closed the front door behind me. My friends were smiling at each other, celebrating their role as matchmaker, so excited to be a part of getting me together with my first boyfriend.

The girls left me alone on the porch so that Jimmy could ask me to go out in private. I waited there for him. I was anxious, nervous, and excited. My stomach uneasy, part of me still wondered if this could be some big joke. For the first time since I broke my leg, I was thankful to have crutches to support me.

I was as white as a ghost, more nervous than I had ever been. Jimmy rounded the corner and stepped up onto the front porch. Oh no. I wanted to hobble back inside and shut the door behind me. What have

I gotten myself into? How could I be so stupid? I was so caught up in Jimmy dreamland that I had neglected to ask Jodie, "Jimmy who?"

There stood Jimmy, so sweet, with a nervous smile and a love struck look. His red-freckled face seemed a little redder than usual. This wasn't my Jimmy. Not my big crush Jimmy. Not Jimmy of my dreams and daytime fantasies. It was the other Jimmy in my class, who I liked as a friend but most definitely did not "like" like.

I heard myself mutter a feeble, "I guess so," when he asked me to go out with him. What else could I do? How could I turn him down after he had prescreened his proposal through Jodie?

We didn't hang around very long on the front porch. As soon as I could, I made some lame excuse about how I had to go back inside the house because my parents would wonder where I was.

Once alone inside the house, I worried about what to do next. I certainly couldn't tell anyone about the mix-up. I'd never live it down. I decided to hide behind the excuse of my broken leg and my life as a social recluse, until I could figure things out. And there was the solution! I would only have to see Jimmy in school, and only in the classroom where we couldn't really talk, and most definitely could not kiss. How on earth could we go out under those circumstances?

I waited what seemed to be an appropriate length of time (about three days), offered my excuse to my girlfriend, Jodie, and asked her to break up with Jimmy on my behalf. I figured that since she helped me get into this mess, she should help me get out of it. Jimmy confronted me, flushed with anger, to confirm the breakup after Jodie told him. Slouching down lower on my crutches, I said something like, "Sorry. I hope that's okay with you." Lame. Lame. Lame.

Rumors floated around about me only agreeing to go out with Jimmy so I could say I had had a boyfriend... and about me breaking up with Jimmy because I was too afraid to kiss a boy. I suffered their laughter in silence and never told anyone about the case of mistaken Jimmy. My big crush remained my big secret, my first true love.

~Karen Lombard
Chicken Soup for the Preteen Soul 2

Who Said There's No Crying in Softball?

Toughness is in the soul and the spirit,
not in the muscles.
~Alex Karras

Our team was playing softball against a team that we were tied with for third place. I was toughing out the position of catcher, and we were winning. However, my knees started to feel not so tough. In the bottom of the second inning they had started to hurt.

I've had bad tendonitis in my knees, and I just couldn't take any more abuse to them that day. So I limped over to the manager, who is also my dad, and told him that my knees were hurting. I asked if he could have the backup catcher, Jill, catch for the rest of the game. He called Jill into the dugout and told her to put on the catcher's gear.

One of the other coaches overheard this conversation and came running over. I could tell that he was mad at my dad's decision because he was steaming like a whistling teapot.

He yelled at my dad, "Are you crazy? Jill can't catch—she has a huge cut on her finger!"

My dad explained to the coach about my knees.

"So what!" The coach rudely yelled at my dad.

Then he furiously walked over to me. His face was red, and I could feel my heart pounding in my chest.

"You'd better get that gear back on and get back out there right now. If you don't, I swear this will be the worst softball season of your life! Every game! Every game you complain about your stupid knees! If your knees keep hurting so much, I don't understand why you even play! You certainly aren't even good enough!" he screamed at me.

I couldn't believe what he said to me. Amazingly, I was able to choke through my tears, "I'm sorry! My knees hurt so bad! If I catch any more I'll collapse!"

"So what! Do you think I care?" he yelled.

By that time I was sobbing hard. The coach stormed off grumbling something over and over, leaving me in tears.

Later that night, I was lying in my bed thinking. A very important question came to my mind.

"Why should I continue my softball season if I don't even have any respect?" I asked myself.

Then, from somewhere deep inside my heart, I found the answer.

It doesn't matter what the coach thinks about me, it only matters what I think about myself. I love softball and I have a right to play, even though I may not be the best catcher in the world. That doesn't make me a loser. But I would be a loser if I believed what he said instead of believing in myself. I would lose my self-respect. No one, even the coach, can make me quit. All I have to do to be a winner is to keep showing up, sore knees and all. And I will.

~Amy Severns
Chicken Soup for the Preteen Soul

One Single Egg

Admitting errors clears the score and proves you wiser than before.
~Arthur Guiterman

I didn't think that I could take much more. I had to keep up with the other girls.

The target loomed closer and closer. Only a little further... ready... aim... splat! I let my missile sail through the air. Then the fear set in—I had to get away! Porch lights were being turned on.

"Separate," yelled Ashley. I passed two homes safely. When I reached the third house, I saw a face peer out of a window in a blur of motion as I sped past. I flew past the last house; I was almost home free. PHEW! I made it. My legs trembling, I watched as Sara, Ashley, and finally Carrie caught up. We hadn't gotten caught! Still, I didn't feel proud of my first "egging." I was filled with fear that we would still be discovered every second of my stay at Ashley's sleepover. Finally, my mom came to get me, and I was unusually silent on the ride home.

My friend Ashley and I had been born only one week apart. We were inseparable until the day her mom and dad decided that they would move to a new neighborhood. I lived for the times that my mom would take me over to her house. Everything went okay at first, but gradually Ashley made new friends and started acting like she didn't need me as much. I no longer felt like I belonged. Carrie and Sara would make it a point to talk about things that I couldn't relate to, like when they went to the mall without me. Slowly, I felt the close bond of friendship slipping away. I wanted to fit in, but I didn't know how.

It had been Sara's idea to go egg the house. She brought a brand new carton of eggs to the sleepover. It didn't seem like a very good idea, but I didn't want to look like a baby, so I decided I had better do it with them.

The day after the sleepover was bright and sunny, and I began helping clean our house, which was a weekend chore for me. My dad was also up, cleaning away. As I polished the furniture, my dad asked me what we had done over at Ashley's house. It must have been the guilt that caused me to tell him.

"You see, Dad," I began, "this is kind of funny, but we went and, uh... egged this house." My dad turned pale. Then he turned red. Then purple.

Please understand a few things here. One thing is that my dad is a cop. Two is that he is a juvenile detective, and he works with kids around my age who have broken the law. Three is that he was currently investigating about ten different kids who had just gotten into trouble for doing exactly the same thing that I had just done.

"Do you think that's funny?" he asked softly. "DO YOU THINK THAT'S FUNNY?!!" he roared. And then he really got mad.

Let's just say that it boiled down to him making me get into the car. As I sat there, sobbing, his purpose became clearer. As we got closer to Ashley's house, I pleaded, "No, Dad, no."

But he replied, "If you are adult enough to go throw an egg at someone's home, then you are adult enough to apologize for it." I gasped. This was even worse than I had thought. He wanted me to knock on the front door of the house we had EGGED! I just sat there in a blind panic.

As we pulled closer, he told me to point out the house.

"There," I said in a shaky voice as he slowed to a stop.

"I want you to come with me," he said.

As we walked toward the door, I was filled with dread. I rang the doorbell once and waited. It seemed like the longest twenty seconds of my life. A lady answered the door.

"Hi, I, uh, just wanted to tell you that I, umm... threw an egg at your house." I watched as her smile of welcome changed to a puzzled look. My dad quickly introduced himself and told her that I would clean up any mess that had been left. As we walked around the side of the house that had been egged, I began searching for damage.

"This had better be the right house," my dad growled. There was nothing visible on the house itself, and I could find no shells on the ground. Desperately, I began poking around in the tall grass. Then I started to wonder if I had been the only one to throw an egg.

Sure enough, I found the remnants of one single egg in the grass. The other girls had all dropped their eggs somewhere else. I picked up the shell of my one egg, but there was no evidence that the egg had ever hit the brick home. I apologized to the poor lady and promised never to do anything like that again.

As my dad and I made our way back home, he explained to me about what he had been putting up with at work from all of the other kids. "You are one of the reasons I can go into work every day and face the problems of others. If it weren't for you, I wouldn't be able to go in and see the children who are hurting and the ones who need guidance. When you make a choice like this, I wonder how I failed as a parent in guiding you the right way. It makes me wonder how anything I do out there could ever make any difference."

With that profound speech, there ended my life of crime. I understood why what I had done had disappointed him so much. More important, I knew that my dad still would love me, unconditionally, no matter what.

I apologized to him for disappointing him and for making a bad choice. I tried to become an example of the good that my dad fights for.

My friendship with Ashley was never quite the same after that, but I learned a valuable lesson and I grew up a little bit. Throughout the years, there were many situations with my friends where I had to make a choice that didn't make me the most popular, but I knew that my dad would be proud of me for making the right decision. That was enough.

I later followed in my dad's footsteps and became a police officer myself. When I first caught a group of kids "egging" a house, I was faced with bringing them home to their parents. One of the boys begged me to let him go... just that one time. He told me that I didn't know what he was in for from his dad. I told him that it wouldn't be as bad as he thought. He scoffed at me, until I said, "Listen, do I have a story to tell you...."

~Cheryl L. Goede
Chicken Soup for the Girl's Soul

Preteens Talk

The Popularity Game

Assumptions allow the best in life to pass you by.
~John Sales

41

Revenge of the Fifth Grade Girls

When sisters stand shoulder to shoulder,
who stands a chance against us?
~Pam Brown

A mother cannot force her daughters to become sisters. She cannot make them be friends or companions or even co-horts in crime. But, if she's very lucky, they find sisterhood for themselves and have one true ally for life. My daughters did not seem likely candidates for sisterly love. They are as different as night and day, and as contrary as any two girls living under the same roof can possibly manage.

My younger daughter, Laura, is smart, athletic, and good at most everything she tries. But for her, friendships are tricky. When, at seven years old, she was thrust into the world of lunch pals and sleepovers, she struggled to survive.

Catherine, on the other hand, sits at the top of the elementary school pecking order. A bright, popular, and beautiful fifth grader, she is usually surrounded by a bevy of adoring girlfriends. When you are in second grade, a word or nod from a fifth grade girl is the greatest thing that can happen. But Catherine and her friends seldom noticed her sister's valiant attempts to be noticed.

One hectic morning, while getting ready for school, both girls began begging for a new hairstyle. Sighing, I gathered brushes, combs, and pins and quickly created new looks. I braided Laura's wispy locks into a snazzy side-braid. I combed Catherine's shiny black hair into a sleek, French twist. They twirled in front of the mirror, pleased with what I'd done.

Laura bounced out the door, swinging her braid proudly. But at school, one girl pointed at her and whispered to the other girls. Then the girl walked up to Laura and asked in a scathing tone, "What's with the stinking braid?"

Laura crumbled. After getting permission from her teacher, she went to the bathroom, where she sat and cried in an empty stall. Then she splashed cold water on her face and bravely returned to the classroom—braid intact.

That afternoon, she broke my heart with her sad tale. How could I have sent her out wearing a stinking braid? How could I have set her back in her meager attempts to fit in with the other girls? I fought back my tears as I drove my girls home. Hearing her sister's sorrow, Catherine sat in stony silence, and as I often do, I wished they had the kind of bond that would allow them to reach out to each other. I barely noticed that Catherine spent more time on the phone than usual that evening.

The next afternoon, when I pulled to the front of the carpool line, I discovered a small miracle had occurred. There stood Laura, surrounded by the smartest, cutest, most popular fifth grade girls. My tiny daughter glowed with utter astonishment as they twirled her around, complimented her, and focused a brilliant light of attention upon her. And, to my amazement, every single one wore a side-braid, exactly like the one Laura had worn the day before. "Ten stinking braids," I thought, as I tried to swallow the lump lodged in my throat.

"I don't know what happened!" exclaimed Laura, clambering into the van. "I looked up, and all the girls were wearing my braid." She grinned all the way home, arms wrapped around skinny knees, reliving her short life's happiest moment.

I glanced at Catherine in the rearview mirror, and I think she winked at me. I'm not sure.

~Carolyn Magner Mason
Chicken Soup for the Preteen Soul

Compassion for a Bully

Kind words do not cost much. Yet they accomplish much.
~Blaise Pascal

My sixth grade year was one of confusion, intimidation, strength, and friendship. There was a girl in my class named Krista. She was taller than me and very skinny, with bony arms and legs. I remember her beady brown eyes and the hard look on her face. Krista didn't like me. In fact, I think she hated me. I was always the smallest in the class and maybe that made me easy to pick on. She would say, "C'mon, little girl, show me what you got! Or are you scared? No one likes you, little girl."

I tried to walk away and act like it didn't bother me. Sometimes it would just get to me, and I would say, "Stop it!" I definitely didn't want her to see me crying in the bathroom. As the year went on, Krista began to get more aggressive. She started coming up to me and punching me in the arm with her bony knuckles. My friends told me to ignore her as we walked away. But those punches hurt. Why me? What did she have against me? I had never done anything to invite this kind of behavior.

One day at recess, I decided to face the bully. I had been imagining this moment for weeks. Oh, how good it would feel to punch her back. I wanted to show her that I wasn't scared. So right as the bell was about to ring, I went up to Krista and kicked her in the leg, and then ran as fast as I could into the classroom. I was safe with the teacher in the room. But Krista beamed an evil look my way and said, "Be scared. I'll get you later."

I worked hard at avoiding her the rest of the year. I remember telling my mom about it, and her consoling me with open arms and kind words. She said, "Nobody can tell you how little you are—you decide how big you will be." I really liked that saying. I would say it in my head often and find strength in these words. Krista continued to punch my arm periodically, but eventually it slowed down. But the thought of Krista and her torment didn't die so quickly in my mind.

A year later, in seventh grade, I received a letter from my temple letting me know the date of my Bat Mitzvah, the biggest day of my youth. Then I read who my partner would be for this special occasion. KRISTA. How could this be? I would stand in front of family and friends and read from the Torah, become a woman, and share this moment on the pulpit with Krista? She was the source of all my anxiety and insecurity and yet this day was supposed to show my strength, pride, and wisdom. I was supposed to become an adult. And she would be there, waiting to belittle me. It wasn't fair.

I practiced my portion for months and planned a wonderful reception. I tried to put the thought of Krista out of my head. When the day came that Krista and I saw each other for the first time in a year, we both acted civil. I could tell she wasn't pleased either. Of course, she couldn't punch me in the temple.

I was all dressed up, standing before a huge audience, wanting so much for things to go smoothly, especially in front of Krista. I would have died if I messed up in front of all these people and then had to deal with the laughing and teasing of this bully. I imagined all the names she would call me.

When I read my Torah portion and my speech, I read loudly and confidently. I knew it well. I had practiced long and hard. I saw my friends and family smiling to me, and I focused just on them.

Then Krista came up. She was shaking. I was shocked at how nervous and scared the bully seemed. I had never seen that side of Krista. She was always so strong. But as I watched her fumble through words and chants, I saw this tough girl become weak, flawed and human. I hadn't thought of Krista as human and emotional. As she sat back down in her seat, she quietly cried in her hands. I suddenly felt something that I never imagined feeling toward Krista—compassion. I had always dreamed of the day I could laugh in her face and make her feel as little as she made me feel. But now that the day was really here, I didn't want to anymore. I sat down next to the sad girl, as her hands remained over her eyes.

"I know I messed up; you don't need to gloat. Go away!" she said.

"You were nervous. Everyone understands. No one remembers the mistakes. They love you and will focus on all the good. That's what family and friends do," I told her.

"Not my family. They love to tell me my mistakes," she answered. And then it made sense to me. This is why she was a bully. This is all she knew.

I put my hand on her shoulder and told her again that she did great. She could barely look me in the eyes, and then she whispered, "Thank you. I don't know why you are being so nice; I was never nice to you."

"I know. But it is in the past; it's over."

"I'm sorry," she finally said. I smiled and gave her my forgiveness. I told her what my mom had told me the year before, "Nobody can tell you how little you are—you decide how big you will be." Hopefully, those words gave her the strength that they gave me.

I truly believe I became an adult that day.

~Melanie Pastor
Chicken Soup for the Girl's Soul

43

Clueless

Fool me once, shame on you; fool me twice, shame on me.
~Chinese Proverb

I fell in love with him because he was the most popular guy in school.

He was the new boy in town, and he and his brothers had become the rage of the whole school. Not only were they all the most handsome hunks we'd ever set our eyes on, they were also musicians. And Peter—he was the lead singer. How cool is that!

I was at home, sick, when he joined our school. My friends would call me up and rave about this great new guy that I just had to see. My curiosity rose even higher when they told me stories of how he'd play the guitar in class, never have any homework done, and wouldn't care about anyone or anything. When his trips to the principal's office had beaten the school record, I was intrigued. This was one guy I just had to meet.

I had gotten sick at the beginning of the school year, so when I came back to school fifteen days later, all the seats in our class had already been assigned—except to Peter and me. Our teacher set up two chairs and a table on the side of the class—a temporary arrangement until she could fit us in.

Our first day was a complete disaster. Not only was he stubborn, selfish and immature, but he made it a point to argue with me about everything.

"What's the circumference of a circle?"

"It's not that!"

"World War II started in 1939, right?"

"Yeah, if history textbooks are all correct."

"What's the capital of Finland?"

"Why? You planning on going there?"

Soon we were in each other's faces all day long. I swear, if it hadn't been for his hazel eyes, I'd have killed him. Finally, our teacher warned us that we'd better start getting along or she'd make us sit together through the entire semester. Not wanting to spend one moment longer than was necessary with him, I decided to give it a try.

Being nice to him wasn't as hard as I had imagined. It was impossible! His atrocious attitude, sarcastic comments, and blatant disrespect for everyone around him was more than I could take. But once he'd start to sing, you'd forget everything in the room. The only thing you'd hear was his voice, the only thing you'd see—his eyes.

With each passing day, we became closer. His atrocious attitude now seemed pretty cool, and the sarcastic comments were kind of funny. It was hard not to like him after getting to know him. Then I went a step ahead and fell utterly head-over-heels in love with him. Little did I know a spark had hit both sides.

A common friend who'd noticed the change of attitude decided to play Cupid. So he asked Peter out for me, without asking me! Then asked me out on behalf of Peter, without asking him! We ended up going out and laughing over what had happened!

A week later, we were officially a couple. I felt so lucky to be with the guy all the girls were literally drooling over. He was charming. He was funny. Best of all, he was popular. I could feel other girls' eyes piercing into my skin as I sat with him and laughed at the latest escapade in his life.

Popularity has its consequences, though. About a week after we'd started going out, I discovered a secret. He'd been going out with another girl, too. And another. He was leading us all along the same sweet path, with none of us having the slightest clue of what was going on. As soon as I found out, I decided to dump him. I wasn't about to take any of this.

The so-called relationship ended in the drain. With so many girls running around trying to impress him, he found it very convenient to play with each one's emotions.

For him, it was a popularity game. The one with the most girl-friends wins. Me, I don't work like that. I wanted exclusivity. In the end, we finished where we had started—detesting each other's guts.

I fell in love with him because he was the most popular guy in school. I fell out of love for pretty much the same reason.

~Mridu Khullar
Chicken Soup for the Preteen Soul 2

44

For Michelle

very day, five twelve-year-old girls waited together for the school bus to take them home. I was one of them. Jessica was the bully. She picked on everyone. Emily and Clarissa were Jessica's sidekicks, because they were afraid if they weren't on her side, they would become targets of her cruelty. Then there was Sarah, a nice girl who didn't like Jessica but was friends with Clarissa. I didn't like anyone except Sarah.

Occasionally, a sixth girl named Brittany waited with us too. She despised Jessica but was liked by everyone else.

One day a new girl, Michelle, started waiting with us. She was shy and plain looking, but very nice to anyone who would talk to her. Although she was a year older, she was in a class with Brittany and me. Nobody else knew her. I sometimes sat with her on the bus and noticed she stuttered and had trouble saying a sentence clearly. She always spoke very highly of Brittany and considered her to be a good friend. She didn't have any friends besides Brittany and me. Most people didn't notice she was even there, but if they did, they made comments about her stuttering.

I was generally accepted in our little group, so when I brought Michelle with me, nobody objected. Things were okay until Jessica suddenly decided she didn't like Michelle and didn't want her to sit with us. Jessica started laughing at Michelle's stuttering. Then the "jokes" got more and more vicious. Emily and Clarissa would laugh along, but Sarah and I did not. We told them to stop. Then Jessica started to make fun of us too, so we backed down.

Meanwhile, I was privately becoming closer friends with Michelle, who confided in me how hurt she felt when everyone picked on her and how it had happened all her life. But whenever I got the nerve to stand up for her, I was always outnumbered, so I stopped trying.

One day Brittany overheard Jessica, Emily, and Clarissa talking about wanting to ditch Michelle. Brittany took it upon herself to be the leader, and so the next day Brittany announced that we all didn't want Michelle to sit with us anymore because we thought she was a freak. Even though I didn't feel that way at all, I didn't say anything. I just sat there, stunned that Brittany had said what she said.

I'll never forget Michelle's expression. Despair, pain, and anger were all mixed together on her face. Brittany, one of the girls she had trusted the most in her world, had told her she was a freak and didn't want to see her again. She silently picked up her backpack and moved to a nearby table with her back to us. I knew she was crying. One of my biggest regrets was that at that moment, I didn't say out loud that I didn't want her to go. I should have called her back—but I was a coward.

So Sarah and I sat there without saying a word, while the others laughed at the thought of Michelle crying in front of us.

Though I was still friendly to Michelle in private, it wasn't the same. Michelle stopped showing the same eagerness when I spoke to her. She started taking the bus less and less frequently until she finally stopped altogether. Her mother drove her home. Then I lost touch with her, because the class we'd had together finished, and she no longer rode the bus. She moved away later that semester.

One year later, Sarah ran up to me at school and blurted, "Michelle died... she committed suicide."

"What?" I asked, not believing what I just heard.

"Her mother put an obituary in the local paper," said Sarah, as shaken as me.

"But... didn't she move to the other side of the country?"

"Yeah, but it was in our newspaper for some reason..."

I went home that day, still not thinking clearly. Had I caused her to kill herself? If I had only stood up for her, would she still be alive today? Those questions ran through my mind over and over. When I got home, I told my mother the whole story, from the very beginning when Michelle first entered my life—to the end, where she left.

Guilt-ridden and miserable, I stayed up that night crying uncontrollably, talking to my mother until 3:00 A.M. When I woke up the next day, my eyes were so swollen and puffy they would hardly open. I felt responsible for her death. I could still picture her face when Brittany told her not to sit with us anymore. It became obvious to me what had happened in her life. She had grown up always being picked on, without any friends to help her. When Brittany and I came into her life, she had clung to us, feeling that we were the only ones besides her family who cared about her. But we both let her down terribly. Moving is difficult for anyone, but for her, it must have been devastating. Not being able to handle it all, without any friends, only enemies, she must have decided she couldn't live with that kind of misery. Perhaps if I had only been kinder to her, she would still be alive.

"Oh, that's too bad," Emily and Clarissa both said, with fake sorrow in their voices when they heard what had happened to Michelle. Jessica just snickered. Their reaction made me sick! How could they act so inhumanely about her, let alone laugh at her, and even her death? After a minute, they forgot their would-be sorrow and went on to make fun of a sixth grade boy with glasses sitting nearby. Sarah was just as shocked as I was at their cold reaction.

Now, two years after Michelle first entered my life, I'm not the same girl that I was. When I see someone—anyone—being picked on or harassed, I always try to help them, no matter what.

Michelle's memory still haunts me, but I will always think of her as a gift... a gift to me and to anyone else who has ever experienced bullying—a gift that reminds me to never make that mistake again.

~Satya Pennington
Chicken Soup for the Girl's Soul

45

Tears in the Bathroom Stall

Be who you are and say what you feel, because those who mind don't matter
And those who matter don't mind.
~Dr. Seuss

s a sixth grader, I began noticing how other kids were separating into cliques. There were the geeks, the jocks, and the popular cool kids. I wasn't sure where I belonged. And I think that was the problem.

Our teacher had assigned "secret buddies" for the coming week. The purpose of this assignment was to do nice things for your buddy without letting them know who was doing it. We could leave encouraging notes on their desk or mysteriously leave a card in their backpack or book. Our teacher wrote each kid's name on a piece of paper and threw them into a bucket, then we each closed our eyes and drew the name of the classmate who we were to secretly befriend and support over the next five school days.

By the middle of the week, everyone, including me, had turned this assignment into a contest to see whose secret buddy could leave the best gift. Instead of encouraging notes, we left stationery sets on our buddy's desk. Instead of giving compliments, we were giving bubble gum, lollipops and even money. It seemed that everyone was getting cool presents from their buddy. Everyone except me, that is.

My buddy followed our teacher's directions without a fault. I received handmade cards, notes with nice thoughts and countless smiley face pictures proclaiming that I was one of the nicest girls in the class. My buddy seemed to think highly of me from the notes that were left, but the lack of gifts made me wonder what was up with whoever had pulled my name.

On the last morning of our assignment, I walked into my classroom and noticed that there was a package on my desk. At last, my buddy had grasped the idea that everyone else had! I ripped open the tissue paper and just stared down at my desk. There sat a canister of perfumed powder. The girls sitting near me giggled and went off about the "old lady" gift I had received. To make matters worse, the powder had already been opened. I felt my face turn red as I shoved it into my desk.

I tried to forget about the embarrassing gift, but when I was in the bathroom before recess, the same girls who had seen me open the powder started talking trash about my secret buddy for giving it to me. I quickly joined in. "How lame," I heard myself saying. "What could my buddy be thinking by giving me such a stupid gift? My grandmother wouldn't even want it."

The girls laughed at my remarks and filed out of the bathroom. I stayed to wash my hands and let the water run through my fingers as I thought about what I had just said. It wasn't normally like me to say mean things like that about someone.

As I turned off the water, I heard a creak. I turned around to see one of the bathroom stall doors open. A girl from my class took two steps out of the stall and looked up at me. There were tears streaming down her face.

"I'm your secret buddy," she whispered to me. "I'm sorry about the gift." Then she ran out of the bathroom. Her sobs stayed with me long after the door had closed.

My secret buddy was a girl named Rochelle, a girl who came from a poor family. She and her siblings were targets at school for those who felt they were better just because their parents had money. Yet through all the teasing and harassment, Rochelle never had a bad word to say back to anyone. She just took the horrible treatment silently.

I was sick to my stomach as my cruel words ran through my mind. She had heard every single thing that had been said. And, once again, she silently took it in. How could I have been so mean?

It took me a few days, but I finally found the courage to face up to Rochelle and apologize. She told me that she had felt bad all week about not being able to leave any cool gifts for me. Her family could not afford it. So finally, her mother had given up the one thing that was a luxury to her so that Rochelle would have something to give. Her mother had assured her that the nice girl Rochelle had talked about would like the powder. Rochelle couldn't wait to get to school that morning and put it on my desk.

And I had ruined everything for her.

What could I say to Rochelle? How could she ever forgive me for making fun of her? Along with my apologies, I told her the truth. I admitted that I had only said those things to be cool, to try to fit in. I didn't know where I belonged, I explained.

Rochelle looked me in the eyes and said that she understood. She had been trying to fit in, too. "We aren't that different from each other, are we?" She smiled. Her simple words, spoken from her heart, found their way straight into mine.

Up until then, like everyone else, I had avoided the "Rochelles" of the world. But after that day, I gained respect and admiration for people like Rochelle—people who give from the heart.

~Cheryl Kremer
Chicken Soup for the Preteen Soul 2

46

So Which Will It Be? Us – or Her?

Jodie was the most popular girl in seventh grade. She was petite and blond and wore black eyeliner and mascara. It seemed like Jodie had an endless clothing budget—she set the style for the rest of our junior high school with clothes that looked like they came straight from a magazine.

Jodie and her friends laughed easily with boys, openly flirted in and out of class, and passed notes back and forth detailing their current crush. All year I had hoped to be included in Jodie's group—the popular crowd. When Jodie invited me to her birthday party, she let me know I should feel honored.

"We'll see how you fit in," she told me. "You're nice, but do you fit?" I desperately hoped I could find a place in the group. After my mother dropped me off at Jodie's party, I discovered that her parents weren't even going to be home for the slumber party I had mistakenly assumed was for girls only. As the music blared, Jodie turned the lights down low, and couples began to dance close together and kiss.

I sat by myself on a couch. All I could think was, "We're only in seventh grade. Do we have to do all this now?"

When a game of Truth or Dare got out of hand, I panicked and called my mom to pick me up early. I wasn't ready to discuss things I'd only read about in books, yet Jodie and her friends already seemed to know about sex and drugs and alcohol. I was relieved to get home and spend the rest of the evening with my puppy. Yet part of me wanted to be like Jodie and her friends—cool and confident with boys, secure in their popular status, superior to the rest of the seventh grade class.

I might have hung around more with Jodie and her group had she not given me an ultimatum. She asked me to dump someone who had been one of my best friends since fifth grade.

Marleigh and I had been friends from the day when she marched up to me on the playground and said, "You can call me M."

Marleigh and I lived in the same neighborhood, both loved to read, and were good students. We were soon in and out of each other's houses on a daily basis. I didn't care that she wore glasses and had kinky-curly short hair instead of long, straight hair like the popular girls. Marleigh and I understood each other and she was a loyal friend.

Jodie's ultimatum caught me off guard.

"Even though you left my party early, we voted to ask you to join our group," she said, tossing her perky head. "There's just one thing, though."

My stomach flip-flopped when I saw several of Jodie's friends pass a knowing look between them. Jodie pointed to the edge of the playground where Marleigh stood.

"She's a problem," Tiffany, Jodie's number-two-in-command, said.

"We don't like her," Jodie said. "She's too weird. If you want to hang out with us, you need to dump her."

I stood surrounded by the most popular girls in seventh grade. I looked at their perfect clothes and confident smiles. I wanted to be like them.

"So which will it be? Us? Or her?" Jodie put her hands on her tiny waist and cocked her head to the side. "We need to know if we can count on you."

"What difference does it make who else I'm friends with?" I asked timidly.

"We look bad if you hang around with us and her. She's a geek," Jodie said.

I couldn't tell if Marleigh was watching us, but I did see that she was standing there all alone. I wanted to be part of Jodie's group so badly I could taste it. I looked at Marleigh—at Jodie—at Marleigh—at Jodie.

"Then I guess I'm a geek, too," I said finally, "because Marleigh's my friend."

Jodie gasped as I turned away from her and "the group." I felt their eyes on my back as I walked up to Marleigh, who seemed to have been expecting me. Her eyes shone from behind her thick glasses and her face became animated as she started telling me about a movie she'd seen on TV the night before. We stood and talked until the bell rang to tell us lunchtime was over.

In the hallway during passing period, I saw Jodie leaning against her locker, chatting with an eighth grade boy. I was surprised when she smiled at me, just as I was surprised that the other girls in her group were friendlier to me than they had been before. I was nice to them in return, but the burning desire to be part of the "in group" was gone. A few years later, Jodie and her friends were also gone—they had dropped out of school or moved to other cities. Marleigh remained a good and faithful friend through high school, college, and into adulthood. And me? I realized that popularity wasn't worth changing who I was or giving up a friend.

~Anne Broyles
Chicken Soup for the Girl's Soul

47

Backfire!

It was spring at last. The sun was high in a cloudless sky. Birds sang. Flowers bloomed. Best of all, it was Saturday—a perfect day to be out playing with friends. The problem was we'd only been in town two months, so I hadn't made any friends. My family moved a lot. It's hard when you're always the new kid on the block.

So here I was, stuck with my baby brother John and Mary, the new sitter, while Mom and Dad were out of town on business. It was not going to be a fun day!

Just as we started lunch, the phone rang. I hopped up to answer it. "Hello, Morrell's residence. Lou speaking."

"Hi, Lou. It's Alicia."

My heart did a rapid pit-a-pat-pat. "Alicia Whitman?"

She giggled. "You know another Alicia?"

"No." There was only one Alicia: the most popular, prettiest, richest girl in my class.

"I called to invite you over to my house this afternoon. We can ride my horse."

"Hang on. I'll ask." Heart racing, I ran to the kitchen. "Mary, can I go play with my friend Alicia this afternoon?"

Mary was trying to scoop peas off the floor faster than my brother dropped them. "Where does she live?"

"Only a few blocks from here," I said, picturing the fancy brick house that we passed on our way home from school. I held my breath.

"Would your mom let you go?"

"Sure, she would. Please, Mary. Please, please, please."

John dumped the whole dish from his highchair.

"Oh, all right," Mary said with a sigh.

I rushed back to the phone. "Alicia, I can come. What time?"

"One o'clock?"

"Great. See ya then."

I was so excited I could hardly breathe. I was going to hang out with Alicia Whitman! Ride her horse. Every girl in class wanted to be Alicia's friend.

"Come eat your lunch," Mary called.

"I'm not hungry. I have to get ready."

I chose my outfit very carefully: my best shorts, clean t-shirt, and brand-new shoes. I even washed my face and combed the tangles out of my hair. When I was satisfied, I called, "I'm going now, Mary."

I set off. The sun beat down on my back and bounced off the sidewalk. Cars and trucks swished by on the highway. I didn't care about the heat or the noise. I was too busy daydreaming about the possibility of becoming good friends with Alicia. I'd liked Alicia from the first day. We were a lot alike. We both loved to read. Our hands were the first up to answer questions. We mostly got A's. We both liked to play sports, although Alicia was always picked first and me last. And we both were horse-crazy. I just knew we could be best friends—if we had a chance.

The sidewalk stretched on forever and ever. It hadn't seemed this far in the car! My shirt was getting sweaty and one heel in my new shoes hurt like crazy. I stopped and pulled down my sock. A big, fat blister had bubbled up. Youch! I kept going, walking on my tippytoes. It couldn't be that much farther now, could it?

Several blocks later, across the highway, I saw the meadow with Alicia's horse, Buttercup, in it. Now all I had to do was cross four lanes of traffic. I sure hoped I wasn't late!

Cars and trucks whizzed past me. I waited for the longest time for a break. When it came, I made a mad dash to the other side. Whew! I was there.

The Whitman house was surrounded by big, old trees. The cool shade felt wonderful. I smoothed my hair and my shorts. My mouth was dry. I hoped Alicia would offer me a cold drink right away. I walked up to the front door and rang the bell.

No one answered.

I rang again, then knocked. No one came to the door.

Maybe they were out back? I walked around on the brick walk. There were no cars in the driveway. No one on the fancy rock terrace either. I knocked on the back door.

Nobody came.

Alicia's tree house was empty, too. I climbed up to check. Except for Buttercup, the whole place was deserted!

I couldn't believe it. Had I heard Alicia wrong? Didn't she say today? Why would she invite me and leave? Maybe she'd gone to pick me up? That was it! Alicia didn't walk to school or ride the bus. A shiny black car brought her and waited for her when school was out. She wouldn't expect me to walk all the way out here. We'd just missed each other.

Happily, I went back and sat on the front steps. I waited and waited and waited. It got later and later. No Alicia. No Whitmans. Nobody came.

I sat there with my head in my hands, growing more disappointed and confused by the minute. I finally decided that Alicia wasn't coming, so I got up and trudged home. I was ashamed of myself. I'd been so hungry for a friend that I'd fallen for her mean trick.

By Monday morning my shame had turned to anger. Being pretty and popular didn't give someone the right to trick people! I spotted Alicia on the playground, surrounded by the usual group of girls. I pushed my way into the circle. "What you did was mean, Alicia Whitman. I don't want to be your friend, now or ever!" I stomped away.

"Wait!" Alicia cried. "What did I do?"

Right there, in front of God and all her friends, I told her.

Alicia was shaking her head. "I didn't call you, Lou. It wasn't me. We were out of town all weekend."

Someone giggled and said, "Miss Brainiac got fooled."

I ignored the name caller. "Then who called me, Alicia? Who played that dirty trick?"

Alicia looked around the group. Her gaze stopped at Morgan, who was trying to hide the fact that she was laughing to herself. "It was a dirty trick, Lou. I don't know who did it—for sure. But that person's no friend of mine."

Morgan turned bright red. "It was just a joke. Can't you take a joke, Lou?"

"Some jokes aren't funny. Right, you guys?" Alicia said, taking my arm.

Everyone nodded and closed in behind Alicia and me. Morgan's hurtful joke backfired. We all walked away, leaving her standing alone on the playground.

~Lou Kassem
Chicken Soup for the Preteen Soul

48

Call Me

Truth is such a rare thing, it is a delight to tell.
~Emily Dickinson

"I know it's here somewhere."

I dropped my book bag to dig through my coat pockets. When I dumped my purse out onto the table, everyone waiting in line behind me groaned. I glanced up at the lunchroom clock. Only three minutes until the bell, and it was the last day to order a class memory book if you wanted your name printed on the front. I did, but for some reason, I couldn't find my wallet. The line began to move around me.

"Come on, Cindy!" Darcy might as well have stamped her foot, she sounded so impatient. "We'll be late for class."

"Darcy, please!" I snapped back. Even though we were best friends, Darcy and I often frustrated each other. We were just so different. Darcy had "budgeted" for her memory book and ordered it the first day of school, while I had almost forgotten... again.

"Darcy, my wallet's gone." I threw my things back into my purse. "My memory book money was in it."

"Someone took it." Darcy, as usual, was quick to point away from the bright side of things.

"Oh, I'm sure I just misplaced it," I hoped.

We rushed into class just before the second bell. Darcy took center stage to my problem and happily spread the news about the theft.

By last period in gym class, I was tired of being stopped and having to say over and over again, "I'm sure I just left it at home." Rushing late into the locker room, I changed then ran to catch up with my soccer team.

The game was a close one, and our team was the last one back into the locker room. Darcy was waiting for me as impatiently as always. She brushed past the new girl, Juanita, to hurry me along.

I turned my back on her to open my locker. "Darcy, I know, I know, we have to go."

There was a gasp behind me, and when I looked back at Darcy, her face was white with shock. There, at her feet, was my wallet.

"It fell out of her locker!" Darcy pointed at Juanita. "She stole it."

Everyone took up the accusation at once.

"That new girl stole it."

"Darcy caught her red-handed."

"I knew there was something about her."

"Report her!"

I looked over at Juanita. I had never really noticed her before, beyond her "new girl" label. Juanita picked up the wallet and held it out to me. Her hands were trembling. "I found it in the parking lot. I was going to give it to you before gym, but you were late."

Darcy practically spit the words "I'm so sure!" at her.

"Really, it's true." Juanita's eyes began to fill with tears.

I reached for my wallet. I didn't know what to think, but when I looked over at Darcy, her smugness made me feel sick inside. I looked at Juanita. She was scared but looked sincere. I knew I held her reputation in my hands.

"I am so glad you found it," I smiled. "Thanks, Juanita."

The tension around us broke.

"Good thing she found it," everyone but Darcy agreed.

I changed quickly. "Come on, Darcy, there's just enough time to order my book."

"If there is any money left in your wallet."

"Not now, Darcy!"

"You are so naive!"

It wasn't until we were standing in line that I opened my wallet.

"It's all here." I couldn't help but feel relieved. A folded piece of paper fluttered from my wallet. Darcy bent down to pick it up and handed it to me. I opened it to see what it was.

"She just didn't have time to empty it yet," Darcy scoffed. "I know her type. I had her number the first day she came."

"You had her number, all right. Well, I have it now, too."

"It's about time," Darcy huffed.

"Maybe that's the problem, Darcy. Maybe you spend too much time numbering people."

Darcy grabbed the note, read it and threw it back at me.

"Whatever!" she said and stomped off. I knew that something had broken between us.

I read the note again.

Cindy,

I found your wallet in the parking lot. Hope nothing is missing.

~Juanita

P.S. My phone number is 555-3218. Maybe you could call me sometime.

And I did.

~Cynthia M. Hamond
Chicken Soup for the Girl's Soul

49

The Cool Girls

I sat in my living room staring out of the bay window. I didn't want to wait outside for the school bus—no, that would seem too anxious. I had decided that I would wait until I could see it coming down the street, and then casually walk out the front door. After all, I was cool now. I was entering the fifth grade.

Much to my dismay, the sight of the bright yellow bus coming toward my house sent me into a knee-jerk reaction, and I found myself running into the driveway—running and tripping. My backpack went flying and I landed on my hands and knees. Luckily, there were no major scrapes and I was able to return to a standing position almost immediately. The only thing I felt was the intense rush of heat to my red cheeks.

As I climbed the bus steps, the driver asked if I was okay. "Uh... yeah," I quietly replied. "It's nothing." I quickly examined all the kids' faces for any type of reaction. Most seemed to be staring out the window. Maybe no one had seen my fall.

I slowly moved toward the back of the bus to find two girls staring at me. As I sat down in front of them, I heard one of them burst out into a full-blown laugh, while the other quietly chuckled. They were whispering—about me, I was sure. I crossed my hands on my lap and pretended not to care.

I felt them watching me, even though my back was to them. They were definitely older—maybe seventh graders—I wasn't sure. I sat frozen in my seat, feeling like the dorkiest kid in the world, as tears formed in my eyes. This was not the impression I had been hoping to make, especially to the older kids. Then, much to my surprise, one of them tapped me on my shoulder and introduced herself.

"Hi, I'm Jessica!" she exclaimed. "Are you going into sixth?" In my mind, I quickly went from dork to super cool. Maybe they thought I was older. Wow! I shyly replied, "No, fifth," as I turned around and smiled. "Oh," the other girl giggled, "Fifth grade!"

I suddenly felt accepted. They knew how old I was, they had seen me fall—and yet they still wanted to talk to me. I had already made two friends and hadn't even arrived at school yet! I was already seeing in my mind how cool it would be, to be walking through the halls and saying hi to my new seventh grade buddies.

As it turned out, I rarely saw them in school, but I was happy enough to just be bus pals. I sat in the same seat every day on the bus, just in front of them, and waited for them to talk to me. One day, they asked to see my lunch box. "Wow, it's really cool," they both commented as they took my pink-and-white checkered box from my hands. I couldn't believe how much they liked me. They returned my lunch box and thanked me for letting them see it. "Oh, no problem," I giggled, filled with smiles both inside and out.

When I opened my box at lunch that afternoon, my lunch was gone. The empty box resembled my heart as it sank to the pit of my stomach. I never even paused to think of another possibility. In one single moment, everything made such painful sense. They were never interested in me, they were not my friends, and this whole time I was some kind of joke to them. I felt like a fool—right back to the moment I tripped in my driveway. That was how they saw me; that's who I really was. Some little dorky fifth grader thinking she was actually fitting in with the older kids.

I never cried. I never said a word. I didn't tell my teacher because I didn't want to get them in trouble. They already thought I was a dork. I didn't want to add "tattletale" to the list. I simply closed the box and sat in silence for the rest of the lunch period. I had no appetite anyway from the thought of having to face them on the bus that afternoon.

When I stepped onto the bus, I only saw Jessica sitting quietly alone in the back seat. I slipped into a seat in the front without making any eye contact with her. There was no sign of Jessica's partner in crime. I held my empty lunch box tightly against my legs and quickly got off the bus as it reached my house. When I got to my room, I finally burst into tears.

The next morning I vowed not to even look to the back seat, which of course I did anyway. It was only Jessica alone once again, not looking quite as cool and confident without her friend. As I sat once again in the front seat, I suddenly felt a presence behind me. "Hey," Jessica quietly muttered as she tapped me on the shoulder. I turned around and managed a slight smile. "Look," she proceeded, "I'm really sorry about the lunch thing." I wanted to just say it was okay, but I couldn't manage to speak. She went on to tell me that Cory had been getting in a lot of trouble lately and had gotten kicked out of school. Her parents were sending her to boarding school and she wouldn't be on the bus anymore. With that, Jessica handed me a brown paper bag filled with a freshly made lunch, as well as some cookies her mom had made. "I hope this makes up for it," she told me, and returned to her seat. So Cory had been the troublemaker, because when she wasn't around, Jessica was really pretty nice.

Jessica and I sat in silence for the rest of the ride. When we arrived at school, I waited for her as she stepped off the bus. "Thanks for the lunch," I said. We smiled at each other and then walked to our own classrooms.

Eventually, Jessica and I became real friends. Sometimes we hung out at each other's houses after school, and there was never a mention of Cory. We had a lot of fun together and the age difference seemed to disappear. I never even thought much about the lunch incident again. All I could think about was how Cory had gotten some free food but, in the process, lost two really nice people as friends.

~Mel Caro
Chicken Soup for the Preteen Soul 2

Danny's Courage

*Believing in our hearts that who we are is enough
is the key to a more satisfying and balanced life.*
~Ellen Sue Stern

I was in seventh grade when Danny transferred to my school and became my first real crush. He had the darkest of brown eyes with a dark complexion and light blond hair. I fell for Danny the first day he arrived, and many of the girls in my class felt the same way. However, that soon changed.

Danny had been going to our school for about a week when his parents picked him up in an old beat-up car that spewed exhaust and made loud banging sounds. The girls who had previously adored him looked disgusted. It was obvious that Danny was poor and that was that. He was no longer boyfriend material.

I had a poor family as well; I just hid it from everyone. I was so ashamed of how we lived that I never had kids come over to my house. Even though I couldn't do a thing about it, I felt like the kids in my class would judge me if they knew the truth. It was a lot of work keeping my secret, but I figured it was easier than it would be to not have any friends.

One day, our teacher, Mr. Sims, announced that the seventh grade field trip would be to an amusement park. The classroom buzzed with excitement as the girls discussed what they would wear and what they should bring with them. I sat back and listened, knowing that my parents did not have the money to send me. It made me angry to feel so left out. But not Danny. He simply told everyone that he wouldn't be going. When Mr. Sims asked him why, Danny stood up and stated, "It's too much money right now. My dad hurt his back and has been out of work for awhile. I'm not asking my parents for money."

Sitting back down in his seat, Danny held his head up proudly, even though whispering had begun. I could only shrink in my seat, knowing those whispers could be about me when they found out I would not be going either.

"Dan, I'm very proud of you for understanding the situation that your parents are in. Not every student your age has that capability," he replied.

Glaring at the students whispering in the back, Mr. Sims spoke again, only louder.

"This year, we're going to do things differently. The trip is not until the end of the month, so we have plenty of time for fundraising. Each student will be responsible for bringing in at least one idea for a fundraising drive. Bring them in tomorrow. If a student does not want to contribute to the drive, then he or she will be spending the field trip day here at the school. Any questions?"

Of course, Shelly, the most popular girl in the class, spoke up.

"Well, Mr. Sims, my parents can afford it. Do I still have to help?"

"Shelly, this is not a matter of being able to afford it. Money is not just something that is handed to you when you get older. This will be a great learning experience for everyone, whether you have the money or not."

While walking home from school that day, I noticed three of the boys from our class talking with Danny. I worried that they were giving him a hard time, but as I got closer, I realized they weren't harassing him. They were all just debating about the best ideas for a fundraiser.

Although not everyone accepted Danny after that day, he won over the respect of many of us. I was especially awed by how he didn't cave under peer pressure. For so long, I could never admit to my friends that I could not afford to go somewhere. Instead, in order to continue to fit in, I lied about why I couldn't do things and came up with excuse after excuse.

By standing up and admitting he was poor, Danny changed my life. His self-confidence made it easier for all of us to understand that what his parents had or didn't have did not determine who he was. After that, I no longer felt I had to lie about my family's situation. And the funny thing was, those who were truly my friends stuck by me when I finally let them get closer.

And Danny, more because of his courage and honesty than his great looks, is someone I will never forget.

~Penny S. Harmon
Chicken Soup for the Girl's Soul

51

A Cheer of Triumph

As I sat in the bleachers surrounded by fifty girls, butterflies did back flips in my stomach. We waited anxiously for the judges to give the final results of the cheerleading tryouts. One by one, each girl leapt from her seat, jumping up and down, ponytail wagging as her number was called out.

Would I be one of them? I wondered.

I was getting more nervous and excited by the second, and each second felt like an eternity.

"Number seventeen," the judge announced. I leaped from my seat and ran over to stand next to the bouncing girls.

We hugged each other and giggled with joy as we each realized we were part of the ten girl junior high cheerleading team. Little did I know my happiness wouldn't last long.

It all began when I showed up to the practice before the pep rally in the wrong uniform. I felt silly. I must have misunderstood. And I was co-captain of the team!

All the other girls on the squad were practicing in their white tops and skirts. There I stood in my blue uniform. It felt like everyone was laughing at me.

"I'll give my mom a call," said Tammy, one of the girls in white. "She doesn't work, and she'll drive you home so you can change."

When we reached my house, I couldn't find my uniform. I looked everywhere. Finally, I opened the hamper, and there at the bottom of a smelly heap of my brother's clothes was my dingy white uniform crumpled into a ball. I quickly put it on and ran out the door to Tammy's mom's car. We had just fifteen minutes until the pep rally started. We barely made it there in time.

"I can't thank you enough," I told Tammy's mom as I bolted from the car. She smiled and waved goodbye.

Humiliated, I ran toward the gym and joined the other girls in front of the school for the opening cheer. I heard waves of laughter ring out from the bleachers as we did the first cheer sequence. We did the cheer again, and the laughter grew even louder.

They must be laughing at my uniform. I felt a sickening feeling growing in the pit of my stomach. But it wasn't the uniform they were laughing at, at all.

The next day, my friend Jay was the one who clued me in.

"Kim, at one point you were doing the cheer with your arms opposite of everyone else. That's why they were laughing."

"I couldn't have been doing it wrong," I said, feeling confused. "The cheer captain taught me herself and said that I was doing it perfectly."

I didn't want to believe that the team captain had done this on purpose. I couldn't imagine why anyone would be so mean in the first place. But the denial that was keeping me from feeling hurt quickly faded away after the next thing happened.

The team captain told me to meet everyone at her house that morning before driving to the away football game. When my mom and I drove up to her house, we noticed no cars in the driveway. When I rang the doorbell, her dad answered.

"They're not here," he said in a gruff tone.

"What! We were all supposed to meet here at nine o'clock."

I knew he could tell by the expression on my face that I was very upset. Anger was sweeping over me as I walked back toward the car. Now I knew for sure that this time it was intentional—and that probably all the other times were too.

Why don't those girls like me? What did I do? The heavy weight of pain hit me like a sledgehammer. I felt like crying. I felt like throwing up.

In those few moments, I gave up on believing in the kindness of people. I felt like the world was against me. I wanted to quit the cheer team.

"Wait a minute, Kim."

I've never met this man before and he knows MY name.

Her dad had been watching me as I walked toward the car. "They're at the McDonald's on Main Street," he whispered, as his eyes caught mine.

I knew he wasn't supposed to be telling me this. To my surprise, there was kindness in the way he was looking at me. It was as if he was saying he was sorry for what they were doing to me. I was deeply touched in the most extraordinary way.

Mom and I went to the McDonald's and joined the other girls. They told us we must have misunderstood where to meet, and they laughed it off, but I knew that it wasn't true.

For the rest of the season, I cheered my heart out on that cheer team and tried my hardest not to let the mean girls get me down. A year later, I learned from another girl that it had been the captain and her mother who caused all the turmoil against me. They believed I was their competition and were trying to get me to quit by leaving me out and being mean. I was shocked because I never thought I was that good. Most of the other girls hadn't had a clue about what was really going on.

It was over the next few years of cheerleading that I began to feel sorry for the team captain and her mom for treating me so cruelly. They continued to act this way until high school graduation.

I had almost lost hope that there were any nice people left in the world until that day I stood in the cheer captain's front yard. The smallest gesture of kindness that had come from my rival's own dad had put a spark of hope into my hurting heart.

A few years later, I did something that surprised me even more. I decided to forgive them.

~Kim Rogers
Chicken Soup for the Girl's Soul

Chapter 6

Preteens Talk

Everyday Superheroes

*We all take different paths in life, but no matter where we go,
we take a little of each other everywhere.*
~Tim McGraw

52

You'll Be Good for Him

The only disability in life is a bad attitude.
~Scott Hamilton

I heard the rhythmic clatter of metal crutches coming down the hallway. I looked up to see ten-year-old Brian smiling at me in the doorway, his blond hair tousled. Every day, Brian arrived at school cheerful and ready to work.

Brian had a great sense of humor and loved his own jokes. He was my first "handicapped" student. Everyone who worked with Brian told me, "You'll be good for him."

Brian worked with the adaptive physical education teacher and swam three mornings a week. He kept a busy school day schedule. Everything he did required more effort than it did for the other students.

One day, Brian agreed to talk to the class about his handicap. The students liked Brian and wondered what he did after school. He told them that he watched a lot of TV, or played with his dog. Brian felt proud to be a Cub Scout and enjoyed being a member.

The students then asked him why he used different paper and a special magnifying lens and lamp when he read. Brian explained that he had a tracking problem, and that he could see better out of one eye than the other. "I'm going to have another eye operation," he said casually. "I'm used to it. I've already had six operations." He laughed nervously, adjusting his thick-lens glasses. Brian had already had two hip surgeries, two ankle surgeries and two eye surgeries.

Brian explained how he'd been trained to fall when he lost his balance, so that he wouldn't hurt himself. I felt bad when he fell, but he didn't fuss. I admired his fortitude.

He said he often felt left out, then somebody asked if people ever made fun of him. He replied that he'd been called every name you could think of, but that he usually tried to ignore it.

I asked Brian if he ever became discouraged.

"Well, to tell you the truth," he said, "I do. Sometimes I get really mad if I can't do something. Sometimes I even cry."

At this point I ended the discussion. I felt the important questions had been answered. The students applauded.

"Can you walk at all without your crutches?" one of the boys shouted.

"Yeah," he said shyly.

"Would you like to walk for us?" I asked him gently.

"Yeah! Come on, Brian. You can do it!" several students shouted.

"Well—I guess," he answered reluctantly.

Brian removed his crutches and balanced himself. He proceeded to walk awkwardly across the room. "I look like a drunk," he muttered. It wasn't smooth, but Brian walked on his own. Everyone clapped and shouted.

"That's great, Brian!" I placed my hand on his shoulder.

Brian laughed nervously while I had to hold back tears. His honesty and courage touched me. I then realized that maybe I wasn't as good for Brian as he was good for me—for all of us.

~Eugene Gagliano
Chicken Soup for the Preteen Soul

The Hidden Treasure

*The greatest discovery in life is that a human being
can alter his life by altering his attitudes.*
~William James

Old Man Donovan was a mean man who hated children. He threw rocks at them and even shot at them with a shotgun. At least that's what we had heard.

His small farm bordered our neighborhood where my younger sister, Leigh Ann, and I lived when we were growing up. His farm was long, narrow, and quaint. It held two treasures. One was his beautiful fruit.

There were many varieties of fruit: pears, apples, and lots more I just can't think of. The fruit naturally drew the children to his land. It made them into thieves. But my sister and I didn't dare to take his fruit because of the horrible rumors we had heard about Old Man Donovan.

One summer day, we were playing in a nearby field. It was time to head back home. My sister and I were feeling very daring that day. There was a short cut to our house that went through the Donovan farm. We thought he wouldn't be able to see us run across his property around the luscious fruit trees. We were almost through the farm when we heard, "Hey, girls!" in a gruff, low voice. We stopped dead in our tracks! There we were, face to face with Old Man Donovan. Our knees were shaking. We had visions of rocks pounding our bodies and bullets piercing our hearts.

"Come here," he said, reaching up to one of his apple trees. Still shaking, we went over to him. He held out several ripe, juicy, red apples. "Take these home," he commanded. We took the apples with surprised hearts and ran all the way home. Of course, Leigh Ann and I ate the apples.

As time went on, we often went through Old Man Donovan's farm, and he kept on giving us more luscious fruit. One day, we stopped by to see him when he was on his front porch. We talked to him for hours. While he was talking, we realized that we had found the other hidden treasure: the sweet, kind heart hidden behind his gruff voice. Soon, he was one of our favorite people to talk to. Unfortunately, his family never seemed to enjoy our company. They never smiled or welcomed us in.

Every summer, we would visit Mr. Donovan and talk to him. He told us all kinds of stories we loved to hear. But one summer, we heard that he was sick. When we found out that he had come home from the hospital, we visited him right away. His voice box had been removed. When he placed his fingers on his throat, his voice came out as a whisper. We couldn't understand him, but through his eyes we could tell what he meant.

The next winter, word got around that Old Man Donovan had died. Leigh Ann and I were heartbroken and decided to go to the funeral. We were scared because we didn't know if the family would welcome us.

When we got to the funeral, the family kindly greeted us and said they were so glad we had come. We all wept mournfully, but our wonderful memories of Old Man Donovan comforted us.

During those summers with Mr. Donovan, my sister and I learned not to judge a heart until you know it. One may just find a hidden treasure.

~Debbie King as told by Ashley King
Chicken Soup for the Preteen Soul

A Bully's Transformation in Room 7

Never look down on anybody unless you're helping them up.
~Jesse Jackson

"**M**rs. Krycia, that song... it's about me. I am the bully. Please, can you help me stop?" The class had already been dismissed for lunch, and I was puzzled about why Tommy had made sure he was at the end of the line when he usually jumped up to push his way to the front. Approaching me with a great deal of obvious discomfort, Tommy looked up at me with pleading eyes. I could not believe my ears!

I was teaching a fifth grade class at the request of the teacher who was at her wits' end with the bullying behavior in her classroom. I had just played a song called "Don't Laugh at Me," sung by Peter Yarrow of Peter, Paul, and Mary. The lyrics really could have been written with this boy in mind. The song described a variety of people who had been bullied and how much it hurt.

Tommy laughed at everyone. He was loud and obnoxious about it. He would stand up, point, and loudly say something derogatory regarding the person's behavior. It could have been as simple as someone misspelling a word in class, or tripping, or perhaps asking a question he considered stupid. "Ha ha!" he would laugh and point at John. "You are so stupid!" John would hang his head and shuffle his feet. Across the room, Scott would be crying; he couldn't stand conflict. Scott spent a good deal of time crying. Everyone ignored him. Tommy got the attention, and he was, by all definitions, quickly earning the title of class bully. The behavior was contagious. The other boys had picked up on it, and now it seemed that the boys in Room 7 were vying for the title of "class thug." Tommy was not a big boy, but he walked big. His fists were always clenched, and his posture said, "I'll get you if you mess with me." He was eleven years old and appeared to be headed for big trouble.

Perhaps it was not until that moment that Tommy recognized the effect his behavior could potentially have on others. Perhaps he had already noticed that he was being mean and searching for a way to change. Either way, here was my golden opportunity to do something with him. Across the nation, educators had to deal with a huge increase in school shootings, and we were scrambling to stop the violence, but the big question still remained: How? So here I stood with a class full of students, and this one boy—who I was very concerned would be at the receiving end of a bullet some day—was asking me to help him stop this behavior that he noticed had spiraled out of control.

I asked the teacher if I could take the boys she considered to be the biggest troublemakers and meet with them twice a week. She was thrilled. She felt when they were gone she could get to teaching. So I began meeting with the boys and asked them each to make one small, obtainable goal—something they could achieve in a week's time. Tommy's goal was to stop laughing and pointing at people. He was to make a mark on a piece of masking tape we had applied to his desk every time he noticed himself pointing and laughing. I was hopeful. I checked in to the classroom and noticed a change. The room appeared calm. The children appeared on task.

The following week, I met with the boys. "How did it go?" I asked.

Alex, not one to ever be serious about anything, responded with a tone of combined disgust and joy: "I can't believe it, Mrs. Krycia! Not only is Tommy not teasing people, he's even getting other people to stop! It's like we're all being nice to each other. It's weird!"

I looked over at Tommy. He was sitting at the table with his school lunch in front of him, hands folded in his lap and looking down as if in prayer. Tommy looked up at me and smiled. His smile was so innocent; his posture had changed. He was relaxed. His eyes, no longer little slits, were wide open and dancing with joy. He reached into his pocket and pulled out what appeared to be a pile of trash—and some of it was—but there in the pile was this beat-up piece of masking tape from the week before. He held it up to me.

"It was so hard at first! But look, Mrs. Krycia!" Tommy said proudly as he handed me the tape with the tally marks. Sure enough, he had tally marks for the first few days, but they had tapered off. I looked at him and saw a child—a little boy, not a bully. I wanted to hug him and run through the halls saying, "He's done it! Look at Tommy!" But I simply smiled and knew that he, indeed, had done it.

As the school year went on, Tommy's character continued to be one of leadership and inspiration. Now, when John trips, or Hannah misspells a word, there is no laughter. There is no hesitation to raise a hand in Room 7. The students know that it is okay to make a mistake and ask questions. Tommy won't allow any teasing.

I was so proud of Tommy that I decided to make a home visit to let his parents know what had been going on at school. I knocked on the door, and his father answered. "I am Tommy's counselor from school. I want to discuss his behavior with you," I said.

His father scowled. "Oh, no, let me get my wife," he started.

I stopped him. "Sir, this is a good thing." Mr. Brown looked at me dubiously. He cleared his throat and called for Tommy and his wife. Tommy came zooming into the room in his stocking feet, took one look at me and smiled. His parents sat down on the couch, and Tommy climbed into his mother's lap. She stroked his hair as I told them what had been happening at school and the changes that had occurred. His mother wiped away a tear. His father proudly said to him, "I knew you could do it, son."

The moment was tender and wonderful. Never again would anyone mistake this boy for a bully! He was kind and compassionate, a born leader who just needed direction. He has been an inspiration to his classmates, to me and to countless others. I am hopeful that Tommy will carry the torch of kindness and pass it on to all those with whom he interacts. Tommy's compassion and kindness certainly proved to be contagious in Room 7!

~Kristin Krycia
Chicken Soup for the Soul: Stories for a Better World

55

Two Tickets to the Big Game

wo tickets. Only two tickets to the big quarterfinals basketball game.

Three pairs of eyes all focused on the tickets in Dad's outstretched hand. Marcus, the oldest, spoke the question running through everyone's mind: "Only two tickets? But, Dad, which of us gets to go with you?"

"Yeah, Daddy, who gets to go?" repeated Caleb, the youngest.

"Dad, can't you get any more tickets?" I asked. I might be the in-between sister, but I was just as eager as my basketball-crazy brothers were for a night out with Dad.

"I'm afraid not," Dad answered. "Mr. Williams only has two season tickets. He was thoughtful enough to offer the tickets to Saturday's game to me when he found out he'd be out of town this weekend."

Dad scratched his head. "Caleb, don't you think you're a little young to enjoy a professional basketball game...?"

"Am not! Am not!" Caleb insisted. "I know all the best shooters! I know the team's record! I know..."

"All right, all right," Dad finally had to agree. He shifted his focus and tried again. "Jill, since you're a girl..."

Before I could respond, Mom came to my defense. "Don't you dare say 'because you're a girl,'" she said to Dad. "Jill's out there practicing at the hoop with Marcus and all of his friends, and she's better than quite a few of them, too!"

"Okay, okay," Dad held up his hands in a "time out" signal. "I guess I'll have to figure out a fair way of choosing between the three of you by tomorrow morning. I'll have to decide who deserves it most. Let me sleep on it—okay, guys... and girls?" he added quickly before Mom and I could correct him.

The next morning, Marcus hurried into the kitchen and plopped down at the breakfast table. "Where's Dad?" he asked as he reached for a box of cereal.

"And 'good morning' to you, too," I responded in between sips of orange juice.

"Sorry, but you can guess what I was dreaming about all last night," Marcus explained. "So—where is he?"

"He and Mom went to pick up some books from the library," Caleb answered, digging his spoon into a mound of cereal.

"And he said we should all get started on our Saturday chores as soon as we finish breakfast," I added.

"Chores! He's got to be kidding," Marcus said as he set down his glass of milk with a thud. "How can we concentrate on chores when the big game is a mere eleven hours away?"

"Parents! They just don't understand!" I agreed, popping the last piece of English muffin into my mouth.

"I'm going for the morning newspaper," Marcus announced. "There's probably a preview of tonight's game in the sports section."

"Wait for me!" Caleb added, slurping the last of his milk and dashing after his brother.

The back door snapped shut as the two boys trotted down the driveway. I looked at the breakfast table in front of me: tiny puddles of milk, bits of soggy cereal here and there, a small glob of grape jelly melting in the morning sunlight. "Well," I thought to myself as I pushed my chair away from the table, "looks like Saturday morning chores start right here."

A few minutes later, as I was washing off the kitchen countertops, I heard the familiar "thump... thump... thump" of the basketball bouncing off of the driveway. I glanced out of the kitchen window and saw Marcus practicing his hook shot while Caleb cheered him on. Frustrated, I knocked on the window three times. When the boys looked up, I meaningfully held up a kitchen sponge and dishtowel.

Marcus casually nodded to me and held up five fingers. Taking his cue from his older brother, Caleb did the same.

"Sure, five more minutes!" I thought to myself. "I'll just bet." I opened the lower cabinet and tossed an empty muffin package into the almost full wastebasket. I reached for a twister to tie up the plastic liner bag and carted it out to the garbage container outside the back door.

"He dribbles... he shoots! If I make this next shot, I get the tickets to tonight's game," Marcus teased as he shot for the hoop. "Hooray! Two points! And I get the ticket!"

"Do not!" Caleb shouted.

"You guys, Mom and Dad will be back any minute," I reminded them as I lifted the lid on the garbage container and placed the full plastic bag inside.

"Okay, we're coming in to help," Marcus said, dribbling the basketball around and around Caleb, who tried again and again to steal it. "Just one more minute."

"Yeah, just one more minute," Caleb added as he finally managed to tip the ball out of his brother's grasp.

I shook my head from side to side as I began to replace the lid on the garbage container. Then a flash of white on the inside of the heavy black plastic lid caught my attention. A white envelope... it must have stuck to the lid by accident. But then I noticed that the envelope was actually taped to the inside of the lid, and someone had written the word "Congratulations!" on the front of the envelope, too.

I lifted the flap on the envelope and pulled out a folded piece of paper. "To the one who deserves to go," the paper read, and inside of it was a ticket to the basketball game!

"I don't believe it," I thought. "I'm the one that gets to go! But how did Dad know?"

Then I thought back to Dad's comment last night: "I'll have to decide who deserves it most." I smiled. Leave it to Dad to figure out who the most deserving kid really was.

By now, Marcus and Caleb had worn themselves out. They shuffled toward the back door. "Come on, little brother, we'd better get started on our chores if we want to have a chance at getting that ticket to the game."

I turned in their direction and held up the ticket, the note and the envelope. "It might be a little too late for that," I said with a sly grin.

Marcus and Caleb looked at each other with question marks in their eyes, as Mom and Dad's car pulled into the driveway.

That evening turned out to be as special as I'd imagined: Two seats at center court, and a dad and his daughter cheering their team to victory. It was a long-remembered lesson in responsibility from a dad who let his kids make their own choices and earn their own rewards.

~J. Styron Madsen
Chicken Soup for the Preteen Soul

56

Annie Wiggle-Do

"**L**ook who's here to see you, Brenda," the nurse said. She led a tired-looking woman to the girl's bedside.

Brenda huddled on her side, facing the wall. When her mother touched her shoulder, she pulled her head closer to her chest, as if making her body smaller would help her disappear altogether.

The nurse patted the mother's shoulder.

"Brenda's still not talking to us," she said in a low voice.

Brenda's mother bit her lip to keep from crying. She remembered exactly how bubbly and happy Brenda had been before the car accident that led to the amputation of her leg. She'd been one of the most popular girls in her sixth grade class.

When Brenda first awakened from her surgery, she had raged at her mother. Why had this happened? Now, she felt like a freak. No one would ever want to be her friend. She would never date, never have a boyfriend. Then, Brenda had just stopped talking.

"I wish I could bring her friends to visit her," said Brenda's mother. "It's just too long a bus trip, though, about three hours each way."

The nurse smiled. "Don't worry. We have a plan."

Shortly after Brenda's mother left, two nurses wheeled in a stretcher.

"Moving day, Brenda!" one said cheerily. "We need this bed for someone who's really sick. We've picked out the best roommate in the hospital for you."

Before Brenda could protest, the nurses had rolled her onto the stretcher and whisked her down the hall. The room was awash with light, posters and music.

"Here's your new roomie, Annie Wiggle-Do," one nurse told a dark-haired teenager in the other bed. "She's just beginning to get better, so please don't kill her with your corny jokes."

Fourteen-year-old Annie grinned. As soon as the nurses left, she hopped out of her bed and sat on the end of Brenda's.

"I lost my leg from bone cancer," she announced. "What happened to yours?"

Brenda was so astounded she couldn't even form a word.

"You're lucky," Annie continued. "You've still got your knee. They had to take mine, hip and all, see?"

But Brenda's eyes had already found the raw scar and empty hip socket. Her gaze seemed frozen, like a magnet held it there.

Annie scooted back to her bed. "I'd like to socialize, but my boyfriend's due any time now, so I have to get ready."

As Brenda watched transfixed, Annie reached up and took off her hair! Her head was completely bald.

Annie giggled. "Oh, I forgot to warn you, the stuff they gave me to kill the cancer also killed my hair. But check this out! My parents, my grandma, my boyfriend, and some kids from school all brought me wigs!"

From her bedside stand, Annie removed a tangle of wigs. Brown wigs and blond wigs, short-haired and long-haired wigs, curly wigs, and straight wigs.

"That's when I thought up 'Annie Wiggle-Do,'" Annie said. "Get it? 'Any wig will do.' Annie Wiggle-Do?"

Laughing at her own joke, Annie chose a curly blond wig and arranged it on her head. She just managed to dab on some pink lip gloss and powder before a group of boisterous teens burst into the room. Annie introduced Brenda to them all. Her boyfriend, Donald, winked at Brenda and asked her to keep Annie out of trouble.

Before long, Brenda began chatting with Annie and her friends. They didn't make her feel like a freak at all! One girl even shared with Brenda that her cousin wore an artificial leg, played basketball, and rode a motorcycle. By the time the nurses shooed all the visitors from the room, Brenda felt more like the old Brenda.

The girls talked into the night. Annie shared her dream of becoming a comedy writer. Brenda told Annie about her secret desire to act in live theater.

"Ladies!"

A night nurse came in and shined her flashlight on Annie and Brenda. "It's after midnight," the nurse scolded. "What do you have to say for yourselves?"

"Nothing, your honor," Annie said. "We don't have a leg to stand on!"

They all laughed, but Brenda laughed hardest of all.

As the nurse's footsteps faded down the hallway, Brenda snuggled under her blanket. "'Night, Annie Wiggle-Do," she whispered. "I can hardly wait 'til morning."

~Kathleen M. Muldoon
Chicken Soup for the Preteen Soul

57

Derek

Time is the wisest counselor of all.
~Pericles

On the first day of sixth grade, all of my classmates and I were sorted into classes. Just as we had hoped, my best friend Hannah and I were in the same class. Lots of other friends were too, including Derek, a boy I've known for a long time. I knew class would be great now, and fun. Derek was the kind of guy who brought excitement into anything and was nice to everyone, regardless of their "status."

For the first few months of school, Derek was, well, Derek. He wore his Maple Leaf jersey to school almost every day because that was his favorite NHL team. He spent all of fall and most of winter playing soccer with the other guys, guarding the net even in a big snowstorm. Once, he brought seaweed to school for lunch. Somehow, he convinced me and Hannah to try it. I spit it out right away—it tasted disgusting! But Hannah kept it in her mouth a little longer—until the seaweed turned her tongue blue. Derek, who actually enjoyed the stuff, laughed at our revolted expressions, revealing a bright, blue tongue as well. Derek always had the best lunches, full of stuff like Pringles and AirHeads, his favorite foods. He never finished what he brought, so he would throw the candy in the air and whoever caught it could keep it.

Then, a few weeks before school ended for the Christmas

holidays, Derek stopped coming to school. I didn't think much of it at the time—I just kept following my busy schedule.

But on the morning of December 19, 2001, my French teacher announced to our class that Derek was very sick and in the hospital. She said he probably wouldn't be back at school until after the holidays.

That night Derek died. I went to sleep not knowing about it.

The next morning, our class was excited because it was the second-to-last day of school before vacation. We planned to do pretty much nothing all day.

Then as we settled down into craft making, game-playing, and chatting mode, our English teacher walked into the class. Her nose was bright red, and I could tell she had been crying. I stopped midfold in an origami Christmas tree. Then the school principal, who was also crying, walked in. She was followed by a bunch of people carrying Kleenex boxes. I later found out they were from the funeral home.

Our principal moved to the front of the class and we immediately fell silent, wondering what possibly could have happened.

"I have some very bad news about Derek."

Suddenly, I knew. I knew in my heart what happened, but I prayed to God I was wrong.

"Last night, Derek died."

A mourning silence fell on the class. No one moved. For a second, there was complete stillness. Then, suddenly, everyone was crying. The counselors moved around the room, attempting to comfort us and hand us tissues.

One counselor approached me and led me out of the room and into the library. I just sat there, crying for Derek. The counselor hugged me like my mom would have had she been at school. Then Hannah came into the room and we clung to one another in disbelief.

One by one, a lot of other students entered the library. Some kids wrote or drew pictures on the big sheets of paper laid out on the table, while others ripped up the paper in anger and confusion. I just sat there, sobbing my heart out.

Derek, I miss you. I hope Heaven is just like I believe it is because it will be the perfect place for you.

Around lunchtime, I went home. I didn't want to be at school anymore, so the secretary called my dad, and he came to pick me up. He was sad, too, even though he never knew Derek personally. He knew that to lose someone at such a young age was painful for everyone.

I went to school the next day, but I was still numb with pain. I don't understand why you had to die, but you probably did. I think you get smarter and wiser when you die.

Christmas passed by the same as usual. Well, almost the same. I knew that part of me would never be the same.

As the months passed, I continued to miss Derek with all my heart. He will miss out on so many things. He won't graduate, get a job, marry, raise a family. It made me feel like I had to live life as much as possible... live for him.

On December 19, 2002, exactly one year after Derek's death, I went to school as always. And just like the year before, our class was excited and happy that school was almost out for the holidays.

I brought my journal to school and wrote in it, oblivious to all the Christmas cheer. My teacher took me out to the hallway and asked me what was wrong. And that was it. I started to sob.

The next year was much the same. It seems like I'm the only one at school who continues to be so upset every year. Not that other people don't care, but they just don't seem to show their pain in the same way I do. I don't understand why I've reacted so differently. Derek and I weren't that close, but his death has affected me in such a deep way. Though the pain lessens a tiny bit with each passing year, I know that I will never completely forget him. I will never completely heal.

Then, one day, I had an idea.

Derek, I have an idea. I'll write a story. Your story. Maybe that will help me heal.

But this story is different. Unlike all the other stories I write, I have no control over the ending. That part is not up to me. It's up to God.

~Karina E. Seto
Chicken Soup for the Soul: The Real Deal School

58

Bobby Lee

If you want others to be happy, practice compassion.
If you want to be happy, practice compassion.
~Dalai Lama

I walked home with my little brother every day the same way, past an oil refinery. Mom always told us to walk together and never to talk to strangers. One day, that walk home changed forever. As my brother and I passed the oil refinery, I heard an old man's voice.

"Hey there, children."

I turned and saw a very old man standing there with a sweet smile on his face.

"Hi," I answered, still keeping my distance.

"Would you like a soda pop? I know you walk by here every day. I don't mean you any harm."

I was already hot from walking and carrying my heavy backpack, but I knew what my mother would do once my little brother ratted on me for talking to strangers.

"No thanks. I'm not allowed to talk to strangers," I replied.

"Oh, I understand. And your mama's right. My name's Bobby. Now run along," he said as he disappeared behind the gate of the refinery.

"What a strange man," I thought. But I also felt bad, thinking I may have insulted him by calling him a stranger.

I went home and reported to my mom what had happened. My mother told me that I was right not to talk to strangers, so I tried avoiding this stranger for the following few days, but it was impossible. Other streets were not as safe to walk on, and every time we passed the refinery, a familiar voice would say, "Hello there, children."

Then one day, my family was taking a walk around the neighborhood. We were just about to pass the refinery when I noticed the gate was ajar. I remember silently praying that Bobby would appear and prove once and for all that he was a "good" stranger. And there he was.

He smiled as he approached my mother, "Well, you must be Little Miss Pretty's mama! And you must be her daddy! It is so nice to meet you."

The genuine smile and surprise on my parents' faces were all I needed to see. They spoke for a few minutes and then, walking home, my parents said it would be safe for us to visit Bobby after school.

My brother and I would stop to visit Bobby after school every day after that. He would invite us into his tiny office to talk about my schoolwork, my friends, and sports.

It wasn't long before I started getting a few friends to walk home with me just to meet Bobby. Before long, a group of about fourteen kids went daily to visit Bobby and receive our sodas and gum. Thinking back, I now realize that Bobby bought all those treats just for us... and there were a lot of us to treat!

We visited Bobby every day after school for about three years! My mother finally decided it was time to do something nice for Bobby. So, with some thought and a lot of effort, she arranged for a plaque-giving ceremony to be held at the refinery on Father's Day. All of the children who visited Bobby, and even some of their parents, were invited. And you know what? Most of them came.

On the plaque, my mother had engraved "To the Neighborhood Grandfather," and all of our names were engraved below that. I remember that Bobby cried when he received it. I don't think he'd ever been surrounded with so much adoration in his long life.

The following holiday, my mother gave Bobby an enlarged

photograph of the "Neighborhood Grandfather Ceremony" with all of us kids standing around him.

One cold afternoon in February, we stopped by as usual, only to be told that Bobby had died. I remember crying for days after hearing the news. He really had been like another grandfather to me.

My mother went with two other mothers to the funeral service. There, right on the coffin, were three items: the American flag folded into a triangle shape (as is customary for war veterans), the plaque we gave him, and the photograph of that memorable Father's Day ceremony with all of us kids standing around him. Bobby had no children. I guess we were his children.

To this day I think about him—an old man with no responsibilities to family, taking in a group of "strange" little kids who ended up meaning so much to him. I know now there was a reason why I met Bobby and why a group of us went to see him every day. He was able to die knowing that somebody loved him.

~Daphne M. Orenshein
Chicken Soup for the Preteen Soul

Teasing Tami

From their errors and mistakes,
the wise and good learn wisdom for the future.
~Plutarch

*I*didn't have the best self-image in junior high, and there were two things that I fell back on in order to be accepted: athletics and humor. I've always been a decent athlete and I have always been able to make people laugh. Unfortunately, sometimes the laughter came at someone else's expense. At the time I didn't fully realize what I was doing to other people around me, especially Tami.

When I found out that she had a crush on me, I did everything possible to get her to stop liking me. While some of the boys in my class were starting to be interested in girls, I just wasn't there yet—in fact, the whole thing kind of freaked me out. Instead of trying to let her know that I wasn't ready for a relationship with a girl yet, I went out of my way to make things miserable for her. I wrote stupid songs about her that made my friends laugh whenever they saw her, and loudly told crazy stories about having to save the world from "Tami, the Evil Villain."

Everything all changed about halfway through the year though, when Mr. Greer, my favorite P.E. teacher, stopped me in the hall one day.

"Hey, Michael, you got a second?"

"Sure, Mr. Greer!" I said. Everybody loved Mr. Greer, and I looked up to him like a father.

"Michael, I heard a rumor that you've been teasing Tami and making her life miserable." He paused and looked me straight in the eye. It seemed like an eternity before he continued. "Do you know what I told him? I told him it couldn't possibly be true. The Michael Powers that I know would never treat another person like that—especially a young lady."

I gulped, but said nothing.

He gently put his hand on my shoulder and said, "I just thought you should know that." Then he turned and walked away without a backward glance, leaving me to my thoughts.

That very day I stopped picking on Tami.

I knew that the rumor was true and that I had let Mr. Greer down with my actions. More important, though, it made me realize how badly I must have hurt Tami for Mr. Greer to want to talk to me about it. He not only made me realize the seriousness of my actions, but he did it in a way that helped me to save some of my pride. My respect for him grew even stronger after that.

Even though I did stop teasing her, I never was brave enough to apologize to Tami for being so mean to her. She moved away the next year, and I never saw her again.

Just because I didn't know how to deal with Tami liking me, I still should have known better than to handle it the way I did. I think I actually did know better, but it took my favorite teacher's gentle guidance to help me change my ways.

~Michael T. Powers
Chicken Soup for the Preteen Soul 2

A Little Coaching

For me, it was normal to feel lost at the inter-camp track and swim meet. Four camps of kids were ready to lead their teams to a blue ribbon and win the day. Not me. I was too little to be a leader and too skinny to be an athlete. I knew this by the time I was twelve, because my camp counselors and the other kids reminded me of it every chance they got. So when our camp needed a fourth runner in the two mile race around the lake, I knew I was no one's first choice.

I hid in the shade of a maple tree as they called the names of the runners. My body tensed as I heard a counselor call, "Noah! Where's Noah? He's in this race!"

It was Bronto. His name was really Alan Bronstein, but everyone called him Bronto. He spotted me under the tree and lifted me up by my elbows. It was more than just his name that qualified him for his "Brontoism."

"Noah, we need a twelve-year-old who hasn't been in other events to run the two-mile."

"But you've got three guys."

"We need four. You're in."

He gave me a push toward the starting line. Trying to save myself from the humiliation of taking last place as four camps watched, I pleaded with him.

"But I don't know the way around the lake!"

"You're in. Just follow Craig." Bronto smiled.

Craig was my friend and the fastest runner in our camp. And then Bronto said, "When you make it to the last stretch on the field, just throw your head back and run."

At the starting line, I stood next to Craig and trembled.

"On your mark... get set..." The gun cracked and sixteen of us took off. Kicking up dust on the dirt road leading to the lakeshore path, I was determined not to get lost. I stayed close on Craig's heels. A little too close for Craig, I guess, because he shouted at me, "Back off!"

I did. Two guys passed me but I kept my eye on Craig.

It was tiring. The distance was widening between Craig and me. We made the turn from the dusty road onto the muddy, wooded trail that wound around the lake back to the field. Through the trees I saw Craig slip and fall out of sight. A runner from another camp passed him.

In a moment, he was up again and running. He yelled to me, "Watch the roots. They're slimy!" Struggling to keep my legs moving, I looked down and saw the tree root stripped of its bark. I puffed over it. Fifty yards later I was out of breath, but I turned up the hill into the sunlight again, which shone on the open field. My energy was spent. I scrambled up, ready to see the rest of the pack crossing the finish line and was about to drop to my knees and quit, when I saw not the fifteen guys that I thought would be in front of me, but three. The crowd was roaring, but I could hear Bronto over the rest of them, yelling, "Run!"

I threw my head back and told my legs to go. I never looked ahead and I never looked back for those last hundred yards. I felt free. Nobody was telling me what I was, or what I wasn't. My legs were running a race against my brain and I was winning.

I didn't know when I crossed the finish line. Bronto caught me and I collapsed—winded, but happy that I finished. Then I realized Bronto wasn't just holding me up. He was hugging me!

"You flew! You flew, man! Second! You passed two guys!"

There was a crowd of kids around me patting me on the back,

giving me high-fives. I had come in second. Craig had finished first... by a step, they said.

They gave me a red second place ribbon. Even with that and all the high fives and cheers of the day, the best prize that I walked away with was my confidence. That year I discovered I could do a lot of things if I put my energy into them.

I never got to say thanks to Bronto right after the race. But during the next events, I spotted him over at the lake. He was coaching a reluctant kid who was going to swim in the freestyle relay. I ran over to cheer him on. With Bronto coaching, I had no doubt that this was going to be another good race.

~Noah Edelson
Chicken Soup for the Preteen Soul

Chapter
7

Preteens Talk

Tough Stuff

Sorrow has its reward. It never leaves us where it found us.
~Mary Baker Eddy

The Day My Life Ended

I had taken my father for granted. Now that I had lost him,
I felt an emptiness that could never be filled.
~Benazir Bhutto

"He only has a few weeks to live."

Try having someone tell you this about your own father.

Try having to watch your father die for two years.

Try having your father die in December, just before Christmas, just a month after your sister got married.

Try being me.

During sixth grade, I loved school. Not because it was fun, but because it was an escape from my home reality—a place where I could forget that back at my house my dad was dying. A place where I could forget that at any time, colon cancer would finally take my dad's life. Try getting good grades while you think about that 24/7.

I hated coming home every day after school and seeing my dad hooked up to an oxygen tank. I hated going to the hospital after school to visit him when he was really sick. I can still remember that horrible smell of death when I walked into his hospital room and seeing my dad not even able to lift his head because he was so weak. I hated knowing that my dad was going to die before Christmas day.

It was a chilly December day, and I woke up to the sound of birds chirping outside as the rays of sunlight poured through my

The Day My Life Ended: Tough Stuff   209

bedroom window. I can still remember the sweet smell of pancakes being cooked, coming from the kitchen. I got up, took a shower, got dressed and went into the kitchen to get some food. As I walked past the front room where my dad was, I stopped and kissed him good morning. It looked like he was sleeping, but he wasn't. For the past two days, he had been hooked up to oxygen and hadn't been able to talk or open his eyes. It was Saturday, so I ate my breakfast slowly since there was no reason to rush. After I finished eating, my mom put my dad's favorite movie on, and I sat down next to him and watched it. After it was over, I decided I needed some fresh air, so I went on a really long walk. Actually, I didn't need fresh air, I just needed to get out of that house since the mood was very depressing and sad.

Later on that evening, my mom, sister, her husband, my aunts and uncles, and my cousins were sitting in the front room with my dad when I heard the phone ring. I picked it up, and it was my friend from down the street. She asked me if I wanted to spend the night with her. I was so happy when my mom said yes. I couldn't stand being in that sad environment. I packed my stuff, said goodbye to everyone and kissed my dad goodbye. My sister, brother-in-law, and cousin walked me down to my friend's house.

I hadn't been there for more than twenty minutes when I heard my brother-in-law's voice coming from the front door. The minute I went into the hallway and saw his face, I knew. Before I could ask, he said, "He went." Those were the two words I had been dreading for two years since my father was diagnosed with cancer. At that moment, my life stopped. Nothing made sense anymore. How could my father die? I should have been there when he went. But I wasn't, and I regret it to this day.

That night I experienced two of the hardest moments of my life. One, my father died. Two, later on that evening, I kissed my dad goodbye, and as I did I whispered, "I love you," for I knew that it would be the last time I would see him. I went into my room because the people from the mortuary were there. When I came back out, he was gone and I had to accept the fact that my dad wasn't coming back.

I wish I had spent more time with my father. Now he won't ever teach me how to cook, drive a car, or walk me down the aisle on my wedding day. I wanted him to be there to see me graduate from high school and go to college. I just wish he could have seen me pass the sixth grade.

Every day I try my hardest at whatever I am doing, because I know up in heaven Dad is watching me. I try because I want him to be proud of me. I'm sure that he is. I loved my dad very much. No matter what happens, I know that will be one fact that will never change.

~Sammie Luther
Chicken Soup for the Girl's Soul

62

Get Over It and Go On

Every day may not be good, but there's something good in every day.
~*Author Unknown*

I was a ten-year-old girl who loved to wrestle, build tree forts in the woods by my house, and spend time with my friends—just like I had done on the night that my life changed. We were on our way home from my sister's birthday skating party, and my seven-year-old sister, Tiffany, and I were both exhausted after skating all night, so we were asleep in the back seat of the car.

I awoke to find myself in the hospital. At that moment, all of our lives were already changed. I just didn't fully realize to what extent things would be different. I soon learned that I had broken my back, which had damaged my spinal cord. I would spend the rest of my life in a wheelchair. My sister, who had two broken legs and a broken arm, would end up in foster care and become separated from me. Mom had some broken bones, but that was mild compared with what would happen to her.

Why?

Because she had been drinking and driving. The police figured that she fell asleep at the wheel and then crashed head-on into a tree while going about 75 miles per hour.

During the time that I was recovering in the hospital, my mom was convicted of drunk driving and child endangerment. They gave her a sentence of three years in prison and she lost her parental rights to us. This news hit me really hard. The courts decided to find my dad so that he could care for us girls, but that didn't go well. My dad was also on his way to prison after lots of problems with the law. He was sentenced to something like twenty-five years, so he wasn't able to do anything but give up his parental rights as well.

So after the accident, my sister and I never went to live at home again. After five months of being in the hospital, I went to live in foster care with a nice couple who were already caring for my sister. Things were fine there, but one day, my sister and I were sent to live with a lady named Paula. Things were all right there for a little while, but then we were split up and my sister went to live with another family. At first, I wasn't that sad about it, maybe because I had so much to deal with after the accident, but I really began to miss my sister. I wondered about her all the time. I wished so much that we could grow up together, but the accident changed all that.

One day, Paula told me that she knew of a family that might want to adopt me. I said that I would meet them and see what they were like. So, I met the family—Sue and Chris and their two sons, Daniel and Josh, and I liked them a lot. I guess they liked me, because they adopted me.

I had to adjust to having two brothers, which was very different for me because I had never had a brother, let alone two. They act like typical boys and pester me sometimes, but overall, they're pretty nice.

My adopted mom, Sue, is a nurse, and she encouraged me to try physical therapy to see if I could learn to walk again. But after struggling with crutches and trying as hard as I could, it didn't work out. That's when I realized that I had a choice to make. I could put all my interests that involved physical activity aside and forget about them, or I could try doing what I could from a wheelchair.

After looking around for something that I'd like to be involved in, I found out about a wheelchair basketball team for nine to eighteen-year-olds in our area. I tried out and I made the team! I'm proud to say that we have been number one in the nation for our age group for the past two years. We get to fly to tournaments in different states where we play against several teams over a weekend. That's the best part of all—traveling and seeing other places. I like meeting new people, too. Every summer now, I also go to two out-of-state basketball camps. The instructors are always really cool and usually teach us some pretty tricky maneuvers. Getting involved in something so much fun and so rewarding has shown me that things are possible, no matter what your situation is.

Just when my life began to level out and get better, my adoptive parents got a divorce, so now I live with my adoptive mom, two brothers and my biological sister. I sometimes wonder what things would have been like if my birth mom hadn't driven drunk and crashed that night. I can wonder all I want, but I guess it doesn't matter, 'cause I'll never know. I just know that life keeps changing, but we have to go on anyway—with or without some of the people that we love. Sometimes, we just don't have a choice. It's definitely not fair, but that's life. You can't let things get you down, because it gets you nowhere to sulk and feel sorry for yourself.

I know some people might get depressed if they had my life, but the way I see it, it's like, what's the point?

You just have to get over it and go on.

~Christina Zucal
Chicken Soup for the Preteen Soul 2

63

Kelsey

Hugs are the universal medicine.
~Author unknown

My little sister Kelsey was two years younger than me. I can actually remember the day she was born. It was beautiful outside. The sun was out and there was a nice cool breeze. I went into the hospital to see my new sister, but I was too young to hold her.

Four years later, my brother Dakota came along, and by then, I was big enough to hold my new little brother.

Since Kelsey and I were so close in age, we did a lot together growing up. We were typical kids and we sometimes fought like cats and dogs. But there were also days that we were really nice to one another. We used to play games on Nintendo once in a while, but most of all, we loved to play outside.

My sister was the most athletic person in our family. She was a lot faster than me. As we got older, we used to race all the time, but she would usually beat me. We especially loved to swim, so my dad got us a membership at the pool at our nearby church. We loved that pool, especially the lifeguards and the people who would often go there. We would race in the pool, too, and sometimes I would actually beat Kelsey.

My family life was going pretty well but when I was about eleven,

I started to notice that my parents argued a lot. My dad was a hard worker and provided well for us, but he drank too much and my mom had no tolerance for alcohol abuse. The madness never did stop, so eventually they divorced.

I thought things would never be the same without my dad living with us and that it would be the hardest thing I'd ever have to go through. I realized that our lives would never be perfect due to the stress and strain that was created. But I tried to stay positive and remember the good times my father and I had. Mom and Dad seemed happier this way, and I knew we'd be okay.

My family and my mom's family have always been a close-knit bunch. My Nana and Pops were the best! Nana is a really sweet lady and cares for us a bunch, but Pops was my favorite person in the world. He was funny and silly, and he loved me and my brother and sister a lot.

One day, my pops wanted me to come over to watch some John Wayne movies that were on TV. We made popcorn and root beer floats that night. We were up pretty late and had a great time together. I was spending the weekend with them, which I loved to do. The next morning, Pops and I were going to get up early and eat breakfast together. Pops usually woke up at around 6:30 A.M. My Nana was up but Pops still hadn't gotten up, so Nana told me to go and wake him.

I went to get him, but I knew something was wrong as soon as I walked in. My Pops had died in his sleep early that morning of a massive stroke. I was totally devastated. My whole family was numb and in shock. For months we were all in a sad fog. Still, I tried to stay positive. My pops was in a better place and although I'd miss him my whole life, I knew I'd see him again.

Things were going along all right, but we had our days when it was tough. We did our best to get through them. Then in November of that year, my mom was diagnosed with an aggressive form of breast cancer. She ended up having a major operation on Christmas Eve. My mom spent her birthday, Christmas, and New Year's in the hospital. I was so worried about her. I didn't know how I should deal with it. I guess I just dealt with it by trying to be as much help as I could around the house.

My mom went through several extensive surgeries and a massive amount of chemotherapy. She went away to Omaha for a few weeks to undergo treatment. I was so worried about her through those times. I was lucky to have such strong and supportive friends and family through it all.

Finally, Mom came home and was doing pretty well. We had several false alarms but nothing serious. By July, Mom was feeling good enough to get out with us and have a little fun.

One afternoon, my mom, Nana, brother, and family friend Tracy went out to play miniature golf and then we went out to eat. We had a really good day. It was the most fun I'd had in a long time.

When we got home, there were tons of messages on the phone machine. My dad's girlfriend left us an urgent message asking us to call her as soon as we got home. When we reached her, she gave us more horrible news. She told us that my dad had died earlier that day of a massive heart attack. My mind was going in all sorts of directions. I had no idea this could happen to my forty-five-year-old father. It was a total surprise to all of us. I did not know what to do or think.

There was a huge visitation for my dad. Then, as a final goodbye, we spread his ashes in Lake Okobji in Iowa where he always used to say he wanted to be put to rest.

After we got things back on track again and going well, I started back at karate, something that I had always loved doing. Kelsey was excited about starting her first year of middle school and I was going to be in eighth grade. By this time, I'd been through more than most kids had, but nothing would prepare me for what happened next.

On September 3, Kelsey and Dakota begged my mom to let them go to the pool. I didn't go because I was mowing the backyard to earn some extra cash. My mom was not going to let them go, but finally they just broke her down. She was very sensitive to the sun from all of the chemotherapy, so she could not go with them. She said they could go for half an hour—just long enough to come back and get me so that I could go to karate.

My mom had just walked through the door and started to change clothes when the phone rang. It was someone from the church. They said there had been an accident at the pool. Mom came running down the stairs to tell our family friend, Tracy, and me. Tracy left with my mom and I stayed at home. I tried to call my nana and ask her if she knew what was wrong. I needed someone to talk to but apparently Mom called her and asked her to come to the pool. So I waited at home patiently for a phone call or someone to come and get me.

Finally, the phone rang and it was my nana saying she was on her way to pick me up. When she got to our house, she sat me down and told me what had happened.

My sister, Kelsey, had been caught in the pool drain. The paramedics came, but they could not pull her out. She was underwater for approximately twenty-five minutes. Finally, they were able to get her out and they rushed her to the closest hospital immediately. When she arrived, they worked on her and found a faint pulse after about thirty minutes. From there, she was rushed to Children's Mercy Hospital and that is where she stayed on life support. I went in to see her. She was not the same at all; she was not my athletic little sister anymore. She only lived for two days.

Knowing that I would never see her again, and having to say a final goodbye to Kelsey was the saddest thing that I've ever been through. We had been together through the toughest times our family had ever known and we had helped each other out. Now she was gone forever and I was on my own. I knew I had to learn how to help myself out, and to help Dakota, too. If it weren't for my family and friends, I would never have made it through the experience of losing her.

I think my family and I might have a new start with our lives now. I know it will never be the same without Kelsey, but I think the tragedies in our lives have stopped. Mom is in remission and has gone back to teaching kids with special needs. I'm studying kickboxing and karate and doing really well in school. As for Dakota, he's following in my footsteps and taking karate, too. So far, so good.

One thing I learned from all this is to treat your family with love and kindness. Always give hugs and kisses to them because tomorrow is not promised to anyone. If you do this, then you won't ever have to wonder if they knew that you loved them.

~Shane Ruwe
Chicken Soup for the Preteen Soul

Getting Better

Never apologize for showing feelings.
Remember that when you do, you apologize for the truth.
~Benjamin Disraeli

I was a nine-year-old girl beginning a journey to a whole new place. My mother and I were saying goodbye to our family, and were on our way to Kent, Washington, where we were going to live. My sisters, brother, and dad were staying in Billings because my parents were divorced. My parents divorced when I was around two, and my dad remarried when I was four years old.

My mother and I were moving to Seattle because she had been offered a job as a special ed teacher. The only reason that I went with my mother was because she had told me so many bad things about my father, and I was too scared to live with him. I didn't even really want to leave because I wanted to stay with my sisters, but I didn't know what to do about my dad.

Let me tell you, it was incredibly scary to be all of a sudden moving to a whole new place where I didn't know anybody. My mother and I moved into an apartment. Just after we arrived and we were unloading our things, a somewhat nice-looking guy came walking down the stairs. He introduced himself as John and offered to help us unload our belongings. He seemed quite nice, so we said yes and just kept on unloading. We finally finished unloading so we began to unpack our things.

Pretty soon, my mother and John began to date, and after about three months, John would come over to our apartment all the time. To me it began to feel like they were married. He would stay until really late, and he loved to tuck me into bed. I was not sure how to deal with all of this because something about him scared me really badly. My mother and John decided to get married. I didn't get excited about it.

After the wedding, John started to come into my room more and more, and would stay for a long time. He began to touch me in very uncomfortable ways and I would get extremely scared. I didn't say anything because I was too scared. Sometimes I would put my hands over my chest and roll over so that my back was facing him. During this particular time, my mother would usually be in her room watching TV, and I did not want to scream. I knew that if I did, he would immediately stop and pretend to be innocent, and my mother would think that I was crazy.

A few months after the wedding, my mother and John found a new house. I was given the opportunity to live with my dad again, and based on what was going on with John, I decided to move back to Billings.

My family in Billings was extremely excited to have me back, but when I got home it was hard for me to get close to them. I found myself having a hard time showing any physical affection toward my dad and stepmom. John had confused me as to what was normal and what was appropriate. Any physical contact made me pull away.

My sister and I would go see my mother during every vacation. Sometimes neither of us wanted to, but we were expected to. I used to cry and beg my parents not to make me go. Every time I was there, John would touch me and I would get more scared about what was happening and whether or not anyone would believe me if I told.

At one point, I told my best friend Lindsey what was happening and she told me to tell my parents. I didn't think that they would believe me so I made her swear to keep quiet, and I didn't take her advice.

My dad and stepmom began to wonder if there was something going on that I just wasn't able to talk about. Then one day, my stepmom decided to have a school counselor come to the house to see if she could help me break through the awkward silence. Rather than tell a stranger what had been happening, I finally burst out and told my stepmom the truth.

At last, I had the courage to tell my family what John had been doing to me. My stepmom, Jean, pulled me close to her and we cried for a long time together.

Soon after that, we contacted an attorney who got in touch with the police in Washington. John was arrested, but it took nine months before we actually went to court. It was really hard on me to face my mother during the trial, but I got through it. All that I have to say is that it was one of the hardest times of my life.

John was found guilty and went to jail, but immediately he hired a new lawyer to appeal the case. Just before he was to be sentenced, he was granted a new trial. He decided to accept a plea bargain and was freed from jail after only five months. As unbelievable as it sounds, he was able to return to his job with the government and is living with my mother. As I suspected, she didn't believe me, even after a jury of twelve adults found John guilty. The family has not had any contact with her in nearly three years.

After the trial, I felt that the attorneys had taken such care with my case and treated me so wonderfully, that I wanted to become a lawyer. I want to defend little kids, or anyone else, who is unfortunate enough to be in the same situation that I was.

I always have hope that one day my mom will see how much she has missed and get back in touch with us kids. There are days when it saddens me and I cry and get furious. I will always love my mother no matter what, and hopefully someday I will be able to accept the choices she has made and the person that she is.

I now live my life the best way that I possibly can. I know who I am inside, and that took a lot of counseling. I also don't think that I would be who I am right now if it weren't for my stepmom and dad and their intuition that something was terribly wrong in my life back then. I can't imagine what my future would have held. Now, it's better than it's ever been, and getting even better.

~Tiffany Jacques
Chicken Soup for the Preteen Soul

The Big Slip

A bend in the road is not the end of the road...
unless you fail to make the turn.
~Author Unknown

I was getting ready to walk out the door after my usual morning routine when my mother yelled for me to get out to the
car—as she often had to do just to get me moving. I grabbed
my book bag, threw on some shoes, and walked through the door to
the garage with no idea what was going to happen that day.

The morning went off without a hitch: math class, English, social
studies. Finally it was 11:30, time for lunch.

I went to my locker, grabbed my lunch, and walked to our gym/
cafeteria with the rest of my friends. The lunchroom was always a
mess when it was our turn, because we were the last ones in the
school to eat—after the kindergarten through fifth grade kids were
done. We had a very small school and it was used as both a cafeteria
and a gym. Dust and dirt often collected on the floor from students'
shoes—not to mention spilled milk, drinks, and dropped food.

I sat down at a table with my friends, ate my lunch, and sat
back to talk with them for the remainder of the lunch period. We
got up when it was finally time for recess. During recess there was
never anyone eating in the gym, so we had the option of using it. We
started playing a game of half-court basketball.

The game was about halfway through, and my team had the lead. I was outside of the key, guarding an opponent, when he shot the ball over my head. I jumped to block but missed. Michael, a teammate, got the rebound and was immediately covered by Andrew. Seeing that I was open and that he had a clear passing lane, he threw the ball to the ground for a bounce pass. I remember the ball hitting the floor only to come back up and hit me in the chest. Then my memory just goes blank. Just like when you fall asleep. You never see it coming—it just happens and there is a gap of memory between that instant and when you wake up.

It turns out that I caught the ball, slipped and bounced on my head. Maybe it was the wet floor or the shoes I was wearing. But either way, I was headed to the hospital.

The next part of this story is a little sketchy because I don't remember it at all. What you are reading now is what I've heard from various sources. I was lying on the ground with blood coming out of my nose, and Jarred asked me, "Are you all right?" There was no reply. The lunch aides ran to my side as I suddenly sat up and began hitting away or waving my arms at anyone who came close to me. I said that I had a really bad headache and the aides suggested that I lie down on the couch in the teachers' lounge. Our principal came into the gym and started to ask me questions. When I hit her with my fist, she realized I wasn't myself and yelled for someone to call an ambulance.

The paramedics arrived and took me to St. Luke's. The doctors, noticing I was going to need an emergency CAT scan, called and told them to rush the person out to make it available for me. Such a call is uncommon. Usually they simply rush the patient up there, hoping it's open. They rushed me to the CAT scan and took the pictures of my brain. The doctors found that I had ruptured a blood vessel inside my skull. I was bleeding inside my head, and the growing amount of blood was applying a lot of pressure to my brain.

The doctors had to surgically relieve the pressure, so I was rushed to surgery where Dr. Shinko would operate. He told my mother that there was a 75 percent chance he could relieve the pressure. My father, who was away in Chicago on business, was frantically awaiting a flight home after hearing about what had happened to me. As I headed into surgery, I have a vague memory of saying to my mother, "Tell everyone that I love them."

Inside the operating room, I have another vague memory of about six people around me, very busy doing things. I remember yelling, "My head hurts like heck, my head hurts like heck!" Then a female nurse kindly said to me, "We're doing everything we can." That's where the memory ceases.

Dr. Shinko had to shave the side of my head to make a clean incision, which begins at the front side of my ear and ends about a centimeter away from my left eye. He cut through a lot of nerves, but he knew they would grow back. He was able to relieve the pressure and close the incision using staples instead of stitches. Then I was taken to a hospital room where the doctors and my parents awaited my awakening.

I remember slowly raising my eyelids. My eyes half open, I heard someone whispering, "He's awake." Then another person saying the same thing. I remember thinking, "What is going on?" There was a machine to my right displaying my heart rate and other information. To my left was an IV bag hanging on a rack. Sitting on a chair to my left was my mother and standing behind her was my father. I asked in a soft voice, "What happened?"

They explained what had happened, and they asked me if I remembered the basketball game. I remembered every detail of it—even who was on my team and who was on the opposing one—everything, that is, except the accident. I stayed in the hospital for about a week, really groggy most of the time. I did more sleeping than anything else.

I woke up one day to find my room showered with cards. A few of my friends visited me to tell me how all the girls cried after it happened. And they asked if I could play in our upcoming tournament basketball game. I knew I wouldn't be able to, no matter how much I wanted to.

After some more tests, I finally left the hospital in a wheelchair, all the while insisting I didn't need one. But I didn't get my way.

It was weird going to church the following Sunday and hearing my name on the sick list to be prayed for. My punishment, as I call it, was that I couldn't run for two months and worse, couldn't play contact sports for six months. It stunk having to be tied down like that, but I got through it.

Dr. Shinko say he fixxxed everythiiing but for ssomme eason me dont realllly belive himm.

~Scott Allen
Chicken Soup for the Preteen Soul 2

Heaven Sent

Making the transition from middle school to high school is always a tough one. Luckily, I had my five best friends, Kylie, Lanie, Laura, Mindy, and Angela, to help me through it. We experienced our most important moments together and shared everything, the good and the bad. Their friendship completed me. With their help, I went from being a shy little girl to a confident and excited young woman. Life without them was unimaginable, or so I thought.

The unexpected all began on a beautiful spring day during my sophomore year. Life was perfect. It was a Friday and the weekend was upon us. After my friends and I made our plans, I said goodbye to each of them and gave them all a great big hug. As always, I told them that I loved them and we went on our own ways.

Laura and I decided to go to the mall and do some shopping before we went out that night. As we returned to her house, I noticed something very odd: both of her parents were home and waiting outside. I knew right away how peculiar this was, since even Laura seemed surprised to see her father home so early. As we approached the door, Laura's father quietly uttered, "Reality is going to hit right now." My stomach sank and my heart began to pound quickly. What was he about to tell us?

Once I found out, I no longer wanted to know what he was trying to say. Seeking comfort, I looked into the eyes of Laura's mother but saw her eyes fill up with nothing but tears. As she tried to speak, she choked on her words. But slowly the words came. The five words that would forever destroy my life were, "There has been an accident."

Images of the people I loved raced through my mind as my heart began to beat faster. My first instinct was to retreat to denial. Nothing was wrong, nothing had happened and no one was hurt. This would all go away and things would be back to normal in the morning. Unfortunately, I couldn't run away from the truth. I sat on the edge of my seat in shock as I was told the news.

My best friends had been in the accident. Lanie and Mindy had walked away. Kylie, however, was in bad shape. I soon realized that no one was telling me what had happened to Angela. As I prepared to ask, I took a deep breath and swallowed hard. Deep down inside, I already knew what I didn't want to hear. I tried to ignore my instincts. After all, Angela couldn't be dead. She was only fifteen!

Then the news came and there was nowhere I could run to escape. Angela was dead. After hearing the news, all I could do was laugh. This had to be some kind of sick joke. My inner refusal to accept what I had been told prevented me from crying. I had no tears. I was in shock, utter shock. From the moment the accident had happened, each of our lives had been changed forever.

As I arrived at the hospital, the first person I saw was Lanie. Even though it truly was Lanie, this wasn't my Lanie. The Lanie I knew was full of spunk. As I looked into her eyes, I thought I was looking into the eyes of a stranger. For the first time in our lives, she was out of my reach. I was devastated to see her in so much pain. She couldn't even speak to me.

As if that weren't hard enough, I was then told that before I could see Kylie, there were certain conditions that I had to agree to. I was to remain calm and tell her that everything was going to be okay. The hardest part, though, was being told that I couldn't cry, because this would upset her. I quickly agreed. I just wanted to see her.

I walked into the emergency room to find Kylie hooked up to many machines. She was screaming and crying. It was beyond difficult to pretend that all was well when all I could see was the hell that she was going through. My heart stopped. She was in agony and I could do nothing but watch. As I told her that I loved her, I felt my eyes well up with tears, so I turned and ran away.

Once I was outside of Kylie's room, I tried to regain my composure. However, I panicked once again when I found out that Angela's father was on his way over to the hospital to check on the other girls. My only instinct was to run, and that is exactly what I did. I ran as fast as I could to the other side of the hospital. I was not running away from him, but from the truth. I just couldn't bear facing him. I knew if I did, I would have to face the truth that Angela was gone forever. I wasn't ready for that truth. Somewhere deep down, I was still hoping that this was really an awful nightmare that I was going to wake up from any minute. Unfortunately, it wasn't.

That night all of my friends gathered at Laura's house. We consoled each other and reminisced about the times we had shared with Angela, times that we would have no more. At this point, I was still not allowing myself to grieve. If I did, it would mean that I believed it was true. I knew it was true but I could not accept it, so I didn't.

Later that week was the viewing. The once vibrant young woman lay lifeless and cold. That was not my Angela; I did not know or recognize that person. What followed was the funeral. That was where the spirit of the Angela that I knew actually was.

It was a beautiful sight to see the community come together to express their love for her. The microphone was open to all of those who wanted to share their personal memories or their love for Angela. Seeing all the people that were there to remember her made me realize that Angela not only touched my life but the lives of everyone she came into contact with. She was my sunshine, and now without her my days were darker. How does a person live without the love, warmth and security of her best friend?

I didn't think my life could get any worse, but I was wrong. Without notice, I was told that my parents were getting a divorce. As soon as I heard the news, I automatically wanted to call Angela. After all, she was the one I always ran to when I needed someone to talk to or cheer me up. But she was gone.

All my friends were still hurting from the devastation of losing Angela, so I didn't think that I could burden them with my new crisis. I ended up feeling completely lost and abandoned. I bottled up all my thoughts, questions, and frustrations inside of me. I thought that meant that I was strong. It took me some time before I realized that there was someone that would always be there for me no matter what happened: God. He always had a way of coming into my life with open arms when I had nowhere left to run. I soon learned that God has a mysterious way of working. This time, he placed a situation in my life path that enabled me to grow as an individual.

Unexpectedly, Brenda Hampton, the creator, writer, and executive producer of *7th Heaven*, came to me and asked if I would be willing to do an episode about "dealing with the death of a young friend." Up until this point, I had not let myself grieve over the loss of Angela. Simply put, I had been acting. I had put up this perfect facade that I was totally happy. When Brenda asked me if I was willing to do this episode, I suddenly realized that I needed to let out my emotions and fears if I ever wanted to get over my pain. As a result, I agreed to what Brenda proposed, and she developed "Nothing Endures but Change."

At first, I wasn't prepared for the emotional tidal wave that would be released. Filming that episode was both emotionally and physically exhausting. Emotions that I had ignored for so long were now being unleashed, and I did not know how I was going to deal with them. Luckily, this time around I felt comfortable enough to turn to my friends and family for the love, advice, and security that only they could offer. I came to the realization that it was okay to hurt. Once the tears came, they didn't stop until weeks after. That was when I realized that even though Angela wasn't physically with us any longer, her spirit had never left my side.

One day, after visiting Angela's grave at the cemetery, I was listening to the radio. I noticed that the songs playing were those that I always associated with Angela and our friendship. Five of "our" songs played back to back. As I came over a hill, I saw a beautiful rainbow. I immediately got chills all over my body. I knew that this was a sign and it instantly caused me to smile. To all of my friends and me, rainbows had symbolized our friendship with Angela. There she was, as beautiful as ever, just reminding me that she was still by my side and had never truly left me. I cried, but this time out of happiness and joy. I knew then that I have an angel watching over me, now and forever, and her name is Angela.

~Beverley Mitchell
Chicken Soup for the Preteen Soul

My Problem

Every man stamps his value on himself...
Man is made great or small by his own will.
~J.C.F. von Schiller

I'm an eleven-year-old overweight boy. I have felt down in the dumps, felt bad about myself, felt left out and confused at one time or another over the past four years.

I've been overweight since I was three years old. My mom, dad, brother, and sisters all worked at different times, and they didn't realize that when they came home and ate at different times, I would eat with each one of them. No one realized what it was doing to me until I was overweight.

When I started school, the kids made fun of me. They called me "fatso," and "fatty, fatty, four by four." This made me feel sad, mad, and upset. Sometimes I wanted to hit them and tell them to leave me alone. Instead, I would walk away, and at times, I would go home and cry with my mom. I never let anyone know this because they would have just teased me for it instead of realizing how much I was hurting.

In sports, I was always picked last, making me feel like I couldn't do as well as the other kids. This, I believe, is part of the reason I don't enjoy sports very much.

When I was eight, my mom and I joined TOPS (Take Off Pounds Sensibly), a weight-loss support group. Since I've been in TOPS, I've learned to exercise and to count calories. While I was in TOPS, I became a Division winner for weight loss for my age group. I was proud to be onstage for this, especially knowing part of my TOPS group was there to support me. I've also learned how great it is to have my family support my efforts, as well. I try to give the same support either by talking to someone who has weight issues or by giving hugs to people who need them.

I now set small goals for myself, and one by one, I find that they are easier to achieve than really big ones. They all add up to a bigger change in my weight eventually. Seeing the success as I go also has helped me to believe in myself more than ever before.

Still, following new ways of healthy eating can be really tough. Sometimes I just want to eat everything in sight. It's hard when we go out to eat or go to functions where there is food. I know I can have some of whatever I want, I just need to watch how much I eat of it. Sometimes it doesn't seem fair being a kid and having to think about this!

I think because of what I've been though, I am more aware of how a person with disabilities feels. I try to help others and talk to them in a way that shows them respect. I never want to hurt anyone's feelings the way mine have been hurt.

My family and TOPS friends have taught me to treat people with respect. If I could say anything to people who make fun of others, it would be not to just look at the outside of a person. You should get to know them on the inside—get to know them for who and what they are.

Also remember, if you can't say something nice about someone, don't say anything at all. I might laugh at your joke about my weight, but inside... I might be crying.

~Allen Smith
Chicken Soup for the Preteen Soul 2

The Perfect Figure

*I finally realized that being grateful to my body
was the key to giving more love to myself.*
~Oprah Winfrey

"Oh my gosh, it looks sooo good on you," exclaimed my best friend. "That color flatters you, and I'm getting it for you for your birthday. After all, it's in two weeks!"

I had gone bathing suit shopping with my best friend. Since we were going into the seventh grade we needed to look cooler. We tried two piece suits in hopes that we would get more attention from the guys. We wound up purchasing them, and the topic of conversation came up about going on a diet. The only reason for going on one would be to lose a little bit of our "baby fat." I thought all the guys would like me if I was pretty and thin.

So I decided to stick to the diet, even though it would be hard because I am a chocoholic. I had always been a big girl. Not necessarily fat, but tall with a solid build. All the courses in school I took were advanced placement and I played many sports. I thought, "A thin, pretty, smart, athletic girl—everyone will love me." When I would come home I wouldn't snack and I cut down on my dinner portions. I had cravings for ice cream, but I just looked at beauty magazines and my bathing suit. The craving disintegrated quickly.

My mom noticed when I dropped five pounds. She told me to stop because I could hurt myself. I promised her I'd stop, but I couldn't. My best friend lost about ten pounds and stopped because she knew she looked good. I started getting complimented by my peers at school. I wore my same clothes which kept getting baggier and baggier. Some people would ask me where my lunch was. I lied to them and made up excuses.

Since I lost weight by dropping lunch, I did the same with breakfast. I tricked my dad into thinking that I ate my bagels, but I fed them to the deer. My weight dropped drastically, and my best friend would threaten to tell my parents if I didn't eat. I fooled her so she thought I was eating, but I wasn't. When I looked at myself in the mirror every day, I saw bulgy thighs that had to go.

My gym teacher confronted me about my immense weight loss. I told her I was losing weight, but that it was all through exercise.

Finally, dark circles formed under my eyes, and I stopped physically developing. It was a struggle for me to even walk up my driveway. I couldn't sleep at night, and I wore layers of clothing in eighty degree weather but I was still cold. That didn't matter. I still needed to be thinner, and I started wondering how many calories were in toothpaste and communion wafers.

About a month and a half after I had bought the bathing suit, I tried it on again and it fell right off me. My mom told me to look in the mirror. I could see my eye sockets, my transparent skin, the dark circles under my eyes, and my cheekbones popping out of my skin. That was the day I realized how skinny I was.

I went to our family doctor and a psychiatrist. My total weight loss was about twenty-five pounds in one month and a week. It took one year for my body to start working normally again.

Sometimes I want to go back to being thin, but I would never do what I did again. It's not worth it. Please don't go on diets when you're young. You will regret them. I know I do. Get help right away because you'll slowly kill yourself and suffer greatly. Don't judge and compare yourself to others. Try to love yourself for who you are, not for how you look. Besides, you probably look fine just the way you are.

~Nikki Yargar
Chicken Soup for the Preteen Soul

Forever Stay in My Heart

~In loving memory of Cassie L. Sweet~

It was late when I heard the phone ring
I didn't know then the grief it would bring.

She was killed by one thoughtless mistake
That a few of her friends decided to make.

I can't understand what they had been thinking
The driver of the car she was in had been drinking.

All I do now is think about her and cry
And ask myself again and then again, why?

I cherish all the memories that we shared
And remember how much she loved and she cared.

She is gone now, and yet it's still hard to part
So that's why she will forever stay in my heart.

~Jillian Eide
Chicken Soup for the Preteen Soul

70

BFF

Death leaves a heartache no one can heal,
love leaves a memory no one can steal.
~From a headstone in Ireland

Whenever something bad would happen to me, I would think that nothing could be worse than when I had to move away from my home and leave my best friends behind. Flying away from my small home in Colchester, Connecticut, at the age of seven, I felt that it was the hardest thing I had ever done—or ever would do. But I was wrong. I was very, very wrong.

I was just about to go out the door, when I heard the phone ringing. "Hello?" I said into the receiver.

"Courtney? This is Mrs. Lynch."

"Oh! Hey, Mrs. Lynch! My..."

Mrs. Lynch cut me right off. "Courtney, please let me talk to your mom."

"Sure, well... she's walking out the door to go to dinner group, but I'm sure she'd want to talk to you!" I went to get my mom. I caught her just as she was pulling out of the driveway with my dad.

"Mom! Mom!" I called, motioning for her to stop the car. "It's Mrs. Lynch, and it sounds really urgent!" I yelled, thrusting the phone at her. I started to walk away but then stopped because I heard the car door open and then slam shut.

I heard my mother say to Dad, "You go ahead and drop off this bread pudding. I have to stay here with Court and the girls." I was really confused. I had never heard Mrs. Lynch sound so... stressed out... or serious... or anything like the way she had been when I just talked to her.

"Courtney, come here, Honey. I have to tell you something."

"Why did Mrs. Lynch sound like that?" I asked, realizing that my mom looked very concerned and like she was choosing her words very carefully.

"Kelly and Jenn..." she trailed off. Then she took a deep breath and started again. "Kelly and Jenn have been in a very serious sledding accident." Her words filtered into my head very slowly. Everything started to feel strange. Nothing was making any sense. I was confused. "What about Christiane? What happened? What do you mean?" All of a sudden, my mind sped up again and everything my mom was saying to me started to sink in and I had a very bad feeling in my stomach.

"We don't know very much except that they both have serious head injuries and they were flown from Colchester to Hartford by Life Star. Then Hartford Hospital transferred them to Boston Children's. They are both still in the air right now, on the way to Boston. Jenn was sent first because her injuries are more serious than Kelly's." Everything was spilling out of her like she was having a talking race with someone. There were tears in her eyes, and as I saw hers I felt a warm stream of tears running down my cheeks as well. I was too overwhelmed to do anything but hug my mom.

My mother told me to call Christiane because she didn't want to talk to anyone but me right now. I didn't want to talk to anyone either. The only thing I could think about was Kelly and Jenn. The three of them were my best friends in the whole world. Christiane and I were like sisters. We had done everything together since... well, forever. Kelly, Christiane, Jenn, and me. That's it. We were all best friends—BFF—best friends forever. Now two of them were almost gone?

I ran to the parlor and cried. I didn't stop. Everything seemed to be blocked out of me. I wanted to run. I wanted to be with Christiane. I had to be with her. We needed each other right now, and we were a thousand miles apart.

As the night wore on, I heard the phone ring. My mom answered and murmured something into the receiver. Then I heard footsteps coming down the hall... my mom's footsteps. Not wanting to talk, I rolled over and pretended to be asleep. My mom came over to my bed and handed me the phone. I pushed it back. I didn't want to talk to anyone. I couldn't. "Courtney, it's Chris. She won't talk to anyone but you. She needs you right now. You need each other," she said quietly but firmly. She pushed the phone back toward me, and this time she didn't allow me to push it back. There I was, trying to think of what to say to my best friend.

"Hi, Christiane," I said very quietly.

"Hi, Court," Chris said back.

"I don't really know what to say. I am so confused. None of this is sinking in right now."

"Yeah. It hasn't sunk in for me either, and the scary part is that I could have been on that sled with them."

"Oh please, Chris! Don't even go there! Please! Please!"

There was a long moment of silence between us. Then I said I had to go, even though I really didn't. I just didn't know what else to say. So we just hung up.

A few hours later, I woke up not realizing where I was or what was happening. I looked at my alarm clock and saw that it was very early in the morning. I had no idea why I was awake. Then I remembered. Tears came into my eyes, and I wiped them away. I climbed out of bed and went downstairs. I saw my mom, just sitting at the table, looking out the window. I knew something was terribly wrong.

She hugged me hard as she gave me the worst news of my life. "Oh, Court," she said softly. "Jenni died this morning."

And that was it. I screamed and ran. Then there was nothing. I wanted to be with Jenn—to laugh with her, do stuff like we used to—just to see her. I never would again.

Now I'm on the plane again. We are going back to Colchester for

Jenni's funeral. I haven't sorted through my feelings enough to understand how to deal with what has happened. I know I will get there eventually, but I'm not there yet. All I can think about is Kelly and Chris and what I will say when I see them. And poor Jenni. I look out the window, and the tears run down my face. I had always thought that plane rides were supposed to be for fun, for an adventure... but never again will I think that.

~Courtney VanDyne
Chicken Soup for the Girl's Soul

71

Celebrate the Good Days

The human spirit is stronger than anything that can happen to it.
~C.C. Scott

Cancer. It sends chills up my spine as I say it. A six-letter word causes so much pain. I didn't think it would happen to anyone that I knew, until it happened to my mom.

It was in April of what seemed to be a great year. I was in fourth grade with the greatest teacher, Miss DeRosear. It was the year everyone looked forward to because Miss D. was the coolest teacher.

I had just come home from school to find Mom at home. That was odd because she never arrived home before me. Mom was sitting on the couch with Dad. A thousand horrible things started flashing through my mind. What if Grandma had passed away? I did not have the chance to say goodbye. What if my brother was hurt? As I crawled up on the couch next to Mom, she gave me a kiss and a huge smile, so I relaxed and went on with my normal after school activities. During the TV show that I always watched after school, Mom started getting phone calls. The calls continued for the rest of the night. Each time the phone rang, Mom rushed to her room. I then knew that something bad had happened.

When Mom came back, I asked, "Mom, why do you keep on leaving the room every time you get a phone call?"

She turned to my sister and me and said, "Girls, I have something to tell you. I have a disease that will make me very sick. I have cancer."

As she said that I felt a sharp pain in my heart. I was thinking, "Why is God taking my mom from me so soon? What have I done?" Little did I know that we were just beginning a very long, painful journey.

The next day on the bus I turned to my friend, Kate. "My mom...." That was all I could say before I started crying. Kate gave me a big hug and whispered, "I know, and I'm here for you." I knew then that Kate would support me.

As other people found out about my mom's cancer, they all had different ways of dealing with it. When my grandma found out about it, she had a difficult time, because to her, cancer was a death sentence. She had lost her husband, my grandfather, to cancer when my mom was only a senior in high school.

Then the time came for Mom to have chemotherapy. Her hair fell out, and she was always sick. I remember all those nights that she was too tired to eat, or she was sick from the chemotherapy.

During the summer, Mom stayed home. On the good days, Mom, Sis and I went down by the pond and made shapes out of clouds. On these days we talked about what we were going to do the next day, week, month, or year with Mom. We never talked about losing her.

Support came from many different people and places. When school started again, Mom had to have surgery. I stayed with one of my teachers, Mrs. Stephens. Mrs. Stephens made me rainbow French toast. It always made me feel better; it let me know that someone cared and made time to make something for me. I would feed it to the dog if I had too much or if I wanted the dog to feel good also. Mrs. Stephens was always there for me with a smile, a hug, or "it will be okay" advice.

Sometimes I lost hope, wondering, "Am I losing my mother just like she lost her father?" I spent hours just ranting at God, telling him that he could not take her away! I needed her! He just could not take her away!

After a long six months of losing her hair and throwing up

because of chemo, my mom took a turn for the better. She slowly started to recover.

On April 5, my mom became a five-year survivor. When that day came, we had a big party. Friends came from far and wide to celebrate how special Mom is and her victory against cancer!

If you know someone who has cancer, you can help by doing little things. You can stay with them for awhile and just chat or do some chores.

Dealing with cancer is so hard. Don't bottle up your feelings. Talk to someone. Chat rooms are available for kids dealing with cancer, and support groups help kids and teens deal with cancer, too. Do not give up!

There will be good days and bad days—some more bad than good. But as I have learned from my mother, celebrate the good days!

~Leslie Beck
Chicken Soup for the Preteen Soul

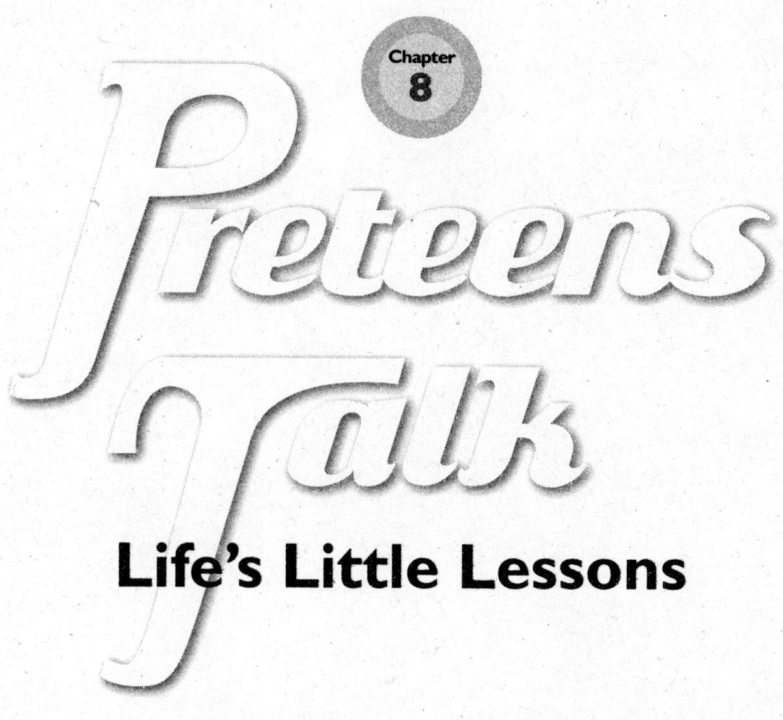

Chapter
8

Preteens Talk

Life's Little Lessons

Man is harder than iron, stronger than stone,
and more fragile than a rose.
~Turkish Proverb

72

Never Put Rocks in Your Mouth

Life is really simple, but we insist on making it complicated.
~Confucius

When I was in the sixth grade, my teacher asked our class the question, "What does 'doing the right thing' mean to you?" She asked us to think about that question over the weekend, and to talk to our parents or anyone else we thought might have a good answer. By Monday, we were to turn in an essay on what "doing the right thing" meant, and be prepared to live up to our answers.

The entire weekend, I wracked my brain trying to come up with something that would impress my teacher and be easy to live by. I talked to my parents, called my grandmother, and asked my next door neighbor. I even asked the mailman! Everyone had good answers, but I didn't feel like I could live up to them.

By Sunday afternoon, I hadn't written my essay. To make matters worse, my parents said we were going to my Aunt Cindy's house. That usually meant that I would have to entertain my cousin Andrea while my parents visited after dinner. Andrea was four and a major pest.

Just as I predicted, my parents told me to play with Andrea while they visited. I turned on the television and found a Disney movie for Andrea, and then I sat down and started to write my essay. I still didn't know what I was going to write about, but it was due the next morning and this was my last chance.

Soon I felt a pair of eyes on me. It was Andrea.

"What are you doing?" she asked.

"I have to write an essay about what doing the right thing means to me."

Andrea laughed. "That's easy," she said.

"Okay," I said, thinking, "What could this smart aleck four-year-old possibly know that all of the adults who I had asked hadn't already come up with?"

"Tell me the answer," I said smugly.

Andrea cleared her throat and stood up.

"Doing the right thing means: Being nice to your family and friends. Doing what your mommy says. Never lie. Eat lots of fruits and vegetables. Don't eat dog food. Take a bath when you're dirty and wash your own private parts. Don't watch icky movies with kissing and stuff. Don't waste water and electricity. Don't scare the cat. Don't ever run away. And never, never put rocks in your mouth."

I stared with astonishment at my little cousin. Then I jumped up, grabbed Andrea and gave her the biggest hug I could. Not only had Andrea answered a very tough question for me, I could easily live by all of her rules. All I had to do was be nice, not lie, keep myself clean and healthy, not scare cats, and never, never put rocks in my mouth. Piece of cake. So when I wrote my essay, I included the story about Andrea and how she had answered my question.

Two weeks later, my teacher returned everyone's essays. I received an A+ along with a little note my teacher had written at the top: "Always do the right thing—and give Andrea an A+, too!"

~Shirley Barone Craddock
Chicken Soup for the Preteen Soul

73

There Is Always Someone Less Fortunate

We often take for granted the very things that
most deserve our gratitude.
~Cynthia Ozick

It's 8:00 A.M., and Mum just called me to get up. I'm lying in bed daydreaming about what I want to do today. I want to stay home and listen to my CDs. I want to work on my tan and then swim in the pool when I get hot. I want to play basketball with my friends and just hang out. I want to watch television and go on my PC and chat with my friends online.

It's 8:30 A.M. now, and Mum is shouting at me to get up. So, I get up, put my swimsuit on, take my CD Walkman outside, and lie in the sun for a little bit.

Then my mum comes out, telling me that I need to get dressed into some nice clothes that are not going to be too hot for me to walk around in. I ask, "Why do I need to do that? I'm staying home, working on my tan and just chilling for the day." But Mum wants me to go out with her. She tells me a lot about this place called Give Kids the World. It's a special place for families to spend a vacation when a child has a life-threatening illness. She sometimes goes and meets families at the airport and escorts them to the village. There are several jobs she does there, including serving ice cream and gift giving. I expect this is a very boring job to do, but Mum says I will enjoy it.

So, I get dressed in suitable clothes, get in the car, and Mum drives to this place. I think it looks really childlike and silly. There is a warehouse at the back of the village that we go into to do our work. I have to put food into boxes. I don't know why, but I do it anyway. Then I have to put some gifts on the back of a golf cart. Mum tells me we are going to deliver a toy to every child in the village. Mum and I then start off on the rounds. We go to the first villa but no one is home, so we leave the gifts for the children to find when they get back.

We pull up to the next house, and I knock on the door and shout, "Gift giving," and a woman answers the door. She tells me I can come in. Sitting in the middle of the living room is a young boy in a wheelchair. I give him the gifts I have for him, and his face lights up with joy. I walk out and think to myself, "That must be a real pain, not being able to jump around or play basketball."

At another villa a bit later on, I knock on the door, again shouting "Gift giving," and another person answers the door. I enter this villa, and lying on a chair is a little girl with tubes in her nose and one coming from her tummy. Her brother is feeding her through a tube. The food is a milky liquid and looks disgusting. I did the same as before—gave them their gifts and walked out. I suddenly thought that it must really be uncomfortable lying there not being able to feed yourself or to be able to eat anything you want, especially sweets and chocolate.

I get to the third house, and I go through the same process again. As I come in with the gifts, it seems a little strange that the child doesn't notice me. Her mum says that she is deaf and only partially sighted, so I need to go and stand in front of her, so she can see the gift. When I do that, she gets very excited and makes a sign with her hands. Her mum tells me this is the sign for thank you. I ask her mum how you say goodbye in sign language. She shows me and I sign to the little girl, and she signs back as I leave the house.

Once back in the cart, I ask my mum what is wrong with these kids. Mum tells me that they all have life-threatening illnesses and that they might not live to see tomorrow. That is shocking to me. Suddenly, I realize that I should be more thankful that I don't have these illnesses—that I am not in the same position as these kids. I no longer want to be at home working on my tan, listening to my CDs, playing basketball or swimming in the pool. I would much rather be doing this, seeing things that not a lot of people really get to see, maybe making a difference in these kids' lives.

My first visit to Give Kids the World was over six months ago, and I now go on a regular basis. I have even taken one of my friends along as well. I do miss spending the time at home and hanging out with my friends, but I wouldn't want to miss the opportunity to make a difference to these kids who are much worse off than I am.

~Amy Mallinder-Morgan
Chicken Soup for the Preteen Soul 2

74

Like Me

I went to my dad, and I said to him,
There's a new kid who's come to my school.
He's different from me and he isn't too cool.
No, he's nothing at all like me, like me,
No, he's nothing at all like me.

He runs in a funnyish jerkyish way,
And he never comes first in a race.
Sometimes he forgets which way is first base,
And he's nothing at all like me, like me,
No, he's nothing at all like me.

He studies all day in a separate class,
And they say that it's called Special Ed.
And sometimes I don't understand what he's said,
And he's nothing at all like me, like me,
No, he's nothing at all like me.

His face looks kind of different from mine,
And his talking is sometimes slow.
And it makes me feel funny and there's one thing I know;
He is not at all like me, like me,
No, he's nothing at all like me!

And my father said, "Son, I want you to think
When you meet someone different and new
That he may seem a little bit strange, it's true,
But he's not very different from you, from you,
No, he's not very different from you."

Well I guess, I admitted, I've looked at his face;
When he's left out of games, he feels bad.
And when other kids tease him, I can see he's so sad.
I guess that's not so different from me, from me,
No, that's not very different from me.

And when we're in Music, he sure loves to sing.
And he sings just like me, right out loud.
When he gets his report card, I can tell he feels proud.
And that's not very different from me, from me,
No, that's not very different from me.

And I know in the lunchroom he has lots of fun;
He loves hot dogs and ice cream and fries.
And he hates to eat spinach and that's not a surprise,
'Cause that's not very different from me, from me,
No, that's not very different from me.

And he's always so friendly, he always says hi,
And he waves and he calls out my name.
And he'd like to be friends and get into a game,
Which is not very different from me, from me,
No, I guess that's not different from me.

And his folks really love him, I saw them at school,
I remember on Open School Night—
They were smiling and proud and they hugged him real tight,
And that's not very different from me, from me,

No, that's not very different from me.

So I said to my dad, "Hey, you know that new kid?"
Well, I've really been thinking a lot.
Some things are different... and some things are not....
But mostly he's really like me, like me,
Yes, my new friend's... a lot... like me.

~Emily Perl Kingsley
Chicken Soup for the Unsinkable Soul

The Unusual Package

Do not judge according to appearance, but judge with righteous judgment.
~Jesus of Nazareth

The glow of the large colored lights illuminated the long strands of silvery tinsel and pinecone angels that decorated the huge tree in our classroom. Desks had been shoved to the back and replaced by rows of brown folding chairs. We had just finished our wonderful Christmas pageant. Now restless family members and friends wanted to head for home on this snowy Wisconsin evening, but they sat waiting. To them it was time to leave, but to each of us it was finally time to exchange the brightly wrapped presents piled under the tree.

Earlier in December, each of us students had pulled a slip of paper with a name on it from an old coffee can. Then it was our job to buy a Christmas present for that person. All of us hoped that we would pull the name of our crush, or at least the name of our best friend.

The moment had finally come. One by one, our teacher handed Santa the presents, and he called out each name. Some of the kids hurried up to the front and then sat down to tear off the paper right away. Others took their time to receive their gift, carefully removing the bow and then trying to take off the paper without ripping even one corner. Soon, all kinds of gifts, from board games, candy, scarves and mittens to small toys and stuffed animals had been opened.

I stood off to one side with my two best friends, Carrie and Megan. Patiently, I oohed and aahed as they each opened their gifts. Carrie's gift was from Kevin. This was no surprise. Everyone in school knew how Kevin had held his brother's head in a snowbank until he finally agreed to give up Carrie's name. Kevin had given her a two-pound box of chocolates, which she generously shared with Megan and me. I think Carrie was secretly hoping for something a little more personal like a bracelet or a ring, but I'm sure Kevin's mother had something to say about what he was allowed to give Carrie.

Megan's package contained a book of 365 crossword puzzles and word searches, "One for Every Day of the Year," the bright red print on the cover proclaimed. This was perfect for Megan, who happened to be the brains of our group. She rushed over to thank Shelby.

As Carrie flirted with Kevin and Megan pored over her book, I stuffed chocolate after chocolate in my mouth. I tried to appear calm and disinterested while, one by one, the pile of presents shrank.

Finally, the last brightly wrapped present was gone from under the tree, and I began to silently panic. I quickly put what I hoped was a brave smile on my face, which wasn't particularly easy to do, because I was thirsty after eating six chocolates and my mouth was already dry from anxiety.

Santa was about ready to get up and distribute candy bags to the kids in the crowd when our teacher handed Santa one more gift. He called out my name, and I hustled to the front of the room, too relieved to even pretend to be disinterested. Santa handed me an old, sort of dirty looking envelope. That's weird, I thought. What an unusual package. Who would wrap something like this? I vaguely remember mumbling "thank you" as someone in the crowd giggled. Red-faced, I hurried back to my friends.

"Who's it from?" asked Carrie.

I turned over the envelope and revealed, "To Barbie from Sarah," written in pencil. My heart dropped down to my toenails when I saw it.

Sarah was the middle child of eleven. Her family had moved here about two years ago. They lived in a house that would have been too small, no matter how few kids would have been in the family. Their yard was strewn with cars that no longer worked and parts of broken toys; a bicycle wheel there, a wagon handle here, a stuffed bear that their dog had probably chewed the legs off of. Sarah was nice enough but terribly shy. She wore strange combinations of clothes and had trouble with her schoolwork, especially reading. Sometimes our teacher asked me to help her.

My mother had instilled in me that I should always be polite and act as if I like a gift (even the time that I got a black and white shirt from my sister that made me look like an escaped convict).

"Feelings are more important than things," she always said. "There is nothing in the world worth hurting someone else's feelings over." So with my mother and the entire roomful of people looking on, I was ready to act as if I had just been given the best present I had ever received.

"Maybe it's money," whispered Carrie.

"I think it's probably a poem," chimed in Megan.

But when I tore open the envelope and reached my fingers in, I knew they were both wrong. I felt something hard in the corner. I pulled out a long silver chain. Dangling from the chain was a teardrop-shaped blue iridescent pendant with a scalloped silver border. It was truly beautiful.

I looked up and saw Sarah's anxious face across the room. I flashed her a big smile and mouthed, "Thank you." She smiled back, revealing pink candy cane-stained teeth.

That night, I received more than the gift Sarah gave me, which I still have. Even more valuable than that pretty necklace were the lessons that I learned that Christmas. I learned not to prejudge others, and that sometimes my turn will come last. And finally, that nice presents and kind hearts can come in unusual packages.

~Barbara King
Chicken Soup for the Soul: Christmas Treasury for Kids

76

In Every Thought

> *Some people come into our lives and quickly go.*
> *Some stay for a while and leave footprints on our hearts.*
> *And we are never, ever the same.*
> *~Unknown*

I don't remember exactly when he came into my life. He was just always there. My grandfather was the most incredible person in the world.

Some days Papa (as I called him) and I would go down to a little creek that flowed into the river and go fishing. He taught me how to cast, reel, and the scariest of all, bait a hook. I remember what it was like to catch my first fish, which Papa called a blue gill. For the first time in my life, I felt I had accomplished something useful. I was proud of myself.

Other days we'd sit on the front porch in the rocking chairs he had made and talk.

But the thing I loved most was when we'd go out to the barn and he'd make things out of wood. He made me my first rocking horse when I was four. It wasn't anything fancy, but like me, Papa believed if it came from the heart, then that alone made it beautiful.

Above all, anything that could bother a seven-year-old was something that I could always talk to him about. Papa would set me on his knee and listen to me cry. He made the world go away with one hug.

Whenever I needed punishment, he always talked to me about what I had done. He'd ask me why I made that mistake, while every other authority figure I knew went straight to physical punishment. He was the one person who had my respect, and who actually treated me with respect in return.

Something else I admired was that he didn't treat me like a girl who only related to pink ribbons and Barbies. He treated me like a person.

When I turned eight, a horrifying fact changed my life forever. That fact was death.

In September, they discovered that my Papa had cancer. It never sank in, even at his funeral the next February, that I'd never see him alive again.

The agonizing six months of his sickness were long and cruel, especially to my grandmother, who could not talk without crying. I didn't know what death was.

Everything was a big, rushing blur. It was too much for an eight-year-old, so I blocked it out. Whatever death was, it wasn't real to me.

Slowly, I learned I couldn't block it out. There were no more rodeos, no more fishing, no more horses and no one left to talk to. When I walked into my grandmother's house, there was no longer the smell of smoke mixed with coffee and sawdust, which was what Papa always smelled like. Everyone around me was sad, and I was learning what it was like to be sad.

It finally hit me that he was gone. Things started getting rough with guys and friends. I knew if Papa had been alive, he could've helped. Instead I faced the world alone, and believe me, there are many pressures from sixth grade to high school. The world had become very cruel to me, or so it seemed, and I missed Papa. Night after night, I would go to bed crying.

In seventh grade, I hung out with the wrong crowd. One morning, in the bathroom, a girl offered me a cigarette. All of a sudden, something clicked in my mind. Cigarettes are what had killed my Papa.

"No," was my simple but strong reply. Regardless of their comments like "good girl" and "too-good," I stuck with my no smoking policy. Since then, I have been offered cigarettes many times, and I have always replied with a simple "no." I wouldn't want my grandchildren feeling the way I did if they lost me to smoking.

I was too young to figure out what a great role model I had around me when he was alive. But I realize it now. Papa is in every thought I have today. I still have all our special memories in my heart. He always made me believe in myself. Anything I do, he has influenced in some way. No one has ever or will ever have the patience he had with me.

His death taught me many lessons, but the one so harshly instilled in me is that no one, even someone as great as him, is invincible.

~Leslie Miller
Chicken Soup for the Preteen Soul

77

A Valentine for Grandma

It was just a harmless prank, that's all that it was. And it wasn't as though Old Lady Hayes didn't deserve it. The way she used to scream at us for borrowing a few of her precious raspberries, like we were stealing gold from Fort Knox... well, she had it coming.

At least, that's the way it seemed to us as George finished tying the string to the red, heart-shaped box. We giggled as Ron added the final touch: two plastic red roses, glued to the lid of the empty valentine box.

"I wonder what will surprise her most," I asked as George and Albert practiced jerking the box out of reach by yanking on the used kite string we had attached to it, "seeing a box of candy on her step, or watching it fly away when she tries to pick it up?"

We laughed as we watched George make Albert chase the empty box around the dusty garage. For a chubby ten-year-old Navajo, Albert did a pretty good imitation of Mrs. Hayes's hunched-over hobble and her seemingly permanent scowl. And we howled when he picked up a broom and pretended to ride it through the midwinter air while shouting, "I'm Old Lady Hayes, the driedest-up old prune in the West!"

Ron was the first to notice my dad in the doorway. Within seconds, Ron's anxiety was shared by all but Albert, who, unaware of Dad's presence, continued to swoop around the garage, cackling and screeching all the way, until he came face-to-belt-buckle with our silent observer.

For a few moments, the only movement in the suddenly quiet room came from mouths. Albert pulled a face, groping in his mind for some way to conceal the evidence now stacked so neatly against him—and us.

Dad broke the stillness by walking slowly to the empty candy box lying on the floor at Albert's feet. He picked it up and dangled it by the string, watching it swing incriminatingly back and forth. Then he looked into the eyes of the six frightened boys who anxiously watched his every move. And, as was his custom, he looked into their hearts as well.

"It doesn't seem so long ago that I was pulling Valentine's Day pranks myself," he said as he laid the heart-shaped box on the work-bench. At first it was difficult to picture my dignified father pulling the kind of prank we were planning. But then I remembered a picture I had seen of him as a child, with fiery red hair, a freckled face, green eyes and wearing a tight, impish grin. It was possible, I thought.

"One Valentine's Day my cousins and I decided to pull a good one on my Grandma Walker," he continued. "Not because we didn't like her. She was the sweetest grandma a boy could ever have, and we loved her. We were just feeling a little devilish and decided to have some fun at her expense.

"Early in the evening we snuck up to her doorstep with a can of red paint. Grandma was hard of hearing, so we didn't have to worry about being very quiet. Which was a good thing, because every time we thought about how funny it was going to be to see Grandma try to pick up a valentine that was just painted on her doorstep, we couldn't keep from laughing.

"It didn't take long to finish. It wasn't very artistic, but for a bunch of farm kids and an old woman with poor eyesight, it would do. As soon as we were satisfied with the painting, we kicked the door and ran to hide behind bushes and trees to watch the fun.

"There was a lot of giggling going on as we waited in the snow for Grandma to open the door. When she finally appeared, she stood in the doorway for a minute, peering into the darkness, her gray hair pulled back tightly into her usual bun, wiping her hand on her usual white apron.

"She must have heard the commotion in the bushes because she looked in our direction as she spoke loudly enough for us to hear: 'Who could be knocking at my door this hour of the night?' My stomach and cheeks ached from trying to hold back the laughter. Then she looked down at her doorstep. Even from fifteen yards away we could see the joy that sparkled in her eyes when she spotted the splash of red at her feet.

"'Oh, how wonderful!' she exclaimed. 'A valentine for Grandma! And I thought I was going to be forgotten again this year!'

"She bent down to retrieve her prize. This was the moment we had been waiting for, but somehow it wasn't as much fun as we had planned. Confused, Grandma groped at the fresh paint for a moment. She quickly became aware of our prank. Her delight at having been remembered by a sweetheart on Sweetheart's Day was short lived.

"She tried to smile. Then, with as much dignity as she could muster, she turned and walked back into her house, absently wiping red paint on her clean, white apron."

Dad paused for a moment, allowing stillness to once again settle over the cluster of attentive boys. For the first time I noticed that my father's eyes were moist. He took a deep breath. "Grandma died later that year," he said. "I never had another chance to give her a real valentine."

He took the candy box from the workbench and handed it to me. Not another word was spoken as he turned and left the garage.

Later that night a red, heart-shaped box with two plastic roses on it was placed on Mrs. Hayes's front doorstep by six giggling boys. We hid behind snow-covered bushes and trees to see how she would react to receiving a full pound of candy and nuts.

With no strings attached.

~Joseph Walker
Chicken Soup for the Grandparent's Soul

78

Cry When You Are Sad

On a sunny Monday in April, I had two loving grandmothers near me, but when Tuesday came, only one was left. One of my grandmothers, who was dear to me, had died. I had a feeling that this awful day was going to come soon, but now that it was here, all I wanted to do was cry. But I wasn't brave enough to shed a tear, for I was always taught that boys should never cry.

Later, as the time came for the funeral activities, I had the hardest time keeping my sadness inside.

My relatives soon arrived from all over the country. I really had to hold back my tears now that my relatives were here, because I did not want to look like a crybaby in front of them. I figured out that my parents, my sister, and I were the only ones who had lived in the same town as my grandma. That explained why her death was hitting me the hardest, while my cousins seemed as though they were here just to get away from home. They really hadn't known her like I had.

Soon, all of my relatives gathered at the funeral home, waiting for the viewing to begin. What I thought was going to be the easiest part of my grieving turned into the hardest.

The moment I walked into the room where my grandma was laying in a coffin, my heart dropped. This was going to be the last time that I would ever see her. At first I was afraid to proceed with the rest of my family up to her coffin, but then I realized that I would have to sooner or later. I grabbed hold of my mother's hand and kept my mind on remembering not to cry.

When I came up to the kneeler, in front of where she was laying, my mother made me do something that almost brought me to tears. She told me to touch Grandma's hand, for that was going to be the last time that I would get a chance to touch her. I reached over to her hand very slowly, afraid of what she might feel like. When my hand touched hers, I was relieved for a moment. She felt the same way she always had, except a little cooler than usual.

When I looked up at my mom, she began crying uncontrollably. I knew this was the time that I really had to be strong. I reached my arms around her and slowly walked with her back to our seats.

During the next few hours, I met many different people. All of them were telling me that they were sorry about my grandma passing away. I just smiled and reminded myself not to cry, because I had so often been told, "Boys should be strong and not cry." I kept reminding myself that soon this night would be over, but the next day would be the actual funeral... the last goodbye.

My mother woke me early the next morning, making sure that I looked my best. I promised myself when I was getting dressed that I would hold back my tears no matter what. I had to be strong and help my grieving parents.

When we arrived at the church, we all waited as they took my grandma's coffin from the big black hearse. We had to follow it in so everyone knew that we were family. Once inside, we took our seats. My family sat in the very front because we were the closest to my grandma. I was surprised to see that even before the service began, my parents were crying. I was trying to hold back my tears, but as the priest began talking about my grandma, it seemed as though not crying was going to be an impossible task.

About halfway through the mass, he began telling the people about how much my grandma was loved by her family and friends. He then mentioned how every night I stayed with her while my parents were working. That reminded me of all of the good times we had together throughout my life. In the summer, we would glide on her swing. In the winter, we would always ride sleds down the big hill behind her house. There were so many good times that went through my mind that I almost forgot where I was. I began to realize that those good times were gone forever. At this exact thought, I began to cry uncontrollably. I didn't care anymore about what other people thought of me. It was something that I just had to do. I could not hold back my sadness anymore.

When my father noticed me sobbing, he leaned me up next to him and we cried together. My father, my mother, my sister, and I sat next to each other, crying as if the world was going to end. At this point I promised to myself that if I ever had a son, I would tell him: "Real boys show emotions. Cry when you are sad, and smile when you are happy." This was the last time I would say goodbye to my grandmother, but I was a better person for letting my tears show everyone just how much I loved her.

~Jonathan Piccirillo
Chicken Soup for the Preteen Soul

79

Lucky

You don't choose your family. They are God's gift to you, as you are to them.
~Desmond Tutu

When you're a preteen, a huge problem might be like when you just have to have this new rock-rap CD that you don't even like, but everybody else says is cool, but your parents won't give you the twenty bucks for it.

Or having this gigantic zit and desperately needing to see a dermatologist right away when nobody else can even see the zit.

I thought life was so unfair when things like this happened—until September 11, 2001.

I was in P.E. when the planes hit the World Trade Center and the Pentagon. As soon as I got home and for weeks after, I saw the disaster unfold on TV. Seeing the innocent people running for their lives as the debris started coming down and the fire and smoke billowed out of the buildings brought tears to my eyes. I couldn't help imagining what the people on the planes and in the buildings were thinking and going through, not knowing what was going on. I admired the courage of the firefighters who rushed in and risked their own lives to save others. It tore my heart apart to watch the desperate looks on the faces of so many people who didn't know if their loved ones were dead or alive while trapped in all the rubble. I felt so sorry for the people whose loved ones were killed and wished that I could help ease the pain of those whose family members died.

Then it hit me: All my life I had thought mainly of myself. I had it easy in life and had been taking it all for granted.

A cold chill ran down my back, and I cried just thinking of the possibility that it could have easily happened to my family. My mom or dad, or both, could have been killed like that, and I would never, ever see them again. I began to evaluate what a real problem in life was.

This tragedy taught me that awful things can happen to anyone at any time. I know now that I have it made compared to others. Now when my mom or dad or sister go somewhere, even if it's just to the store, I try to remember to tell them that I love them because I know there is a chance that I may never get to tell them that again.

Not getting a new CD or having a zit is not going to make or break my life. I can live with those kinds of problems. But losing someone I love would truly make my life miserable.

9/11 showed me just what I am.

Lucky.

Very lucky.

~Molly McAfee
Chicken Soup for the Preteen Soul 2

80

Think Before You Act

I t was a cold evening, the night before Halloween, when something happened in my town that no one will ever forget. During lunchtime at school, some girls who were my brother's friends told him about a plan that they had to toilet paper a guy's house. They had already been playing pranks on this guy, and they were laughing about what his house would look like when they were through with it. My brother told me later that he knew what they were planning on doing was wrong, but he didn't say anything to the girls. Now, he wishes he would have.

That night my brother's six friends stayed overnight at one of the girls' houses. In the middle of the night, they sneaked out of the house. They piled into one of the girls' small blue car and set off to play their little prank. When they got to the guy's house, everything went as planned—until they got caught. The guy that they were playing the prank on came outside and saw them. Laughing, they all ran to the car and hopped in, hoping to get away. The guy got into his car and chased after them, trying to identify them. He was right on their tail, and it scared the girls really badly. They were not sure what he would do to them if he caught them, so they went faster.

Then, when they were turning on a blind curve in the road, they lost control of the car and hit a tree head-on. Three of the girls were ejected from the car and were killed instantly. The other three girls were seriously injured. One of the girls had just enough strength to get out of the car and go to a nearby house. The people who answered the door were afraid of her and didn't even believe that there had been an accident. They said, "Yeah, right, you really got into a wreck," and they would not call the police.

The three girls that died were all honor roll students and were looking ahead to doing something great with their lives. But all of their dreams were shattered when they hit the tree on that cold night. Only one of my brother's friends was wearing a seat belt, and she was one of the survivors. Now whenever I get into a car, I think about the accident and put on my seat belt.

The guy that chased them went to court. All he got was a ticket for running a stop sign and for speeding. I often wonder if he feels anything at all about the death of the girls in that car that he chased. My brother feels bad that he didn't say anything to his friends that day when they told him what they were planning on doing. They still might have gone on their mission regardless of what he said, but he might have saved his friends' lives. We'll never know. So many people have suffered because of a stupid act that was never meant to go wrong.

The only good thing that came from this tragic event is that the mother of one of the deceased girls is setting up a teen center in town in memory of the girls who died. Now there will be a place for teens. Maybe that will keep some of them from getting into situations like this by providing a place to hang out and have fun, to talk to each other, and hopefully give them a chance to help them think before they act.

~Lauren Wheeler
Chicken Soup for the Preteen Soul

Ramon

You learn something every day if you pay attention.
~Ray LeBlond

It was an average April day when the phone rang. I rushed to answer it.

"Hello," I answered.

"Hi, Emma, it's Kim. Is your mom home?"

Kim is my mom's friend, and she sounded like something was urgent.

"She's out of town but should be back this evening," I replied, wondering what had happened.

"Well, is your dad home?" she asked quickly.

My dad was in the shower, so I told her that he couldn't talk at the moment. She told me to tell him to call her as soon as possible. I hung up the phone thinking, "What could be that important?" Had something really gone wrong? Had something happened to her son, Bain, who had been in my class since kindergarten?

I sat down to read, but I was shaken.

A while later, I was reading and had forgotten to tell my dad about the phone call, even though he had been out of the shower for quite some time. The sky was dimming, and it was getting to be dinnertime. I was jolted from my story by the ring of the phone. I hopped up to get it.

It was Kim again. I handed the phone to my dad, who had come into the kitchen to see if it was for him. I went back to my chair to read, but of course I wasn't really reading, but rather pretending to read while I listened intently to their conversation.

My dad's voice became serious and solemn, and as I listened, it seemed to become more so. I heard things like, "I'm so sorry," and "He was a great kid."

My stomach became queasy. What did my dad mean by, "He was a great kid"? Who was he talking about? I felt nervous and scared.

I heard my dad say a quiet, "Goodbye," and a click. The floorboards creaked as my dad headed across the kitchen toward me. I braced myself for whatever news I was about to hear. Dad came to stand next to me and was silent for a moment before he spoke. He seemed very nervous and things felt awkward.

"Emma," he began. I stared up at him, dreading the news, yet wanting to hear it.

"Ramon's dead," he said quietly.

My stomach lurched. I shook. Had I heard wrong? This couldn't be right, but my dad wouldn't joke about such things.

Ramon had been in my class since grade one, and had become an important part of my school. He had come from Germany, not knowing a word of English, but he learned the language rapidly since reading had become a passion of his. He had loved the outdoors, excelled in soccer, and had been quite a gentleman. He had been my teammate and classmate. At one point, I had even had a crush on him. And now he was gone.

I thought back to that day at school when he and Shane had been playing roughly. Ramon hit his head, but he had seemed all right afterwards, though not in the best mood.

"He hit his head pretty hard at school today when he and Shane were fooling around," I told my dad, wondering if the accident had been more than it seemed. I tried hard not to cry.

"That wasn't quite the reason for his death," my dad said. "It seems that he hanged himself."

That made it even more horrible. How could someone who was

so full of life just take it away? So what if he had been suspended? That was no reason for him to do this. He had been a very emotional guy; when he was happy the world was heaven, but when he was mad, the world was... well, you know.

"Oh," I responded, not knowing what else to say.

"I'm really sorry," my dad told me—truly meaning it.

At that moment, I really wished my mom were there. I love my dad dearly, but my mom was so much more comforting. I stood up and wrapped my arms around my father, and he returned the embrace warmly.

A few minutes later, my mom came through the door calling to us happily and talking about her trip. My dad and I didn't say much until she had gotten up the stairs. We then told her what happened. Tears rolled down her cheeks as my dad told her the horrible news. I held her close and cried.

The next morning, my teacher told us to come to school with our parents, and that it would be a half day in which we would grieve together. That day we shared stories and experiences that included the happy Ramon. I saw people cry who had never cried in front of me before. That day brought my class together in a way nothing ever had.

Weeks later our class went to Ramon's house to plant a garden in his honor. We planted cloves (his favorite) and wild plants. His mom watched with tears in her eyes, touched by what we had done in his memory.

I have learned so much from this, but most of all, to be kind to people, for even if it seems what you are doing and saying is harmless, it may not be so harmless to the person you're aiming it at. Be kind and think before you act—you may save a life with your kindness.

I hope that Ramon has found peace and happiness where he is now, which he was unable to find here. And, although I may not pass to Ramon in soccer anymore, I'll always remember his big smile.

~Emma Fraser
Chicken Soup for the Preteen Soul 2

82

The Reason for Living

Perfect love sometimes does not come until the first grandchild.
~Welsh Proverb

I'm only twelve years old, but I know sadness and the fear of death very well. My grandfather has been smoking since he was a young teenager, and now he has a terrible disease called emphysema that ruins the respiratory system.

Ever since my grandmother died, my grandfather has been depressed—mad at the world. He is a very ornery man and has said some hurtful things to nice people. But when he is around me, it's like a whole soft side of him becomes exposed.

Recently, my grandfather got very sick. He underwent surgery on his throat and had to use a machine called a respirator to help him breathe. The doctors thought that his days were numbered, but miraculously he recovered. He was taken off the respirator, but still he couldn't talk. It strained his voice badly to make the slightest noise.

While my grandfather was in the hospital, my mother and I flew to Pittsburgh to be with him. We were very fearful we wouldn't see him again.

When we reached my grandfather's hospital room, I was shocked by his condition. He looked so sickly. He was hardly able to even grunt. Somehow though, he managed to mumble, "I... you."

"You what, Grandpa?" I whispered. He didn't have the energy

to answer me. He had exhausted all his strength with those two syllables, "I... you."

The next morning my mother and I had to leave. I kept wondering just what it was he had tried so desperately to tell me. It wasn't until I was back home in Georgia that I learned what he had tried to say.

A week after we returned home, my family received a phone call from one of the nurses in the hospital. She told us that my grandfather had said, "Call my granddaughter and tell her 'love.'" At first I was a little confused, thinking why he would just say, "love." Why not "I love you?" Then it hit me. The day we were in the hospital he had been trying to say, "I love you." I was really touched. I felt as if I was going to cry, and I did.

After many painful weeks, my grandfather was finally able to talk. I called him every night. Normally he had to stop after about five minutes because he was too weak. No matter what, though, every time we hung up he would say, "I love you" and "I'd do anything for you." These, along with his moving words, "You're the only reason I live," are the best compliments I have ever received.

My grandfather is still very ill and I know our time is limited. I feel very honored that he has shared his feelings with me. I have learned a lot from this experience. But the most important thing I've learned is that a simple "I love you" is really not simple. It's a reason for living.

~Lauren Elizabeth Holden
Chicken Soup for the Preteen Soul

Chapter 9

Not-So-Random Acts of Kindness

You cannot do a kindness too soon,
for you never know how soon it will be too late.
~Ralph Waldo Emerson

83

Just the Two of Us

Sometime in your lifetime, you may be lucky enough to come across a person who knows exactly how you feel and is always there for you. Someone who loves you for who you are and doesn't judge you. Someone who believes in you and urges you to listen to your heart, no matter what anyone else thinks. This person helps you through your hardest days and assures you that tomorrow is always another day, a fresh beginning.

I didn't have anyone like this, until a stranger moved into my house and became my sister.

When I was seven years old, my mom died, and my life changed forever. My dad became a widower and our family was left without a mother. Then, about two years ago when I was twelve, my father remarried. My stepmother, Shelly, moved from New York to our small house in Missouri. She also brought along her daughter, an energetic and lively eleven-year-old named Ariele. With her beautiful blue eyes and winning smile, Ariele was always the center of attention. I never thought that I could bring myself to love her as a sister, because we didn't know each other at all.

It's amazing how opposite we are. I am a perfectionist and a neat freak. I say what I think people want to hear, and I hide what I'm really feeling. Ariele is so full of life, she lights up the room. She's extremely funny and cheerful, celebrating every moment of life. She always manages to crack my frown, figure out my problems and decode my weird moods. I hate to admit it, but even though I am one year older, she knows more about what really matters than I could ever hope to. There was one experience where I really found out how important it is to take each day as a blessing, and how to make the best of it.

Only a year and a half after Ariele came to live with us, my father accepted a new job as head of a private school. The benefits were great, but the only problem was that we would be forced to move across the country to Boston. I was going to have to leave all the people that I had grown to love and care about. I felt helpless. My life was a roller-coaster ride of mixed emotions, and I was stuck aboard, unable to make decisions or get off. But the one person who really helped me through my pain was my stepsister, Ariele. She had the best attitude from the start. She had just left her life in New York and moved when our parents got married. And although she had grown to love her new home, she realized that Boston was good for the family.

A few months later, after selling our home and packing up, we drove with our parents from St. Louis to New Hampshire, where both of us would attend camp. We had to leave for the summer, knowing we wouldn't be back for a long time. But the ride across the country was one of the most memorable few days. We were on the road in a stuffed minivan, filled with luggage and food, but Ariele and I loved it.

Because the car ride was so long, our parents went out of their way to stop at places to show us some of the country. At Niagara Falls, after observing the magnificent display, we decided to get even closer to the edge and climb to the point where people get soaked by the freezing waters. As Ariele and I neared this breathtaking waterfall, and as I watched my sister laugh with joy and shriek from exhilaration, I saw everything in a new light. I hadn't been living each day fully with the excitement or joy that Ariele demonstrated to me.

With soaked jeans and high spirits, we climbed even higher, so that the foggy mist blinded us, and we huddled together to keep ourselves warm. Her shaking arms hugged me, and she told me that she loved me. Then she stood before the mighty waterfall, eyes closed, and arms spread out wide, to let the water soak her... giggling as dripping strands of hair tickled her face. She looked so beautiful. There was something so magical about that moment that it will always remain in my memory.

As I looked at her, I thought of how drastically my view changed when Ariele came into my life, and I remembered all the things she urged me to try. There were so many times she made me feel like a little kid, just having fun, like the time in a park a few months ago. We went on a walk and passed a large, sloppy puddle of mud created from the rain the day before. She started playing in it, covering her hands and legs with the mud, and urged me to do the same. I hesitated, because there were so many people around, but then I thought, "Who cares?" So, together, we slipped and slid in that mud and had the best time.

I thought of the many times we've been at the mall, and I've seen something I have really liked but didn't want to spend my money for it. Her mouth will turn up in a mischievous grin, and she will say, "You only live once!" Then I end up buying the shirt or CD that I wanted so badly. And during these moments, I can't help realizing how much I owe her for giving me another shot at life, another chance.

Before Ariele moved in, I was so scared of risking things and too shy to express myself as I wanted to. I was reluctant to step out of my preteen mind and enjoy those little pleasures. Even though she may not be aware of it, she has taught me that the person who risks nothing will gain nothing. Pain and disappointment may be avoided, but one will simply never grow or learn. Without risks, one misses out on the incredible opportunities and experiences that make life worth living.

I owe everything to her. She is my better half and my best friend in the world.

So whenever we fight about our shared room, boys, or simply how we've been acting toward each other, I remember all the times we've spent together and realize that no matter how hard and impossible it seems at times, we always find a way to work it out. And through all of our family ups and downs, we'll be in it and stay in it—together. Two sisters who bring out the very best in each other, every single day... and in every possible way.

~Miriam Bard
Chicken Soup for the Preteen Soul 2

Nice Catch!

From the moment Kyle heard the loud crack of the Red Sox bat, he was sure the ball was headed over the fence. And he was ready for it. Without ever taking his eyes off the ball, he reached up and pulled it out of the air.

"I caught it!" he yelled to his dad and his grandpa. "And I caught it with my bare hands!"

It was opening day of spring training and they had come out to the ball field to watch the Red Sox play. Kyle's grandma and grandpa lived near Ft. Myers, Florida, where the Boston Red Sox come in late February to prepare for the season.

Later, on the way home to Grandma's house, Kyle kept his head down. He tried to think of a way to convince his parents to stay a few more days.

"Wish we could go back to the ballpark tomorrow," he said. "Maybe I'd catch another ball to put with my Little League trophies and stuff. And maybe I'd even get some autographs."

"You know that's not possible, Kyle," his dad said. "We're flying out early tomorrow morning."

"I know, I know," Kyle said, rolling the baseball around in his hand. "I just thought you and Mom might decide to stay a few more days. We don't go back to school until Monday, and tomorrow's only Thursday."

"We were lucky to get that flight!" his dad said firmly. "The airlines are booked solid this week."

That night, a huge snowstorm moved into the Northeast. When they arrived at the airport early the next morning, they were told that all flights into Logan Airport in Boston had been cancelled for the day.

On the drive back to his grandparents' house from the airport, it was obvious to Kyle that his dad was upset. It was definitely not a good time to bring up going back to the Red Sox ball field.

But by the time they were back at Grandma and Grandpa's house, Kyle's dad began to joke about the cancelled flight.

"Another day in sunny Florida isn't so bad," he said. "I'm in no hurry to get back to Boston, where my car's probably buried in snow."

"We could go out to the ball field again," Grandpa said. "Unless there's something else you'd rather do."

"The ballpark's fine," Kyle's dad said with a grin. "I'd never go against the wishes of anyone with so much power over the weather."

It was mid-afternoon when another loud crack of the Red Sox bat sent a ball flying over the fence. Again, Kyle reached up and caught the baseball in his bare hands.

As he rubbed his fingers around the ball, a small voice from behind him called out, "Nice catch!"

Kyle turned around to see a small boy in a wheelchair. Without a moment of hesitation, Kyle handed him the baseball.

"Here," he said. "You can have it. I already got one."

The grin on the boy's face was a mile wide.

"Thanks," he said. "I never held a real baseball before."

Kyle's dad and his grandpa looked surprised—very surprised.

But they were no more surprised than Kyle was himself. He couldn't believe what he'd just done. But he wasn't sorry. He could never forget the happy look on the small boy's face. It was worth a million baseballs.

"I'm gonna get some autographs," Kyle said, rushing off to meet the players as they came off the field.

With three Red Sox autographs in hand, Kyle walked back to the parking lot.

"Think the Red Sox will have a good season?" Grandpa asked.

"They looked pretty good today," Kyle said. Kyle's dad tapped him on the shoulder.

"You looked pretty good today yourself, son."

And three avid Red Sox fans left the training grounds, each carrying with him a special feeling of pride. The proudest of all was Kyle.

~Doris Canner
Chicken Soup for the Preteen Soul

A Friend's Secret

When I was a kid, every Thursday night was my mom's night out (usually she went to choir practice at church) and my dad's night to take the kids to dinner. We'd go to Red Lobster (Dad loved seafood) and order popcorn shrimp and hush puppies.

Suddenly, when I was in the seventh grade, my mom started going out almost every night of the week. After dinner, she'd kiss my sister, brother, and me and say, "Good night. See you in the morning."

"But where are you going?" I asked, incensed that she would just leave us, even when my dad wasn't home from work yet. My sister, Carla, was fourteen, but still....

"I'm going to see a friend," Mom would respond vaguely. "Someone who needs my help."

But I could see the signs. She'd put on a skirt, touch up her mascara, add another misting of perfume to her neck, grab her purse, and head out the door.

Mom was having an affair. On top of that, my own mother had lied to me. A friend who needed her help—ha!

I was furious.

I didn't tell anyone my suspicions, not Carla, who was too busy talking on the phone to her new boyfriend, and not Charlie, my eight-year-old brother, who barely looked up from the TV to tell Mom goodbye. Dad just acted like there was absolutely nothing wrong with his wife leaving the house after dinner to go on a date.

Apparently, everyone in my family had gone crazy.

Then, one day after school, Mom came to my room.

"Honey," she said, "there's something I need to talk to you about."

I knew what she was going to tell me. There would be a divorce, then a custody battle, then for the rest of my life I'd be packing up a suitcase to go from Mom's house to Dad's for the weekend. My stomach dropped to my ankles.

"What?" I demanded, surprising even myself by how hostile I sounded.

"It's about Christy."

Christy was one of my best friends. We didn't go to the same school—I went to public school and she went to private. We'd met at church and our parents were friends and we had grown up together. We played tennis on the weekends and then made chocolate chip cookies together. We both knew the recipe by heart.

The year before, Christy's family had moved to a new house on a hillside with a spectacular view. It had a long flight of steps down the back that led to a swimming pool and hot tub. I was jealous when Christy got to live in such a luxurious house. I shouldn't have worried, though, because I got to enjoy the new house too. Now after a hot game of tennis, we could go back to Christy's house for a dip in the pool, followed by lazy sunbathing.

"Well, what about her?" I finally asked.

Mom took a deep breath. "I just want you to be really nice to her for a while."

I rolled my eyes. "I'm always nice to her. She's my friend."

"I know, and you're a good friend. But things might be hard for her for a while, and she'll need your friendship more than ever."

"Mom, what are you talking about?"

"Maybe I'd better just tell you, Bethany. Christy's parents are getting a divorce."

It felt like the time during a soccer game that someone kicked the ball right into my stomach. I couldn't breathe. Then the guilt set in.

"You mean, when you said you were going out to help a friend...?"

"I was seeing Christy's mom. She needed to talk through some things."

I closed my eyes, feeling guilty for my suspicions, feeling even guiltier for the relief that flooded through me once I knew it wasn't my parents getting divorced.

"But, Bethany, you have to promise me you won't say anything to Christy. She doesn't know yet."

"She doesn't know?"

"Her parents still have some things to work out. They're not ready to tell Christy and Robbie yet." Robbie was Christy's little brother. "Promise me?"

"Yes, Mom, I promise."

That was a hard promise to keep. For weeks, I made a special effort to hang out with Christy and do fun things with her. Mostly we did the same old things: played tennis, swam in the pool, made cookies, went to the mall or the movies. It was summer and school was out, so we spent lots of time together. Christy didn't say anything about her parents, so I didn't either.

One day, Christy and I were lying on lounge chairs next to the pool at the beautiful house of which I had once been so jealous. While I read my book, Christy dozed. But she must not have been asleep, because suddenly she spoke. "Bethany?"

"Mm-hmm?"

"I have to tell you something."

My heart skipped a beat. "What?" I lifted my eyes over the edge of my book. Christy lay on the chair, her eyes still closed.

"My mom and dad are getting a divorce."

Knowing this information for weeks should have prepared me to say something profound when this moment came. But it hadn't. I couldn't even figure out how to act surprised.

"Christy, I'm so sorry."

"Thanks." A tear rolled out from underneath one of Christy's closed eyelids.

"That really sucks."

"Yeah." Christy turned her head in the other direction, so that she faced away from me.

"Do you want to talk about it?"

"Not really."

For a few minutes, silence floated between us like sunlight on the surface of the pool. "Christy?"

"Yeah?"

"Want to stay over at my house tonight?" I held my breath. "Mom has choir practice, so Dad's taking us out to eat."

Christy turned her head to face me again and smiled. "I'd like that," she said.

In that moment, I realized something. I couldn't make things better for Christy. I couldn't keep her parents from splitting up. I couldn't make Christy's pain go away. But if I kept being Christy's friend, even when she had to move to a new house with her mom, a house without a pool or a spectacular view, even when she got angry and threw things across the room, even when she needed to cry but didn't want to talk about it—if I could stick by her through all those things, then she would know that I loved her and cared about her.

And maybe that would help... just a little.

~Bethany Rogers
Chicken Soup for the Girl's Soul

86

The Note

Love me and the world is mine.
~David Reed

When I was in the fifth grade, I fell in love—real love—for the very first time. It only took about a week into the school year for it to happen, and I was completely, head-over-heels crushing on Mike Daniels. No one ever called him just Mike; it was always one word—Mike Daniels. Blond hair that stuck up in every direction and blue eyes that crinkled in the corners when he laughed—visions of Mike Daniels occupied my every dream.

To say I wasn't the most popular or prettiest girl in our class would be an understatement. In fact, I think I must have been the original geek. I was so skinny that I still had to wear days of the week panties and dorky undershirts when most of my friends were starting to wear bras and more grown-up undergarments. My mom made me wear brown orthopedic lace-up shoes to school every day, because I had a foot that turned in and my parents wanted to "correct it before it was too late." Right smack dab in the middle of my two front teeth was this giant space that even gum surgery the year before hadn't fixed, and the two teeth on either side of my front teeth over-lapped, making me look like I had fangs. Add a pair of thick glasses, thin baby-fine hair (with a home permanent from my mom—help!), knobby skinned-up knees and elbows—and what do you get? A kid that only a parent could love.

I wouldn't—couldn't—tell my friends that I was in love with Mike Daniels. It was my secret to write about in my journal. In my dreams, Mike Daniels would suddenly grasp what a beautiful soul was hiding inside my gawky body and realize that he loved me for who I really was. I spent hours writing poetry for him and stories about him, until one day I got up the nerve to actually write to him about how I felt.

Our teacher, Miss Finkelor, was really awesome about most things, but the one thing she was majorly serious about was not writing notes to each other during class. Everyone did it anyway. Except me. My only shot at self-esteem was being teacher's pet, and I excelled at it. I loved it so much it didn't even bother me when kids teased me about being the teacher's favorite.

It was a huge decision for me to go against the one thing that Miss Finkelor detested—note passing. But I knew that there was no other way to tell Mike Daniels about how I felt—and I also knew that if I never told him, I was going to burst... or maybe even freak out. I vowed to do it on Monday morning.

So, first thing Monday morning, in my very best printing, I wrote, "I love you." That was it. Nothing else—no flowers, no poetry—just, "I love you." I passed it to Dianne, who sat between me and Mike Daniels, and whispered, "Give this to Mike Daniels," trying to look really casual, like it was a request to borrow a book from him or something. I held my breath as I watched him open and read it—then read it again. Then he folded it up and put it into his pocket. Oh my God, what have I done? What if he shows it to his buds at recess? They'll all laugh their heads off. I'm a fool. An idiot. Why did I tell him? I felt like I was going to throw up.

I was so involved in feeling like I was going to hurl, that I didn't even feel Dianne punching me in the arm. Then she shoved a note in my hand. Slowly, I opened it. It was my own note. "Great, he thought it was so stupid that he sent it back to me," I thought. Then it dawned on me—he had written something on the back of it:

"I like you, too. I'm glad we're friends."

I didn't know whether to laugh or cry. I was so relieved that he didn't trash me—that could have easily happened if Mike Daniels hadn't been a really nice guy. With that one little gesture of kindness, Mike Daniels made me feel special—and, not only that, but I felt that somehow, he had seen the real me hidden in the body of a fifth grade geek.

I kept that note for years—all the way through the eighth grade. Whenever I felt bad about myself, I would reread Mike Daniels' note and remember that act of kindness. It didn't matter to me what inspired him—if it was pity, or the recognition of things to come—that note gave me strength to go through the challenges of the tough years that followed fifth grade.

~Patty Hansen
Chicken Soup for the Preteen Soul 2

87

Tag

"You're it!" I screamed while slapping my classmate, Hunter, on his right shoulder. It was a kind of ritual to play tag at recess. Even in third grade, social standing was critical and tag was just another way of proving yourself. I wasn't too fond of the game. I'm not saying that I wasn't good, but it was rather tiring.

About ten minutes into our ritual, my attention was brought to the kickball field. A group of kids were huddled in a circle shouting malicious names. Curious to see who the poor victim was, I started to make my way over. As I was getting closer to my destination, our teacher Mrs. Smith started to get involved.

"What's going on here?" Mrs. Smith asked in a stern voice.

The circle was immediately broken and there sat a short, brown-haired girl. Mrs. Smith's eyes studied the crowd for a moment and then, bending down, she started to help the girl to her feet.

"Are you all right, sweetheart?" Mrs. Smith asked in a softer tone. The girl nodded and then began to walk away. "Would you all like to not play at recess for the rest of the year?" The children remained silent.

"Then stop tormenting Angelina. She's done nothing to harm you," Mrs. Smith said. "If I ever see any of you teasing her again, I will double your homework and you won't see this playground until next year. Do you hear me?"

"Yes, Mrs. Smith," the children said in unison. Just as it had started, it was over. None of the kids who were involved in the attack had any remorse. They quickly restarted their game as if nothing had happened.

I began to survey the area to see where the girl had gone. Her name sounded familiar, but I couldn't figure out where I had heard it last.

"Tag! You're it!" Hunter yelled.

"Can't you see I'm not playing anymore?" I said, irritated.

"You can't just stop playing. You're breaking the rules," he argued.

"Well, guess what? I just did," I said with a smirk on my face.

"You're a butthead," he responded cruelly.

"I am not!" I shouted. "Hey, do you know who that Angelina girl is?" I asked, changing the subject.

Hunter glanced at her. "That retard?"

"Yeah, didn't she used to be cool or something?" I asked, staring at her.

"She used to be until her mom died. After that, she got really stupid and quiet," Hunter said, trying to squish a grasshopper he had found in the grass. "You're not going to go play with her, are you? 'Cuz if you do that, you'll become stupid, too, you know. Stupidness rubs off on people. Well, that's what my dad tells me."

"I don't want to play with her. I was just asking," I said pitifully. After a moment of thinking, I turned around and hit Hunter in the back. "You're it!" I screamed as I bolted away toward the sandbox with Hunter close behind.

Spring was coming in full bloom. The flowers were starting to come alive, the trees were waking from their dark spell and the sky was finally clear and a beautiful blue. As the bus sped away, I took in a deep breath of fresh air. As the sweetness filled my lungs, I smiled and walked through my front door.

My mother was sitting on the floor filling out paperwork, while my brother was on the couch eating a peanut butter sandwich. I dropped my book bag and headed for the kitchen.

"Hey, Hon," my mom said softly. "How was your day?"

"Good, I guess," I said, kneeling down to find the peanut butter in the cabinet.

"I have to tell you something," she said quietly.

"What is it?" I asked, not even looking at her. I found the peanut butter and placed it on the table. She was silent for a moment, then began to speak.

"As you know, I went to the doctor the other day. He did a lot of tests because of some problems I've been having," she explained. "Well, the doctor called today. The cancer is back." I immediately stopped what I was doing. At the time, I didn't know a lot about the disease. My grandfather had died of cancer a few years before, and as soon as I heard the word come out of her mouth, I thought of death.

I ran out of the house in tears. My mother followed me to the porch. She embraced me and cradled me in her arms. "Erin, it's gonna be all right. Dad's going to come home, and I'm going to start taking medicine that's going to get rid of it," she said reassuringly. I look back at that moment in astonishment at how confident and determined she was.

I was relieved when my father came walking through the door. He was the strong one, the man of the house. But you could tell just by looking in his eyes, that he was petrified.

My mom had gone through cancer once before. She had gone to several doctors to find out why she wasn't feeling well. They did many CAT scans and tests, but all of them came out negative. After months of searching for the answer, they discovered what was going on. She had ovarian cancer.

I cried a lot during that time. I was so confused about the whole situation. I felt betrayed by God. I remember asking over and over why it had to happen to my mother. I even asked my mother. She would always just say that "everything happens for a reason," or that "good always comes out of every situation."

Meanwhile at school, I became distant from my friends. I would try to play games, but I would get frustrated and quit. I was starting to get ridiculed by even my closest friends.

"Why don't you ever want to play anymore?" Hunter asked me one day while I was sitting down watching a game of tag.

"'Cuz I don't want to, all right? Just leave me alone," I said angrily. I felt bad for yelling at him, but he didn't know what I was going through. He couldn't even conceive of it. Hunter looked at me, rolled his eyes, and left to go play.

Days went by, then months, and soon my mother was back to the doctor for another appointment. She came home and told us the great news: She was allowed to stop her treatment. She was in remission for the second time. I began to feel like myself again.

Recess had just begun when I walked up to Hunter. He turned to me just as I tickled him in the stomach and said, "You're it!" He gave me a huge smile and started to chase me. I had never laughed that much before. I was relieved. It was over; my mother was back.

"Ha! You can't catch me!" I screamed. I ran until I couldn't breathe. I bent down to catch my breath, and as I started to get up, my attention was again focused on the kickball field. There was another circle being formed, and in the middle was Angelina. I gathered up my strength and ran over.

"Leave her alone," I hollered.

I quickly turned around. Mrs. Smith was standing behind me. "All of you inside," she scolded. She looked at me and smiled. Then she started to follow the kids inside the school.

I looked at Angelina, smiled, and started to walk away.

"My mother used to call me her little angel," I heard a voice say quietly in a sweet whisper.

"My mother calls me Baby Bear. She had cancer, but she's better now," I said, turning around so I could face her.

She took her eyes off the ground and said, "My mother had cancer, too, but she died last spring." I stared at her. Her eyes were plagued with the innocence only a young child has when she's lost the only thing dear to her.

"Hey, would you like to play tag with me?" I asked with a smile on my face.

"No, that's all right," she said.

I started walking toward the sandbox. As I was looking at the playground to find Hunter, I felt a tap on my shoulder. I quickly turned around and saw Angelina with the biggest smile on her face. Her soft green eyes were no longer dark and empty, but instead filled with light and hope. She looked at me and said, "You're it."

~Erin Gandia
Chicken Soup for the Teenage Soul on Love & Friendship

The Fall and Rise of a Star

I was sure everyone in my junior high drama class saw the paper in my hands shaking when I stood up to audition for a lead role in the annual Christmas play. I was there, not by choice, but because the teacher wanted each of us to try out for a part.

As a "good" student, I did what I was asked, even if it was scary. I was small for my age, wore secondhand clothes, and cried easily. At school, I was often the brunt of jokes and taunts and had no friends. I wanted desperately to shrink back into my seat and be invisible. But there I was, onstage. Reading was, at least, something I loved. So I read.

Within moments, the fear was gone. I entered the beautiful world of make-believe. So much better, I thought, than the real and cruel one. I was reading the part for the main character, "Star." She was poor—like me. But unlike me, she had a positive outlook on life even though she was an orphan. I wasn't an orphan, but I felt like one. My dad had disappeared. My mom worked days, went to school at night and spent her weekends doing homework. I ached for more time with her. In the play, Star was a lonely child who longed for parents, a few kind words, and a home. It was easy for me to feel that her words were also mine.

I finished reading and rushed back to my seat. The spell was broken. I was just me again, wanting to curl up and disappear. When the teacher read the cast list and called my name, I wasn't paying attention. No one ever chose me for anything.

"Patty," she repeated, "you are Star. Come and get your script."

This is impossible! How can it be? With a pounding heart and cold, moist palms, I felt nearly faint, but incredibly happy. I stumbled up to get the papers.

The cutest boy in class was playing the other lead. I didn't know him, but I wanted to. I was even hoping a little that some of his popularity might rub off on me. I was eager to learn my lines and wanted to do my best. So, I practiced every day—while walking to school, at lunchtime, before bedtime, even on weekends. At first, I was worried about forgetting parts of a long monologue that took place in one scene, but I managed to memorize it. I felt more confident after that.

Then we started to work on blocking, which is when the actors must touch, move, and learn to use the props—in other words, really "act." The cute boy played a Scrooge-like character who refused to spend even a dime to put a candle in his window, so that the light would show passersby the slippery ice on the path below. On Christmas Eve, Star comes along, falls on the ice and sprains Her ankle. The "Scrooge" finds himself helping her up, and in gratitude, she kisses him on the cheek.

One day, right before our drama class started, some of the kids were standing in front of the blackboard, snickering and looking at me. When they moved away, I saw a grotesque, cartoon like drawing of a girl with a huge behind and enormous, ugly lips. Above it were the words, "Falling Star."

I had been teased so often in the past that I had a sort of shield over my heart, which I tried to keep up in order to shut out the pain. But I wasn't very good at it, and this time, I was taken off guard. It really hurt. I was too embarrassed to even cry. Calmly, the teacher erased the picture. "Who did this?" she demanded. No one answered... of course.

We started to rehearse. I said my lines, but my heart wasn't in it. At the end of class, the teacher pulled me aside and told me not to pay any attention to the silliness. It probably wouldn't happen again. But she was wrong.

Every single day after that, a "Falling Star" picture, each one uglier and more embarrassing than the last, appeared on the board. Our teacher, who always had to rush from another class to ours, never caught the culprit. Each day it felt like I was entering a torture chamber. My dreams of being liked by my classmates were shattered. They all laughed at the pictures. I was sure that each and every one of them hated me as much as the person who drew the picture did.

In spite of that, at first, I refused to give up. I had worked too hard. Then I began to forget my lines, and I started to have nightmares about being onstage and unable to make a sound, while the audience laughed at me. Finally, I told the teacher to use my understudy for the part; I felt like I would be a terrible flop. She said, "No, you won't. You can do this. I know you can. I'll help you. If you want to, we'll use the auditorium, so you can feel comfortable there."

After that, we met several afternoons each week after school. She taught me to use my voice to show the emotions I was feeling and to fall without hurting myself. I had never worked so hard in my life at anything so terrifying... yet so much fun.

At last, it was the day before the show, time for the dress rehearsal. I was excited, even confident. I really felt and looked like Star when I had on my stage makeup and the old-fashioned, long, soft-flannel green dress. With the full skirt, thick petticoats, knit hat and muff, the transformation was complete.

Everything went smoothly at the dress rehearsal until the scene where I slip on the ice and Scrooge helps me up. When I kissed him on the cheek, a loud, ugly noise sounded from behind the set, like someone farting, followed by loud laughter.

I ran to the stairs, dashed down the aisle into the empty auditorium, collapsed into a seat and started to cry.

"I can't do it. Get someone else!"

Suddenly, I felt gentle hands on my arms. I heard voices and a soft, warm hand took mine. I looked up through my tears to see concerned faces. Four girls, my classmates, had come after me.

"Please, don't drop out," they said. "You're really, really good! Don't pay any attention to that scum, Peter. He's an idiot!" So, he was my tormentor... the boy that everyone said was a bully. No one even liked him very much.

"You've got to go on," the girls said. "Our play will be a flop without you!"

One of them handed me a tissue. I wiped my eyes and blew my nose. "Okay," I said, giving them a shy smile. I went back onstage and finished the scene with no further interruptions.

The following day, two performances were scheduled for the whole school plus an evening show for families and friends. During the first show, everything went perfectly, and people even applauded in the middle of the play after my monologue! I was flying, dancing, filled with the greatest joy you could imagine.

During the second show, in the first act, part of the scenery fell down. The audience laughed, but I didn't care. I knew they weren't laughing at me. Applause was tremendous at the end of that performance—but the crowning event was the evening show when the parents attended, and my mom got to see me perform.

In the weeks that followed, kids at school came up to say, "You were good," even "great" or "terrific." Although frustrations and failures have come my way since then, along with them, I have also had great joy and success. At times I've felt discouraged, and I still do. But it helps to remember that I was once a fallen star who managed to rise and sparkle, through my own efforts, with the loving guidance of a great teacher and the help of a few unexpected friends.

~Patty Zeitlin
Chicken Soup for the Preteen Soul 2

Scott

*I discovered I always have choices,
and sometimes it's only a choice of attitude.*
~Judith M. Knowlton

t was time for the ice cream social fundraiser that my small youth group had awaited for many months. The group consisted of five boys; one of them was Scott.

Scott always had a positive attitude. He looked on the bright side of things and never criticized anyone. But Scott was different from the rest of us. He had a disability. Oftentimes, he was unable to participate in activities. No one ever made fun of him to his face, but at times, people would snicker or stare in his presence. But Scott never worried; he just kept his head up high and ignored them.

Finally, the night of the ice cream social came. We rushed to the church basement and waited with scoopers in hand for the guests to arrive. One by one, people filed in, all hoping to get a nice, creamy glob of ice cream. But what they ended up getting was a hard, frozen mass. We waited for awhile for the ice cream to thaw, and eventually it did.

Once the ice cream thawed, we had another problem. It had melted into three pools of vanilla, chocolate and strawberry. But we persisted in serving it. We all had our chance to serve, except for

Scott. So, being as kind as possible, we gave Scott a chance to scoop and serve.

As soon as Scott gripped the scooper, our ice cream troubles turned into the World's Greatest Ice Cream Massacre. Milky ice cream was flung in every direction. Scott wouldn't stop. He kept scooping and scooping and scooping. Then, suddenly, in the thick of the chaos, Scott stopped. We looked at Scott. Scott looked at us. And that's when I realized why he had stopped.

Scott was looking at a small, cute girl who entered the basement. Scott stated, "That's m-m-my friend." Our jaws fell open. The most beautiful girl we had seen all night was Scott's friend.

We pushed Scott out of the way, hoping that we could get to serve her. But Scott just looked at us and said, "I-I-I want to scoop the ice cream for her." We backed off.

The girl slowly approached him. Scott stood poised, ready to scoop again. The girl said, "Hi, Scott."

"H-h-hi," stuttered Scott.

She began to make conversation with him by saying, "Look. I got my new braces today." She looked up and gave a wide, bright smile to show off her gleaming braces.

"Th-th-they're neat," responded Scott. The two carried on a short conversation and then the girl sat down.

That night I realized that somebody had overlooked Scott's problems and had seen him as a friendly, normal human being.

I realized something else, too. It was time for all of us to see Scott the same way.

~David Ferino
Chicken Soup for the Preteen Soul

Mother's Christmas Stocking

You can give without loving, but you can never love without giving.
~Author Unknown

My sister Trudy and I snuggled close and giggled at our predicament. We were too big to fit under the Christmas tree, especially with all the piles of presents, so we slept around the Christmas tree instead. Actually we were more in the middle of our mobile home's modest living room floor. But it was tradition—we just had to sleep under the tree on Christmas Eve—even if we were ten and twelve. My eight-year-old brother, Ashley, was already asleep. He had pretended to be too grown up to be excited about sleeping on the living room floor. And being the lowest in the pecking order, he had been assigned the spot farthest from the tree—squashed between an older sister and the coffee table that was pushed to the side to make more room.

Trudy was the most likely to have her head between brightly wrapped boxes with fragrant cedar boughs scratching against her cheek. I was happy to be protected on both sides by warm bodies, and of course Breanna, our three-year-old baby sister, was given the safest and most comfortable spot of all. Breanna was sleeping soundly, curled on the couch hugging an oversized teddy bear.

Trudy and I lay whispering to each other, discussing what we expected to get in our stockings the next morning and guessing what was in each of our already well-shaken packages. We gazed at the four flannel stockings hanging limply by the fireplace, and we realized that one was missing. Weren't there five people in our family? How come Mommy didn't have a stocking?

She had told us that when she was a little girl her family didn't hang stockings on Christmas Eve because they were a "no-nonsense family." We were glad our family was a "nonsense" family, and we figured Mommy deserved to be a part of the tradition she had created for us. It was then that an idea hatched between us that would forever change the way we would see Christmas and, more importantly, giving.

Quickly Trudy woke Breanna, and I hurried to wake Ashley. Trudy piled our pillows to one side and smoothed out the quilt for us to have our conference. Her enthusiasm sparked our own. Amidst smothered giggles and excited exclamations of "Oh—yes," and "That would be perfect," we planned Mother's stocking. For several minutes we scattered to go on a treasure hunt through our possessions, returning with only our very best. Now began the task of assessing their potential significance to Mother.

Breanna brought her candy box. We picked through the half-sucked peppermint sticks and found a handful of unwrapped Santa chocolates and a mammoth fruit-striped candy cane. Trudy suggested we write explanations on Post-It notes and stick one on each gift. I wrote in neat, rounded letters, "For your sweet cravings," and pressed it on Breanna's carefully wrapped, but crinkled, package of chocolates. We put this into the toe of an old, oversized, red wool sock Ashley found in the coat closet and stuck the candy cane inside so that the neck hooked over the side.

Ashley brought two of his favorite toy cars and told us they were for when Mommy's car broke down. Now she would always have two extras. Trudy wrote the explanation for him.

I brought a package of cabbage seeds and wrote around the packet edge, "So you will always have fresh seeds of Inspiration." I put the packet in a small terra-cotta pot that I had painted at school and slid it into the red stocking on top of the toy cars.

Trudy crafted a little creature out of a round river rock the size of a hazelnut. She painted face features, glued wiggly eyes, wrapped it in a miniature plaid blanket and wrote a set of tiny adoption papers for "Herman Periwinkle." That was so Mommy would always have a baby, because she often complained that her real baby was growing up too fast.

After adding a few loose coins, pretty bird feathers and a small peach-scented sachet for good measure, we hung Mom's sock on the highest nail and left Trudy's stocking on top of the wood box. Then we stepped back to admire the lumpy sock—only one thing was missing. Trudy climbed back up on the wood box and safety-pinned a note to the outside of the sock that said, "To: Mother Santa Claus—From: The T.A.A.B. Elves." She was proud of her acronym for our names, and we were all so excited we could hardly sleep.

In the morning, we rushed right past our now-bulging stockings, straight into Mom's bedroom. In our excitement we forgot to knock and tumbled, yelling "Merry Christmas!" onto her bed. Mother was sitting up against the headboard, her treasures spread about her, and tears running down her face. She was holding Herman Periwinkle. When she looked up at us, she smiled her biggest smile and formed the words "Thank you," though they were too soft to be audible.

We clambered over each other to get to her, and she kissed us all and hugged us, laughing and crying at the same time. It was so unlike her usual calm manner. But we understood. It was her first ever Christmas stocking.

~Amberley Howe
Chicken Soup for the Mother's Soul 2

The Christmas Care Bear

May no gift be too small to give, nor too simple to receive,
which is wrapped in thoughtfulness and tied with love.
~L.O. Baird

I began to lose hope. The most treasured person in my life was slowly slipping away. My blind, ninety-four-year-old great-grandmother was sleeping soundly in the hospital bed. As I sat quietly with my family, I listened to the constant buzzing of the machines that kept her alive. Her face was pale and empty. No longer was she the cheerful and jubilant person I had always known.

Thoughts flooded my head. It seems like every day she gets worse. She might not make it through Christmas. I tried to think of a present to give to her. Since she was blind, I would have to get her a gift that she didn't have to see to appreciate, but that she could feel with her hands.

I remembered that when she lived with us she always wanted to touch and play with my stuffed animals. Her favorites were my unique collection of bears. I knew right then what to get. She's always wanted one for herself! I would have a teddy bear made especially for her.

"Grandma's Bear" is what I named the brown, furry animal... "Bear" for short. He was quite charming with his tiny black button nose and his big chocolate eyes. I looked forward to visiting her on Christmas morning and seeing the look on her face when I gave Bear to her.

The day came quicker than I thought. I clutched Bear in my

arms as I walked to Room 208 with my family. There was Grandma, propped up in her bed. Her eyes were wide open. I think she was sensing that we were coming. A grin grew on her face as we sat on her bed, close to her frail body hidden under the covers.

"Merry Christmas!" my dad said. Our family chatted for a while with Grandma until it was time at last to give her the gifts we had brought. My mother gave her fresh-smelling baby powder because she could never have enough of it. My father brought her favorite caramel candies, and my brother brought her a new nightgown. Now it was my turn. I placed the fuzzy bear in her gentle, skinny hands. Her face was suddenly filled with joy. The last time I had seen her that happy was many months earlier.

She cooed and hugged the stuffed animal the whole time we were there. She absolutely loved Bear, and she didn't want anyone to take Bear from her because she feared they'd lose him. Before we left, she thanked me numerous times. She said that it would never leave her side. From that day on, she gradually started to heal. Everyone said it was a miracle.

One month later, my great-grandmother moved back into the nursing home where she had lived before she was sent to the hospital. The nurse said that she slept with Bear every single night and never forgot him. One day when I visited the nursing home, the nurse informed me that my great-grandmother was one of the funniest and happiest residents in the nursing home. She also said that she's taking very good care of Bear. I replied, "No, he's taking good care of her."

Ever since my great-grandmother got Bear, her health improved. Bear was the perfect gift. She made it through Christmas when all of us believed she wouldn't.

Months later, when I turned eleven, my great-grandmother passed away peacefully in her sleep. The nurse said that she found her in the morning, still hugging Bear. It might not have been the bear that was the miracle that prolonged her life and helped her to live the rest of her life in joy... but I believe it was.

~Molly Walden
Chicken Soup for the Soul: Christmas Treasury for Kids

92

Kindness Is More Powerful

If we don't change, we don't grow. If we don't grow, we aren't really living.
~Gail Sheehy

"Is she coming?" my shaky voice cracked. I didn't dare look behind me. My sister, Kayleen, turned to see the front of the middle school where eager seventh and eighth graders were pushing their way to carpools or making their way down the sidewalk toward an evening of television and homework.

"No," she whispered, "but if we walk faster, maybe we'll miss her completely. I'll bet she's still waiting for you outside the gym door."

I walked faster with my head bent down because tears were stinging my eyes and my nose had started to run. My heart was beating furiously and I had a sick feeling in my stomach.

"Who was 'she?'" you might be wondering. Her name was Sabrina, and she was a bully. We were in gym class together, and I was less than athletic—more like pathetic! I didn't run very fast and I was afraid of being hit by a ball, so I was a ducker, not a catcher.

That day during gym class, we had played soccer. I not only embarrassed myself, I also made Sabrina mad—basically because she was on my team, and we didn't win. So, in the shower, she threatened me! "I'll meet you after class," she sneered, "and you will wish you and I had never met!"

I didn't need to wait until after class, I already wished we had never met!

As soon as class was over, I snuck out the teacher's entrance and ran to my locker where Kayleen was already waiting for me, so we could walk home together.

"What's up with you?" she asked, noticing the look of panic in my eyes. "Sabrina!" I choked. "We lost the soccer game in gym and it was my fault. She was on my team."

"Oh," Kayleen simply stated, but she patted my back in understanding. "Well," she said, "we'll walk down Seventeenth South instead of Harrison. It's out of the way enough that Sabrina won't have a clue."

Kayleen and I lived straight down the hill about a mile from Clayton Middle School. Sabrina lived somewhere in the middle. She had followed us most of the way chanting harassments since the first day of school. I couldn't figure out what I had ever done to her. She couldn't have had an idea of how bad I was at sports on the first day of school!

My mother said that because I was quiet and kind and non-confrontational, I was an easy target for bullies. I just felt like a loser! I was grateful for Kayleen, though. I always knew I could count on her. I think because she was my older sister, she felt like she needed to be my protector, and she was, always thinking of ways to avoid Sabrina or any of her sidekicks who enjoyed harassing me on a daily basis.

"Slow down!" Kayleen gasped. "You're practically running. We're far enough away now to be safe."

I looked up and Kayleen noticed my tears. "What about tomorrow?" I sobbed. "She'll just make it worse tomorrow!"

Kayleen stopped dead in her tracks, causing me to stop as well. I turned to look at her. She stood there with her hands on her hips. "Well, then," she said in her favorite grown-up voice, "I guess you just might have to tell someone, then!"

"It will just make it worse," I mumbled.

The next day arrived in record time. As Kayleen and I made our way up the steep Harrison Avenue hill, I felt sick. "I still think you should tell somebody," Kayleen chirped every few minutes.

I never replied until she had said that at least ten times, and then I burst out, "Tell somebody what? That Sabrina is mean and scary and just creeps me out? She's never actually done anything! Am I supposed to just tell them I am a big, fat baby who can't handle seventh grade because she is in it, too? What am I supposed to say?" Kayleen didn't respond. We walked the rest of the way in silence.

In homeroom, Sabrina's best friend passed me a note that stated, "At lunch, you will pay for running away!" I didn't even look up, but I accidentally swallowed my gum and choked until Mr. McKonkie excused me to go and get a drink.

Walking down the hall, I felt a slight sense of relief and freedom. Still, the note had me scared, and I ducked into the girls' bathroom and just cried. When I calmed down enough, I washed my face so I could go back to class without it being totally obvious. As I made my way down the hallway, I had a sick feeling that I was being followed.

Suddenly, someone kicked me in the back of the leg, hard. I almost fell over. "You little chicken!" Sabrina's voice sneered. I didn't turn around, I just walked faster. Why wasn't she in class? I wondered in my panic. I turned to go into Mr. McKonkie's class, but Sabrina blocked me. I turned again and started running down the hall. I had no idea what she was going to do, but three months of constant harassment was weighing heavily on my mind, and I was really freaked out.

Sabrina was now chasing me. At last, she caught up with me enough to kick the back of my legs, trying to knock me down. In a panic, I swung around to the staircase that led to the science and math department. Sabrina was so close to me by then that my sudden shift in direction knocked her off balance and she toppled down the stairs. I stood there watching her fall.

At first, I felt a sudden independence and victory. I turned to walk away from her when I noticed she hadn't stood up yet. Instinct took over, and I suddenly wasn't afraid of her anymore. I practically jumped down the stairs and touched her shoulder. "Can I help?" I asked. When she looked up, I could tell she was in pain. "I can't walk," she moaned. I helped her into a standing position, put her arm around my shoulder and together we hobbled to the nurse's office.

Sabrina never harassed me after that. We never became friends, but from that moment at the foot of the stairs, I knew I had earned her respect. She still hated being on my team in gym class, but things were different. Her best friend would still start in on me sometimes, but Sabrina would shake her head and quietly say, "Leave her alone."

And she always would.

~Janalea Jeppson
Chicken Soup for the Preteen Soul 2

93

The Act of Love

"I hate pulling weeds!" I thought. "It's hot. It's sticky. And it's Saturday!"

Still, I made sure to pull every stinking weed out of that flower garden. My dad was Mr. Perfecto Lawnman. He could detect a single weed a mile away. And if he spotted so much as one little clover, I'd be back pulling weeds for the rest of the day.

"Dad, I'm done," I shouted from the garden, feeling sure that I had done a good job.

Dad stormed out of the house. "Don't be yelling outside, Kathy," he grumbled. "Use those two feet of yours and come get me."

Suddenly, a sick feeling came over me. It was the kind of feeling I had when my dad was going to find that one stinking little clover.

"Geez," Dad said, waving an irritated finger, "you missed a spot."

I sighed, went to the spot and pulled the weeds. Afterward, I looked back at Dad, still standing there with a scowl on his face.

"Okay," he said, turning away, "I guess you're done."

As Dad walked back to the house, I wondered if I'd ever done anything good enough or right enough for him. Sometimes, I wondered if he even liked me.

Like the night I had taken out the trash without being told. That was a big deal for me. But Dad didn't see it that way. He was mad because I didn't put the trash can lid on tightly enough to keep our dog out.

"Well, I'm sorry," I thought, "but I can't help it if Sugar's a trash picker."

The other day, when I was in a rush to get to school, Dad stopped me at the door. In his hand was a topless tube of toothpaste, the same one that I'd used just moments before.

"Where's the cap to the toothpaste?" he asked, his eyebrows bunching in the middle. "And how many times do I have to tell you? Squeeze from the bottom!"

"At least I brushed my teeth," I thought.

Just then, a sloppy, wet tongue washed over my face, breaking me from my thoughts.

"Sugar!" I said, hugging her tightly. "Where did you come from?"

Sugar looked at me, her big sloppy tongue hanging to the side. I smiled.

"At least you like me." Then standing up, I brushed the dirt from my knees and headed for the house.

Two weeks later, on the morning of another weed picking weekend, I was sick. I was sweaty and feverish and I ached all over.

"Let's go," Dad said, lifting me from the bed. "You need to see a doctor."

"Please, no," I said, in a shallow, sickly voice, "I'd rather pull weeds."

He took me anyway, and the doctor said I had pneumonia. The only nice thing about it was that I didn't have to pull weeds. I didn't have to take out the trash. And since I had to stay in bed, I didn't have to brush my teeth. If having pneumonia was ever good, it was good then. And as I rested, Sugar stayed with me, lying down beside my bed. She liked me.

That night a noise woke me from my sleep. I opened my eyes just a sliver, and I saw a tall, slender form. Enough moonlight shined through my window so that I could see it was my dad. But why was he there? I didn't say, "Hi, Dad," or anything like that, I don't know why. He came up to me and put his hand against my forehead. When he took his hand away, I saw him lay something on my nightstand. He looked at me again, then left.

When he was gone, I reached over to the nightstand and picked up a necklace. It wasn't like any I'd ever seen before. Dangling from a golden chain was a puppy in a basket, and the puppy looked just like Sugar. With shaking hands, I held that necklace to my heart and cried. My dad, who never gave hugs and never said, "I love you..." had just said it all.

~Kathy Kemmer Pyron
Chicken Soup for the Preteen Soul

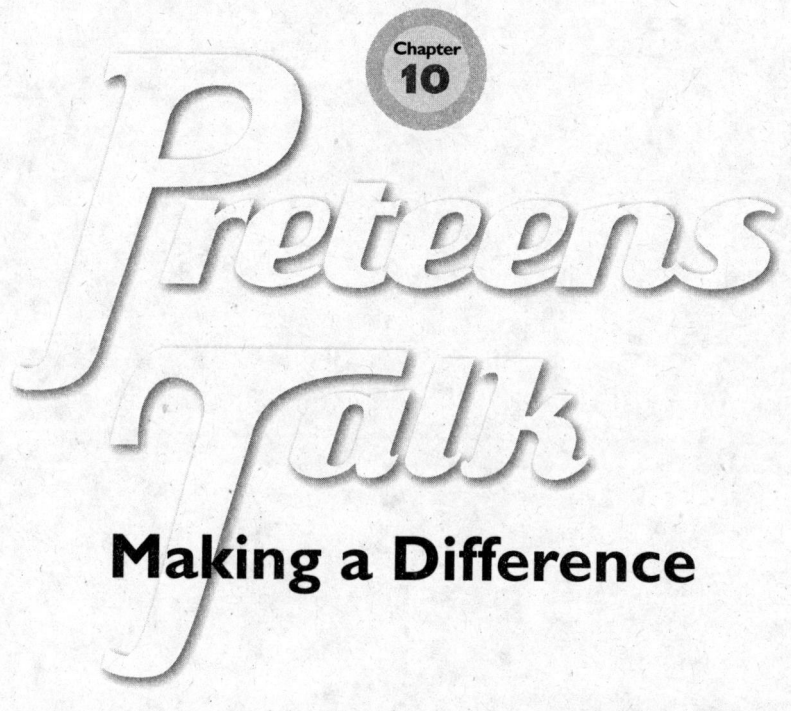

Chapter 10

Preteens Talk

Making a Difference

Actions, not words, are the true criterion of the attachment of friends.
~George Washington

94

To a Different Drummer

Put your future in good hands— your own.
~Author Unknown

"Come on—put up your hands and fight!"

I groaned. Why was this happening to me? My mother had said, "No fighting," right before I left the house. After coming from London, England, to Kitchener, Canada to live with her, I was starting a new life. During recess, this kid wanted to scrap with me, and now it looked like I wouldn't even be able to get through my first day of school and keep my promise to my mum.

"Naw," I replied.

"You're just chicken," he yelled. "Is that it? Are you chicken?" The kid's red hair blazed in the winter sun and his freckles seemed to jump out of his pale skin. At twelve, I was tall for my age, but I was kind of skinny and lanky. He was taller than me, and with his heavy parka on, he looked heavier than me, too.

"No. I'm not chicken. My mother just told me to stay out of trouble."

"I don't care... I want to fight with you, anyway." He pushed me in my chest. Then he put up his hands. "Come on!"

So, I hit him. Down he went into the snow. Other kids on the playground started to circle around us. He got up. He put up his hands—and I hit him again. He went down for a second time. All the kids were yelling, "Fight! Fight!" This time, I kept my hands up just in case someone else in the circle of kids wanted a taste of me, too. I waited, and the kid got back up again.

He walked toward me, stuck out his hand and said, "Shake. I just wanted to see how tough you are. Wanna be friends?"

I heaved a sigh of relief and shook hands with him. I figured that I would need a friend. The snow, strange country, new school, the way that people spoke—different from my London street slang—and being the only black kid for miles around, all of this added up to being a weird new world for me.

I was born in London, England, and lived there with my mother until I was about eight years old. My mum wanted to find a better life for us, so she went to Chicago, in the United States. She left me with friends in London until she got settled enough to send for me. Mum ended up not staying in Chicago but moved to a small town in Canada because she had a friend there who helped her get a good job.

Meanwhile, back in England, I was getting into trouble. I had always felt like an outsider, different from the other kids. They didn't want to play with me. That made me mad, so I got into fights and ended up getting expelled for being a danger to the other kids at my school. The people I was staying with were upset with me and felt they couldn't manage me. So, after living with them for almost two years, they sent me to a home for kids—kind of a boarding school. I lived there for a year. I felt alone and bored, the food was gross, and I really missed my mother. Finally, she sent for me.

My mum met me at the airport in Toronto with a smile on her face, a warm hug, and huge parka to put on. When we went outside the airport, there was snow all over the ground, the cars—everything! I didn't know what it was. I asked my mum, "What is this?" I touched the snow and was amazed by how cold and fluffy it was. It was different from anything I had ever seen before.

The weather was different, my school was different, the country was different, but some things were still the same—I was still getting into fights. Other kids picked on me about my accent, the color of my skin, my grades, or whatever. I was different, still left out. It didn't matter; I hated getting picked on, and I let them know it—with my fists. All through grades seven and eight, I was sent to the principal's office so often that he and I became friends. Instead of punishing me, he would counsel me. He told me that I would be better off using the energy I had in more positive ways and encouraged me to play football and basketball after school. He also suggested that I check out boxing—maybe I could learn to use my fists in a constructive way instead of being on the destructive path I seemed to be headed for.

Even though I was an outsider and a loner, I liked going to school dances. At one of the dances, some of the guys wanted to fight a group of guys from another school. We agreed to meet them on neutral ground—the police boxing gym downtown. We showed up, but they didn't. While we were hanging around waiting for them, one of the boxing trainers called out to me, "You, come over here."

I walked over to him and he asked me, "Do you want to go a few rounds with him?" He pointed to a guy getting into one of the rings. I was pretty full of myself and figured I could take him because he was small, so I said, "Sure, why not?"

I just couldn't hit the guy. He danced all around me while I tried to hit him. Then that little guy really connected with my nose. Not only did that make my eyes water, but it bruised my ego and made me realize that there was more to the sport of boxing than just swinging my fists. The coach put me into the ring with another fighter who was about my size, and I did pretty well. That was a moment of decision in my life. I remembered what my middle school principal had told me and everything clicked. The boxing ring was where I belonged.

All through high school, I played football, basketball, and soccer, and I was on the track team. But from that day on, boxing was the sport that I liked the most. Because it's an individual sport, it's more challenging and exciting to me. I found that I enjoyed the thrill of one-on-one competition. I also liked the fact that it was up to me whether I won or lost—that I was the determining factor. I think I've always been a competitor, and winning would give me a glow of satisfaction and a good feeling about myself. There was always a bad feeling if I lost, and I didn't like that. I wanted to win—every time.

I started training with the man who got me into the ring that first time. He became my boxing coach, friend, mentor, and a father figure for me to look up to. I learned that boxing is a sweet science where I could use my brain as well as my strength and size. I used my ability to focus under pressure. Under his training, I went from being a street fighter to a gold medal-winning Olympic champion.

Though I was basically an outsider, even as a little boy I wanted to be first in whatever I set my mind to. Once I went professional, I worked hard and got what I wanted. I have earned millions, but for me, it's not just about the money. I made my dreams come true. I did it my way. I stayed away from bad promoters and bad managers and upheld my integrity. Throughout my career, I have gained, regained, and retained the WBC and IBF heavyweight belts, the most prestigious in the boxing world. I want my place in history, and I know I will have it.

A couple of years ago, I was given the title, Member of the Order of the British Empire, an honorary title bestowed by Queen Elizabeth II for distinguished achievement. I have come a long way from being a brawling London street kid to the man I am today—the man that my mum raised me to be.

~Lennox Lewis
Former WBC Heavyweight Champion of the World
Chicken Soup for the Preteen Soul 2

Just Do It

Good fortune shies away from gloom. Keep your spirits up.
Good things will come to you and you will come to good things.
~Glorie Abelhas

When I started junior high, my only expectation for myself was to stay invisible. I was shy, sensitive and intimidated by the rest of the school. Everyone seemed so much older, more educated and experienced. Basically they were everything I wasn't but wanted to be. So it's strange how I aspired to run for sixth grade secretary.

The announcement was broadcast on the intercom that anyone interested in running for student council should see the math teacher for qualification forms. Even though I'm normally a cautious person, I followed the massive crowd to the math classroom. Without even thinking twice, my mom and I filled out and turned in the forms, but I had no idea what I had gotten myself into.

The only thing you could see in the sixth grade hall were neon posters adorned with pictures of winning-obsessed pupils. Buttons, bookmarks, and flyers littered the hallways and cafeteria. Most found a permanent home in the trash can.

Meanwhile, my printer lazily spit out what seemed like a million bookmarks. I cut them out, punched holes in them and finished them off with ribbons, finally bringing them in to school. That week my friends and I passed out the bookmarks. Everything was going as planned... until it was time for my speech.

I had never been afraid of being on television before. In fact, I had been on my school's morning news program for two years. But as I got ready to present my speech, my hands clammed up and my sweat glands went into overdrive as the camera fixed on my face. My short, page-long speech hadn't taken more than a minute to read, but I felt as if I had been on that musty old stage for an eternity. Anxious thoughts spun in my head like a tornado. What did my hair look like? Did I look at the camera? And most of all, did I look as petrified as I felt?

Somewhere between handing out bookmarks and delivering my speech, I asked myself one question: "What the heck are you doing, Laura!?" I felt trapped, enclosed. But in the midst of the fury and panic was something unexpected. I had learned some amazing things about who I was. Not only did I give a speech in front of 300 kids, but I'd introduced myself to people I'd never even met before while actively campaigning. In fact, I felt incredibly confident. I could do anything!

After that, things happened so fast that I can't remember every little detail about the election. But what I do remember so vividly is the one thing everyone now knows. I won! It wasn't that easy, though. I actually tied with another student, but in the end, my class picked me! Me! The shy and quiet girl! Destined to be invisible? NOT! Why be invisible when you can shine?

I'm already planning my re-election campaign. And I've learned the importance of taking a chance, going out on a limb, and believing in yourself. And next time there's something I want to do but am a little intimidated, I'm going to just do it!

~Son Truong Nguye
Chicken Soup for the Soul: The Real Deal School

96

Taking a Stand

Courage is what it takes to stand up and speak;
Courage is also what it takes to sit down and listen.
~Winston Churchill

The summer before fifth grade, my world was turned upside down when my family moved from the country town where I was born and raised to a town near the beach. When school began, I found it difficult to be accepted by the kids in my class who seemed a little more sophisticated, and who had been in the same class together since first grade.

I also found this Catholic school different from the public school I had attended. At my old school, it was acceptable to express yourself to the teacher. Here, it was considered outrageous to even suggest a change be made in the way things were done.

My mom taught me that if I wanted something in life, I had to speak up or figure out a way to make it happen. No one was going to do it for me. It was up to me to control my destiny.

I quickly learned that my classmates were totally intimidated by the strict Irish nuns who ran the school. My schoolmates were so afraid of the nuns' wrath that they rarely spoke up for themselves or suggested a change.

Not only were the nuns intimidating, they also had some strange habits. The previous year, my classmates had been taught by a nun named Sister Rose. This year, she came to our class to teach music several times a week. During their year with her, she had earned the nickname Pick-Her-Nose-Rose. My classmates swore that during silent reading, she'd prop her book up so that she could have herself a booger-picking session without her students noticing. The worst of it, they told me, was that after reading was over, she'd stroll through the classroom and select a victim whose hair would be the recipient of one of her prize boogers. She'd pretend to be praising one of her students by rubbing her long, bony fingers through their hair! Well, to say the least, I did not look forward to her sort of praise.

One day during music, I announced to Sister Rose that the key of the song we were learning was too high for our voices. Every kid in the class turned toward me with wide eyes and looks of total disbelief. I had spoken my opinion to a teacher—one of the Irish nuns!

That was the day I gained acceptance with the class. Whenever they wanted something changed, they'd beg me to stick up for them. I was willing to take the punishment for the possibility of making a situation better and of course to avoid any special attention from Pick-Her-Nose-Rose. But I also knew that I was being used by my classmates who just couldn't find their voices and stick up for themselves.

Things pretty much continued like this through sixth and seventh grades. Although we changed teachers, we stayed in the same class together and I remained the voice of the class.

At last, eighth grade rolled around and one early fall morning our new teacher, Mrs. Haggard—not a nun, but strict nevertheless—announced that we would be holding elections for class representatives. I was elected Vice President.

That same day, while responding to a fire drill, the new president and I were excitedly discussing our victory when, suddenly, Mrs. Haggard appeared before us with her hands on her hips. The words that came out of her mouth left me surprised and confused. "You're impeached!" she shouted at the two of us. My first reaction was to burst out laughing because I had no idea what the word "impeached" meant. When she explained that we were out of office for talking during a fire drill, I was devastated.

Our class held elections again at the beginning of the second semester. This time, I was elected president, which I took as a personal victory. I was more determined than ever to represent the rights of my oppressed classmates.

My big opportunity came in late spring. One day, the kids from the other eighth grade class were arriving at school in "free dress," wearing their coolest new outfits, while our class arrived in our usual uniforms: the girls in their pleated wool skirts and the boys in their salt and pepper pants. "How in the world did this happen?" we all wanted to know. One of the eighth graders from the other class explained that their teacher got permission from our principal, Sister Anna, as a special treat for her students.

We were so upset that we made a pact to go in and let our teacher know that we felt totally ripped off. We agreed that when she inevitably gave us what had become known to us as her famous line, "If you don't like it, you can leave," we'd finally do it. We'd walk out together.

Once in the classroom, I raised my hand and stood up to speak to our teacher. About eight others rose to show their support. I explained how betrayed we felt as the seniors of the school to find the other eighth graders in free dress while we had to spend the day in our dorky uniforms. We wanted to know why she hadn't spoken on our behalf and made sure that we weren't left out of this privilege.

As expected, instead of showing sympathy for our humiliation, she fed us her famous line, "If you don't like it, you can leave." One by one, each of my classmates shrank slowly back into their seats. Within seconds, I was the only one left standing.

I began walking out of the classroom, and Mrs. Haggard commanded that I continue on to the principal's office. Sister Anna, surprised to see me in her office so soon after school had begun, asked me to explain why I was there. I told her that as class president, I had an obligation to my classmates to represent them. I was given the option to leave if I didn't like the way things were, so I did. I believed that it would have been a lie for me to sit back down at that point.

She walked me back to class and asked Mrs. Haggard to tell her version of the situation. Mrs. Haggard's side seemed to be different from what the class had witnessed. Then something incredible happened. Some of my classmates began shouting protests from their desks in response to Mrs. Haggard's comments. "That's not true," they countered. "She never said that," they protested.

It was too much of a stretch for them to stand up and walk out with me that day, but I knew something had clicked inside of them. At least they finally spoke up.

Perhaps they felt that they owed me. Or they realized that we'd soon be at different high schools and I wouldn't be there to stick up for them anymore. I'd rather believe that when they spoke up that day, they had finally chosen to take control of their own destinies.

I can still hear their voices.

~Irene Dunlap
Chicken Soup for the Girl's Soul

97

For the Best

It was two days after the tragic school shooting in Colorado, and I was feeling bad about what had happened to the students there. My school began having a lot of bomb threats and it seemed that police cars were there often. I was standing with my friend, Amberly, and her boyfriend when he casually said, "I'm gonna blow up the school and kill everyone." I asked, "Why would you want to do that?" and he said, "I just do," and walked away.

I was scared because no one had ever said anything like that to me before. I found out when talking to other friends that he also bragged about this to other people. My friends told me that I should tell an adult what he had said, but I was too scared and I made them promise not to tell anyone either.

One day, Amberly and I were talking about what he had said when the teacher overheard our conversation. She took me out into the hallway and made me tell her who had said it and what they had said. At first, I refused to say a word. She told me it really was for the best, so I told her. I felt awful for doing it. I was angry with her for making me tell who said it. I wasn't sure he really meant it and didn't want him to get into trouble.

He got suspended for two days and had two days of in-school detention after that. I sometimes wonder if I had not told, would he have done what he said he was going to do? The guys in Colorado seemed pretty normal to a lot of people. The bottom line is, you should never joke around about something as serious as killing people. If you do, responsible people have no choice but to have you checked out to ensure everyone else's safety.

After he was suspended, the whole sixth grade had an assembly. The principal and counselors told the students that there was a kid who was making threats and that he was suspended. I decided later to tell him that it was me who told on him so he wouldn't speculate about who did it. I was surprised to find that he was not angry with me for doing what I did. He was able to get help for his feelings and behavior.

Many people are in the same situation that I was in. If your friend is saying threatening stuff like my friend was, then they obviously need help—soon. It seems like when one school shooting happens, then another one occurs not too long after that. If there were any way that you could prevent one school shooting it could perhaps save your own life and many others as well. If I had to do it over again, I would—because it really was for the best.

~April Townsend
Chicken Soup for the Preteen Soul

98

Pyramid Surprise

Nellie and I have been best friends for as long as I can remember. We were born only a few days apart, so every year we plan a combined birthday party. The year we were in seventh grade, we were especially excited. Our moms said we could finally invite boys. Our theme, we decided, was "Discover the Pyramids."

Nellie was writing out the invitation list when my mom came up and peered over her shoulder.

"What about inviting John?" Mom asked.

John had been in our class for only a few months, but he was already getting better grades in math and science than anyone else in class. He was a loner, though, and hadn't made very many friends.

I wrinkled my nose. "Mom, he wears the same pants to school every day. How could he even afford a costume?"

Mom frowned. "The same pants?"

"Yes. Brown corduroy ones." I felt a twinge of guilt. My family didn't have a lot of money either, but my mom was a whiz at bargain shopping. I never had to wear the same thing twice in one week.

"Hmm," said Mom. Her office phone rang, and off she went.

After school the next day, as Nellie and I were cutting paper for party decorations, Mom waltzed up and handed me an envelope.

"What's that?" I asked.

"Nellie's mom and I thought it would be nice for you two to give this to John," Mom said as she headed back to her office.

I opened the envelope delicately and gasped. Inside was a gift certificate for our favorite department store.

"Wow," said Nellie. We both knew how many cute clothes that would buy.

I stared at the certificate in awe. "So, are we going to just hand it to him?"

"How embarrassing would that be," Nellie scoffed.

She was right. John would be totally humiliated if we gave him money for clothes. "What if we slipped it into his desk when no one is looking?"

"He'd probably give it to the teacher, and then we'd have to say it was for him in front of the whole class." Nellie rolled her eyes. "Triple embarrassing. We have to think of something else.

"Hmm. What if we ask our teacher..."

"Wait a second. Stop everything. I have an idea." Nellie snatched the envelope and started hopping up and down.

"What? What?"

Still bouncing, she sang, "I'm not going to tell you!" I pestered, I wheedled, I glowered. But Nellie wouldn't budge.

For days I watched Nellie and John carefully. No new pants.

Maybe he's saving them for the party, I thought. Or worse, maybe Nellie was going to give them to him there! For just one tiny second, I wondered if she might have confiscated the gift certificate and used it herself.

"She wouldn't do that," I told myself. But I watched in vain for new pants to appear.

On the day of our party, kids arrived dressed in white sheets, black wigs and snake bracelets. John arrived in a dingy sheet, with—no surprise—the brown corduroy pants underneath.

Nobody seemed to care, though. We danced, ate Mediterranean snacks, and divided everyone into teams for a mummy wrap contest and a hieroglyphic scavenger hunt.

"And now for the grand prize game," Nellie announced. Grand prize? My mouth dropped. This was not in the plan.

"Get your pencils ready! The grand prize game is the following riddle: Osiris and Isis were building pyramids. Osiris' bricks were 4 feet cubed, and he worked at the rate of 8 bricks per hour. Isis' bricks were 3 feet cubed, and she worked at the rate of 12 bricks per hour. They both started with a base 60 feet square. If their pyramids had to be 60 feet high, who finished first?"

A math game. Of course! Nellie winked at me. Neither one of us was surprised when John came up with the answer way before anyone else and walked off with the envelope.

Everyone ooohed and aaahed when our moms brought out an enormous chocolate pyramid cake. I noticed John took particular delight in slicing off the very top.

The next week, he wore a new pair of pants every day, and even a couple of new shirts. The whole time he had a big grin on his face.

And so did we. I have never been more proud to be Nellie's best friend.

~Holly Cupala
Chicken Soup for the Preteen Soul 2

Raising a Star

From the very first meeting that I attended, I knew that raising a guide dog puppy was the project for me. My dad had other ideas. He thought the responsibilities required were too much for a sixth grader to handle. After months of my lobbying, begging, sobbing, and working my tail off to convince him, he finally agreed that I could raise a puppy. And so I began my journey as a guide dog puppy raiser—a journey that lasted six years.

After I turned in my application, I still had a long time to wait before a puppy would be available. In the interim I began to puppy-sit. When the dogs I cared for dug holes in the yard, I thought, "Oh... my puppy will be different." I was in a euphoric (and definitely ignorant) state. The days seemed to pass so slowly without a puppy to raise.

On Christmas Day, after all the presents under the tree were unwrapped, I still had the gifts in my stocking to open. I pulled candy, brushes, and Silly Putty from the overflowing stocking, but when I reached the bottom, my fingers closed around something unlike anything I had ever felt in a stocking. It was a piece of fabric. I pulled it out and saw it was a tiny green puppy jacket. Attached to the jacket was half a sheet of paper with a note written on it:

Dear Laura,

You will need this on January 6 when you come to get me in the Escondido Kmart.

I am a male yellow Lab and my name begins with B.

When I finished reading the note, I burst into tears. My puppy! I could hardly wait for the day when I would meet the newest member of my family.

On January 6, I received my first puppy: a yellow Lab named Bennett. He was the first of a series of guide dog puppies—Hexa, Brie, Flossie, and Smidge, to name a few—that I raised over the next six years. Each of the puppies holds a special place in my heart, a place each won as soon as I saw him or her. Who could resist that small, bouncy bundle of fur placed into your arms for you to love and care for?

I found raising guide dog puppies to be a deeply rewarding service project, yet sometimes I wondered who was raising whom. Each one of my canine teachers imparted lessons of love, pain, separation, forgiveness and patience. Four legs and a tail motivated me to do things I would have never attempted on my own. And when you know you'll have just 365 days to spend together, you learn to cherish each moment.

During that year, I organized my time carefully, making sure to include all the required training, such as obedience, grooming, and socialization. To help these future guide dogs acclimate to many different environments, I had to take each puppy with me just about everywhere I went, sometimes even to school! I admit that at first this special privilege was the main reason I had wanted to raise a guide dog puppy, but the meaning of the project grew much deeper as time passed.

The many hours I spent in public with each dog turned out to be a fraction of the time and energy I spent with him or her at home. It's then that the individual raiser adds his or her own personality to each dog. In my experience, it was the minute or two that I took before leaving for school or going to bed—just to stop and pet my puppy or tell him that I loved him—that created the strongest bond.

And that love flowed both ways. Every time a puppy would jump up onto my lap and kiss me one last time for the night, I'd forget all about the unhappy manager who threw us out of the grocery store that day, the hole being dug to China in the backyard and the potty calls at three in the morning. It takes so little extra time to raise not just a well-trained dog, but a loving dog—a dog who will bring such light into a nonsighted person's life.

At the end of the year, it is time for the puppy to leave. The day arrives sorrowfully for me, even though she suspects nothing. The whole day I'm filled with memories of the year we spent with one another: long days at school together, hours spent swimming in the pool and cuddly moments watching TV. But the time has come for the puppy to move on, to do what I have raised her to do. Tears fill my eyes and rush down my cheeks as I say the final goodbye, then take off her leash and hand her over to her new school. Before she even leaves, I miss her, wondering if the important work I have done is worth the anguish. The squirming, brand-new puppy placed into my hands cannot be compared to her. I know I will soon be filled with the same love for this new little one, but I will never forget the one that's leaving.

For six long months, I wait for her weekly school reports, opening them eagerly when they arrive. Finally, she has made it: she graduates from school and is matched with a blind person.

The long trek to San Francisco would be worth it just to catch a glimpse of her, but I usually get to spend the whole day with her and the person she will help. Before that day, I feel as if no one could deserve her love and affection, but I always change my mind as soon as I meet her new partner.

Seeing them together, once again my perception of the project is lifted to new heights. The puppy who pulled me across the yard is now a sleek, gorgeous, grown-up dog who guides a nonsighted person across the busiest streets in America. They are no longer a human being and a dog, but a single unit that moves with more grace than a world-class ballerina. To know I have been a part of creating this team is enough to erase the last vestige of the pain of missing her. She has a new job now. She has matured from the puppy who comforted me, loved me, and was my best friend, to become a guide dog: a lifeline for someone who needs her. And though a single star is missing from my sky, she has opened up a whole universe for another.

~Laura Sobchik
Chicken Soup for the Dog Lover's Soul

More Than I Had Dreamed Of.

rom the time I was seven, I had a dream of becoming a member of my school cabinet. I always admired my school leaders for taking responsibility for all of us. They gave instructions, conducted school activities, proudly wore their cabinet badges, and carried our school flag for parades. They represented us and gave speeches on school issues. Our school cabinet members were our role models.

So, for the next few years, I dreamed—dreamed of being a leader. Dreamed of being the person addressing issues of students. Finding solutions. Making a difference.

Years flew by, and soon I was eligible to participate in the elections. When I was twelve, I entered my name as a junior member. I prepared my election speech and then, on the afternoon that we all gave our speeches, everybody voted. My close friends pledged their votes for me. I was hopeful and I prayed that I would win.

The next morning, we all assembled at the school grounds and our principal announced the results. I waited anxiously for my name to be announced. I was all set to fulfill my dream.

One by one, the names were announced and the whole school cheered as the girls with the highest votes walked up to the stage. I closed my eyes and waited for my name to be called. The last name was read and my name wasn't among them. I was totally brokenhearted.

My dream had been shattered, and I just wanted to run home and cry my heart out.

And then the reality struck that I hadn't had a chance to win. I wasn't well known, flamboyant, or stylish. I wore braces and wasn't too pretty. Girls across the school hardly knew me. I just did not have what it took to win a school election.

I was depressed because I had nurtured this dream for a long time. I went through something that a huge majority of preteens face—rejection. My whole world began to cave in and suddenly it seemed as if I had no friends.

As I cried in my room that evening, I suddenly took a deep breath and decided I was going to stop seeing myself as a failure. So what if I had lost an election? There were many more things in life to accomplish. I would work hard to make my dreams a reality. I wouldn't stop dreaming.

It didn't matter if I wore braces or if I wasn't too pretty. That didn't give me a reason to give up. I decided that I would stand for elections again in my final year at school—and I would win. I sat at my study table and began to write down my thoughts.

I recognized that my competitors had a lot of things in their favor. Their flamboyant personalities were their biggest strength. What were the points that would work in my favor? I had good grades, and I was friendly and helpful. And my biggest strength was the faith I had in myself to be a good leader. I would not allow my plain appearance or my braces to hold me back from putting my best foot forward. That evening, I began my election plans a whole year in advance.

First, I realized that I would have to work for each vote. Girls would have to get to know me as a person and recognize that I had the ability to represent them. I loved making friends and I liked being helpful, so I decided that perhaps I could use these qualities to work to my advantage. I began to make new friends and help them out in different ways. Slowly and steadily during the year, I made friends across the school. When my official campaign began, they helped drum up support for me.

In order to learn how to present a great election speech, I

attended a course on effective public speaking. At twelve, I was the youngest participant in the course. By the time the election rolled around, I had a good speech and was well prepared as I delivered it with more confidence than I had the year before.

The day after the election took place, every minute seemed like an hour while I waited for the results. Would my efforts pay off? Would I accomplish my goal? Would I be one of the five senior school leaders?

During the assembly, when the principal announced, "Lin Rajan has been elected to the school cabinet with the second highest number of votes in the school," the students cheered as I walked up to the stage. The joy on the faces of all my friends showed me that my victory was also their victory.

Suddenly, I realized that I had accomplished much more than I had dreamed of. The path I had chosen had given me more than the cabinet badge; I had made many new friends and had helped people along the way. I had won the acceptance and love of my schoolmates and they knew me as somebody who would stand by them. I was able to put a smile on their faces and brighten their day.

I realized that just by being me and going for my dream, I had already made a difference.

~Lin Rajan
Chicken Soup for the Preteen Soul 2

The Little Girl Who Dared to Wish

I wish they would only take me as I am.
~Vincent Van Gogh

As Amy Hagadorn rounded the corner across the hall from her classroom, she collided with a tall boy from the fifth grade running in the opposite direction. "Watch it, Squirt," the boy yelled, as he dodged around the little third grader. Then, with a smirk on his face, the boy took hold of his right leg and mimicked the way Amy limped when she walked. Amy closed her eyes for a moment. "Ignore him," she told herself as she headed for her classroom. But at the end of the day Amy was still thinking about the tall boy's teasing. And he wasn't the only one. Ever since Amy started the third grade, someone teased her every single day, about her speech or her limping. Sometimes, even in a classroom full of other students, the teasing made her feel all alone.

At the dinner table that evening, Amy was quiet. Knowing that things were not going well at school, Patti Hagadorn was happy to have some exciting news to share with her daughter. "There's a Christmas wish contest at the local radio station," she announced. "Write a letter to Santa and you might win a prize. I think someone with blond curly hair at this table should enter." Amy giggled and out came pencil and paper. "Dear Santa Claus," she began. While Amy worked away at her best printing, the rest of the family tried to figure out what she might ask from Santa. Amy's sister, Jamie, and Amy's mom both thought a three-foot Barbie doll would top Amy's wish list. Amy's dad guessed a picture book. But Amy wouldn't reveal her secret Christmas wish.

At the radio station WJLT in Fort Wayne, Indiana, letters poured in for the Christmas Wish contest. The workers had fun reading about all the different presents the boys and girls from across the city wanted for Christmas. When Amy's letter arrived at the radio station, manager Lee Tobin read it carefully.

Dear Santa Claus,

My name is Amy. I am nine years old. I have a problem at school. Can you help me, Santa? Kids laugh at me because of the way I walk and run and talk. I have cerebral palsy. I just want one day where no one laughs at me or makes fun of me.

~Love, Amy

Lee's heart ached as he read the letter: He knew cerebral palsy was a muscle disorder that might confuse Amy's schoolmates. He thought it would be good for the people of Fort Wayne to hear about this special little girl and her unusual wish. Mr. Tobin called up the local newspaper.

The next day, a picture of Amy and her letter to Santa made the front page of The News Sentinel. The story spread quickly. Across the country, newspapers and radio and television stations reported the story of the little girl in Fort Wayne, Indiana, who asked for such a simple, yet remarkable Christmas gift—just one day without teasing.

Suddenly, the postman was a regular at the Hagadorn house. Envelopes of all sizes addressed to Amy arrived daily from children and adults all across the nation, filled with holiday greetings and words of encouragement. During that busy Christmas season, over two thousand people from all over the world sent Amy letters of friendship and support. Some of the writers had disabilities; some had been teased as children, but each writer had a special message for Amy. Through the cards and letters from strangers, Amy glimpsed a world full of people who truly cared about each other. She realized that no form or amount of teasing could ever make her feel lonely again.

Many people thanked Amy for being brave enough to speak up. Others encouraged her to ignore teasing and to carry her head high. Lynn, a sixth grader from Texas, sent this message:

> *I'd like to be your friend, and if you want to visit me, we could have fun. No one will make fun of us, because if they do, we will not even hear them.*

Amy did get her wish of a special day without teasing at South Wayne Elementary School. Additionally, everyone at school got an added bonus. Teachers and students talked together about how teasing can make others feel. That year, the Fort Wayne mayor officially proclaimed December 21 as Amy Jo Hagadorn Day throughout the city. The mayor explained that by daring to make such a simple wish, Amy taught a universal lesson. "Everyone," said the mayor, "wants and deserves to be treated with respect, dignity and warmth."

~Alan D. Shultz
Chicken Soup for the Unsinkable Soul

Chicken Soup for the Soul

Share with Us

We would like to how these stories affected you and which ones were your favorite. Please write to us and let us know.

We also would like to share your stories with future readers. You may be able to help another teenager, and become a published author at the same time. Please send us your own stories and poems for our future books. Some of our past contributors have launched writing and speaking careers from the publication of their stories in our books!

The best way to submit your stories is through our web site, at

www.chickensoup.com

If you do not have access to the Internet, you may submit your stories by mail or by facsimile.

Chicken Soup for the Soul
P.O. Box 700
Cos Cob, CT 06807-0700
Fax 1-203-861-7194

About the Chicken Soup for the Soul Authors

Chicken Soup for the Soul

Who Is
Jack Canfield?

Jack Canfield is the co-creator and editor of the Chicken Soup for the Soul series, which Time magazine has called "the publishing phenomenon of the decade." Jack is also the co-author of eight other bestselling books including *The Success Principles™: How to Get from Where You Are to Where You Want to Be*, *Dare to Win*, *The Aladdin Factor*, *You've Got to Read This Book*, and *The Power of Focus: How to Hit Your Business and Personal and Financial Targets with Absolute Certainty*.

Jack has recently developed a telephone coaching program and an online coaching program based on his most recent book *The Success Principles*. He also offers a seven-day Breakthrough to Success seminar every summer, which attracts 400 people from fifteen countries around the world.

Jack is the CEO of the Canfield Training Group in Santa Barbara, California, and founder of the Foundation for Self-Esteem in Culver City, California. He has conducted intensive personal and professional development seminars on the principles of success for over a million people in twenty-three countries. Jack is a dynamic keynote speaker and he has spoken to hundreds of thousands of others at more than 1,000 corporations, universities, professional conferences and conventions, and has been seen by millions more on national television shows such as The Today Show, Fox and Friends, Inside Edition, Hard Copy, CNN's Talk Back Live, 20/20, Eye to Eye, and the NBC Nightly News and the CBS Evening News.

Jack is the recipient of many awards and honors, including three honorary doctorates and a Guinness World Records Certificate for having seven books from the Chicken Soup for the Soul series appearing on the New York Times bestseller list on May 24, 1998.

To write to Jack or for inquiries about Jack as a speaker, his coaching programs, trainings or seminars, use the following contact information:

Jack Canfield
The Canfield Companies
P.O. Box 30880 • Santa Barbara, CA 93130
phone: 805-563-2935 • fax: 805-563-2945
E-mail: info@jackcanfield.com
www.jackcanfield.com

Who Is
Mark Victor Hansen?

Mark Victor Hansen is the co-founder of Chicken Soup for the Soul, along with Jack Canfield. He is also a sought-after keynote speaker, bestselling author, and marketing maven. For more than thirty years, Mark has focused solely on helping people from all walks of life reshape their personal vision of what's possible. His powerful messages of possibility, opportunity, and action have created powerful change in thousands of organizations and millions of individuals worldwide.

Mark's credentials include a lifetime of entrepreneurial success. He is a prolific writer with many bestselling books, such as *The One Minute Millionaire*, *Cracking the Millionaire Code*, *How to Make the Rest of Your Life the Best of Your Life*, *The Power of Focus*, *The Aladdin Factor*, and *Dare to Win*, in addition to the Chicken Soup for the Soul series. Mark has had a profound influence in the field of human potential through his library of audios, videos, and articles in the areas of big thinking, sales achievement, wealth building, publishing success, and personal and professional development.

Mark is the founder of the MEGA Seminar Series. MEGA Book Marketing University and Building Your MEGA Speaking Empire are annual conferences where Mark coaches and teaches new and aspiring authors, speakers, and experts on building lucrative publishing and speaking careers. Other MEGA events include MEGA Info-Marketing and My MEGA Life.

He has appeared on Oprah, CNN, and The Today Show. He

has been quoted in *Time*, *U.S. News & World Report*, *USA Today*, *New York Times*, and *Entrepreneur* and has had countless radio interviews, assuring our planet's people that "You can easily create the life you deserve."

As a philanthropist and humanitarian, Mark works tirelessly for organizations such as Habitat for Humanity, American Red Cross, March of Dimes, Childhelp USA, and many others. He is the recipient of numerous awards that honor his entrepreneurial spirit, philanthropic heart, and business acumen. He is a lifetime member of the Horatio Alger Association of Distinguished Americans, an organization that honored Mark with the prestigious Horatio Alger Award for his extraordinary life achievements.

Mark Victor Hansen is an enthusiastic crusader of what's possible and is driven to make the world a better place.

Mark Victor Hansen & Associates, Inc.
P.O. Box 7665 • Newport Beach, CA 92658
phone: 949-764-2640 • fax: 949-722-6912
www.markvictorhansen.com

Who Is
Amy Newmark?

A my Newmark was recently named publisher of Chicken Soup for the Soul, after a thirty-year career as a writer, speaker, financial analyst, and business executive in the worlds of finance and telecommunications.

Amy is a graduate of Harvard College, where she majored in Portuguese, minored in French, and traveled extensively. She is also the mother of two children in college and has two grown stepchildren.

After a long career writing books on telecommunications, voluminous financial reports, business plans, and corporate press releases, Chicken Soup for the Soul is a breath of fresh air for Amy. She has fallen in love with Chicken Soup for the Soul and its life-changing books, and found it a true pleasure to conceptualize, compile, and edit the "101 Best Stories" books for our readers.

The best way to contact Chicken Soup for the Soul is through our web site, at www.chickensoup.com. This will always get the fastest attention.

If you do not have access to the Internet, please contact us by mail or by facsimile.

Chicken Soup for the Soul
P.O. Box 700
Cos Cob, CT 06807-0700
Fax 1-203-861-7194

Acknowledgments

Chicken Soup for the Soul

Thank You!

Our first thanks go to our loyal readers who have inspired the entire Chicken Soup team for the past fifteen years. Your appreciative letters and emails have reminded us why we work so hard on these books.

We owe huge thanks to all of our contributors as well. We know that you pour your hearts and souls into the stories and poems that you share with us, and ultimately with each other. We appreciate your willingness to open up your lives to other Chicken Soup readers.

We can only publish a small percentage of the stories that are submitted, but we read every single one and even the ones that do not appear in a book have an influence on us and on the final manuscripts.

As always, we would like to thank the entire staff of Chicken Soup for the Soul for their help on this project and the 101 Best series in general.

Among our California staff, we would especially like to single out the following people:

- D'ette Corona, who is the heart and soul of the Chicken Soup publishing operation, and who put together the first draft of this manuscript

- Barbara LoMonaco for invaluable assistance in obtaining the fabulous quotations that add depth and meaning to this book
- Patty Hansen for her extra special help with the permissions for these fabulous stories and for her amazing knowledge of the Chicken Soup library
- and Patti Clement for her help with permissions and other organizational matters.

In our Connecticut office, we would like to thank our able editorial assistant, Valerie Howlett, for her assistance in setting up our new offices, editing, and helping us put together the best possible books for teenagers.

We would also like to thank our master of design, book producer and Creative Director, Brian Taylor, at Pneuma Books LLC, for his brilliant vision for our covers and interiors.

Finally, none of this would be possible without the business and creative leadership of our CEO, Bill Rouhana, and our president, Bob Jacobs.

www.chickensoup.com